JENNI CA

CHRONICLES
OF CONSCIENCE

*A Study of George Orwell
and Arthur Koestler*

"all through history, mind limps after reality"
Leon Trotsky

SECKER & WARBURG · LONDON

First published in England 1968 by
Martin Secker & Warburg Limited
14 Carlisle Street, London, W.1

Copyright © 1968 by Jenni Calder

SBN 436 08120 2

Parts of this book were the substance of a thesis which the University of London approved for the
degree of Master of Arts.

Printed in Great Britain by
Billing & Sons Limited, Guildford and London

CONTENTS

I

LIMPING AFTER REALITY

The period between the World Wars, particularly the decade before the outbreak of the second, brought into focus the problem of the writer who is also, through choice or necessity, a man of action. Men who had been through experiences of war and physical hardship felt a compulsive urge to record these experiences. They wrote as actors and witnesses. In many cases experience, even if second hand, generated social awareness and political understanding, and the writing was directed by criticism and construction. As those professionally concerned with words became involved in deeds, and as the doers sought to express themselves in words, a growing concern with the violent reality of the modern world was inevitable.

The period was pre-eminently one in which the witness and the chronicler played, if not a more important, a more immediately relevant part than the philosopher or the man of imagination. The journalist, the man trained in precise description and immediate response, came into his own. But immediacy and rapidity of judgment often indicate a short life: we do not often remember the reports of tragedy or the analyses of tension in last week's papers. The recorder of events turned to fiction as a half-conscious means of deepening and toughening the significance of his response. He was usually content to accept the traditional forms of fiction as a convenient vehicle for political writing, but he frequently interfered with its traditional content and characterisation. As his relevance came to be acknowledged critics grew uneasy at his tamperings. There seemed to be a danger that political events and social facts would supplant the hero's conventional sensitivities.

CHRONICLES OF CONSCIENCE

V. S. Pritchett, in an article on Arthur Koestler, described the function of the journalist in this way:

The digestive process of journalism is coarser than that of art, and we have lived through a period when coarse digestion became indispensable. The journalist has had the task of accommodating violence to the private stomach and of domesticating the religious, revolutionary and national wars in the private conscience. He has become the intermediary between our private and public selves and, in doing this office, has become a hybrid and representative figure, the vacillating and tortured Hamlet expressing our common disinclinations and our private guilt.[1]

The function of intermediary was clearly both vital and responsible. In almost every case, however, there was a third factor involved in the communication of public events to the private conscience: the beliefs that inspired and grew out of the bringing together of words and deeds. For most of these writers social consciousness grew into socialism. (The apologists of the right were many; those who interpreted specific details of reality in the light of right wing beliefs were few.) Many wrote in order to present socialist belief and the sources of this belief to as wide an audience as possible.

The strands of communication and creed are closely bound. It is hard to disentangle them and hard to establish precisely how one influenced the other. There are two writers who provide a useful focus of an investigation into the relationships between conscience and political fact, between language and political allegiance, between words and deeds: George Orwell, who owed his allegiance to no party and wrote entirely as his conscience dictated, and Arthur Koestler, a member of the Communist Party, who for a time was rigidly committed to propagandising Soviet Communism and afterwards suffered the effects of this commitment. Both these writers reflected and described the social atmosphere of their own times. They each represented a kind of experience that was more widely shared in the Europe of the 1930s than at any other time.

For most of the writers who felt compelled to act, action meant war. Between the outbreak of the First World War and the end of the Second there was hardly a pause for peace. There were four years of world war. In Russia the Revolution of 1917 heralded five years of civil war. In Germany the Spartacist Rebellion and the revolt in Bavaria, in reaction against a monstrous war and the hesitations of a pseudo-socialist government, followed the peace. In Hungary, Arthur Koestler's native country, the Bela Kun commune of 1919 collapsed amidst the confusion and violent rivalries of the central European countries. In 1927 and 1934 the workers of Vienna rose in revolt. Throughout the twenties and thirties China was being torn apart by revolution and civil war. In 1931 Japan invaded Manchuria. The thirties were punctuated by acts of violence—Mussolini's invasion of Abyssinia, the Spanish Civil War, Hitler's grabbing of Austria and Czechoslovakia. These were the large events. Against them was a background of growing violence and hysteria as totalitarian régimes came to rely increasingly on force to maintain their power : Hitler in Germany, Mussolini in Italy, Stalin in Russia.

Jean-Paul Sartre posed the problem of the writer who recognises his involvement with events but whose position as writer becomes almost a liability when having to confront reality. "The man of letters writes while others are fighting : one day he may be proud of the fact, feeling himself to be the recorder and guardian of values; the next day he may be ashamed, finding that literature resembles a kind of special affectation."[2] It is necessary to keep open the lines of communication, to have witnesses who will record and explain events, interpret and relate them. But in times of emergency language may seem to be irrelevant and action the only appropriate response. Sartre himself says that the writer must make words actions. He must give to language all the force and direction of physical achievement. He sees words as loaded pistols. "If the writer speaks, he fires. He may be silent, but since he has chosen to fire, he must do it like a man, by aiming at targets, and not like a child, at random, by shutting his eyes and firing merely for the pleasure of hearing the shot go off."[3]

The writer whose reaction to political events fashioned a political commitment often did not fully recognise his profound and difficult responsibility. Commitment logically demands propaganda; the committed writer must have a target. At the same time commitment should result from a reaction to fact, and a propagandist intention must not wipe out the original inspiration.

Both Orwell and Koestler were acutely aware of the pitfalls of propaganda. Both condemned propaganda. Both were propagandists. They were writers who found themselves, both literally and figuratively, with loaded pistols in their hands, and they felt compelled to pull the trigger. Orwell, in reaction against the decay of his own social class and the hollowness of its values, attacked apathy, insincerity and hypocrisy of every kind, and, initially in reaction against his experiences of imperialism in Burma, attacked social injustice. Koestler, confronted with the physical annihilation of his class, his family and his friends, attacked first the origin of that annihilation—Fascism; second the faith that betrayed him—Communism.

Conor Cruise O'Brien has written, about the present time, "This is an age of propaganda; all of us who work with words are awash with propaganda, our own and that of others, open and covert. One can hardly fail to have—unless one has ceased to be moved by any human cause—what J. B. Yeats called 'a touch of the propaganda fiend' in one's writing. And yet one also feels the need for an effort of decontamination, the elimination of the lies, not merely of one's political enemies but also of one's political friends and—a more difficult and longer term task—of one's own. One can come to feel that this effort of personal intellectual survival is a tiny part of the human effort of survival, in which intellectual integrity must remain an essential element."[4] Orwell and Koestler were, for the greater part of

their lives, striving for "personal intellectual survival". It is this
that distinguishes them from other writers who entered the
political arena. Their beliefs and their propaganda were, perhaps paradoxically, a genuine and necessary part of this effort.
At the same time as they sought personal decontamination they
argued for public decontamination. Propaganda infected the
1930s as it infects the present. Extreme events breed extreme
responses, and extremity by its very nature bred blinkered out-
looks of all kinds. Orwell challenged the contamination of propaganda with his own honest versions. Koestler purged his infection by an exact demonstration of how he caught the disease.

The initial reaction to extremity in this period was one of
baffled shock. The First World War leapt at the throat of a protected culture. Artists and writers were forced into a grim appreciation of their surroundings. A single sentence from a letter
written by Paul Nash recreates the scenery of war. "The rain
drives on, the stinking mud becomes more evilly yellow, the
shell holes fill up with green-white water, the roads and tracks
are covered in inches of slime, the black dying trees ooze and
sweat and the shells never cease."[5] Such was the background to
violent useless death. In the same letter Nash writes: "I am no
longer an artist, interested and curious, I am a messenger who
will bring back word from the men who are fighting to those
who want the war to go on for ever. Feeble, inarticulate, will be
my message, but it will have a bitter truth, and may it burn
their lousy souls."

There were few men who immediately took upon themselves
the role of messenger in this way. Exceptions were the poets
Siegfried Sassoon and Wilfred Owen, who wrote with a consciousness of message. The first attacked with vicious irony the
war, its hideous and unnecessary mistakes, and the bureaucrats
of war. The second wrote about innocent, useless and pitiful
death and about reluctant, uncomprehended killing. Poetry, or
rather the quality of these particular poets' sensitivity and
craftsmanship, could accommodate a rapid response. But on the
whole the reaction to the First World War was delayed.

There was little attempt to convert the facts of war into fiction. The war fiction that did emerge, such as H. G. Wells's *Mr Britling Sees It Through*, was generally placed at a distance from the trenches. R. H. Mottram's *The Spanish Farm Trilogy* was an exception. It deals with the effect of war on the people of Flanders and Northern France, and the bewildered, part-cynical, part-naïve, part-opportunist reactions of the soldiers. Ford Madox Ford in the four volumes of *Parades End* (*Some Do Not . . .*, *No More Parades*, *A Man Could Stand Up* and *The Last Post*) wrote of the War and its effects, but this was almost incidental to his theme. The symbolic value of Christopher Tietjens (perhaps one of twentieth-century fiction's first and most genuine anti-heroes) is enlarged but not differently emphasised by the encroachment of war on his life. Ford shows how the particular horror of modern war hastened the break-up of a group of traditions but makes it quite clear that the disintegration had begun long before.

Some Do Not . . . did not appear until ten years after the start of the War, and generally war experiences forced a more direct and more intense response than fiction could handle. The great number of autobiographical accounts also revealed a more gradual response. Most of these were not written and published until ten years or more after the end of the War. In these accounts the rendering of personal experience inevitably becomes a chronicle of events, and documentary reports become centred on personal experience. For the first time the literary intelligentsia had their noses forcibly rubbed in a grim reality. The result was an irresistible urge to present the facts, to come to grips with them, to try and make sense of them, and also to examine the private response to extreme danger and intense horror.

One of the first, and most extensive, of these documentaries was C. E. Montague's *Disenchantment* (1922), written in a tone of relentless truth-seeking with a touch of journalistic solemnity yet with an ironic sense of humour and a sure eye for the tiny ridiculous incident as well as the monstrous blunder. Montague was a journalist who volunteered at the age of forty-seven.

Younger men often wrote in a tone near to jauntiness, a kind of self-defence. Robert Graves, in *Goodbye to All That*, is egotistical; he did not allow the facts to dominate him. Although he details the horror of the trenches he makes it quite clear that his personality survived it. (Whether it was in fact undamaged is another question.) Sassoon, in *Memoirs of a Fox Hunting Man* and *Memoirs of an Infantry Officer*, is good-natured but profoundly sympathetic. His gentle, wry humour and enjoyment of small things are periodically blasted by spasms of blank anger and outraged futility. Guy Chapman's *A Passionate Prodigality* describes the process of war destroying the ability for any normal kind of life. When peace came the world he had been forced to accept disintegrated. "The whole of our world was crumbling. Presently we could not find a rugger fifteen; not even a soccer eleven. There were no drums to beat retreat. . . . Our civilisation was being torn to pieces before our eyes. England was said to be a country fit only for profiteers to live in. . . . Many of us were growing bitter. We had no longer the desire to go back. It was an island we did not know. . . . England had vanished over the horizon of the mind. I did not want to see it."[6] But there were also records whose tone was predominantly complacent—Ernest Parker's recently published (1964) *Into Battle 1914-18*, for instance. It was not, however, the quality of the reaction that was of such significance. It is the fact that never before had autobiographical documentary become so legitimate and common a means of reflecting the stresses of the times. Men became conscious of the value of witnessing and recording the events that contributed to the movement of history.

In German, too, the literary reaction was intense. The most famous German product of the War was Erich Maria Remarque's *All Quiet on the Western Front* (1922). There is a deliberate destruction of sensitivity in this novel, a dwelling on appalling facts and the cultivation of their acceptance. The hero has to be converted to the mores of war and the only way he can retain his humanity is by clinging to comradeship. And yet the continual conversion of man to horribly mutilated flesh threatens comradeship above all. The film, in spite of its harrowing battle-field shots, loses something of the book's impact, for the hero retains his fresh boyishness throughout, while the book demonstrates his deliberate attempts to destroy his youth. A very different book, whose implications are much wider, is Arnold Zweig's *The Case of Sergeant Grischa*. This is probably the best of a number of Zweig's novels in which the First World War features. It is an ironically controlled measurement of the chaos and inhumanity of war at a distance from the battlefield. The fact that Grischa, a Russian and an escaped prisoner of war, is surrounded by the indestructibility of a character from folk-lore and is yet destroyed quite straightforwardly by the bureaucratic machine is both simple and superbly complex. Grischa is totally insignificant in terms of war and profoundly symbolic. We recognise the irony of the immense time and trouble that is taken over the life and death of one man. The military authorities can kill or save a single man but have no control over the events of war. Not only does Zweig present a broad spectrum of the effects of war with much more confidence and understanding than other war novelists, he changes the focus on his characters with a controlled sympathy and sadness. We see them, general and prisoner alike, large and intimate in personal relations, feeble and insignificant against the war itself. As Grischa is led out first to dig his own grave in the frozen earth, then to be shot, he grows as a symbol but seems to shrink in size until, dead, he is something less yet more lasting, than the anonymous members of the firing squad.

Few other novels of the War had this steady, measured approach. Zweig makes sense of war because his pessimism accepts it as a dominant part of history and the character of humanity. He is not outraged, yet he has the power to stun his readers. In France Barbusse's *Le Feu* was a rapid, angered reaction similar to that of *All Quiet on the Western Front*. It was a reaction against the bumbling, hypocritical conductors of the War and the horrible ignorance of those at home as much as an indictment of modern war itself. His fighting men, threatened not only by virtually certain death but also by the thought that their living comrades will be confronted by the ghastly remnants, have a quality of humanity that Barbusse suggests is more real and more valid than that of both the actionless hypocrite and of anyone who has not known this particular experience.

The memoirs of the German writers Ludwig Renn, Ernst Toller and Gustav Regler describe not only the War itself but its aftermath and its longer lasting effects. There is a tumultuous and confused intensity in Renn's *War* (1929) and Toller's *I Was a German* (1934) which is more tormented than anything the English reminiscences produced. Regler's *The Owl of Minerva* (1959) gives the impression that the facts were almost too overwhelming for the author to handle. He was grappling with events that threatened to drown him. The tone of his response is closer to that of Wilfred Owen than that of Graves. He did not have the meticulous journalist's eye of C. E. Montague, but was concerned to establish the quality of his experience as much as the bare facts. For Renn, Toller and Regler the intensity of war was not relieved by peace. All three were involved in the Spartacist and Bavarian revolts. And this was just a prelude to their activity. The climate of violence persisted. It was the climate in which Arthur Koestler learnt his politics.

There is something more deliberate about the reaction of some American writers to the War. Some, like E. E. Cummings, participated in ambulance services or volunteered before the United States had entered the War. In *The Enormous Room* Cummings wrote about a situation that was an offshoot of war, and he condemned not war itself but bureaucratic confusions and middle-class fear. The Americans missed the stagnant trenches, and it is the trenches above all that dominate the European war literature. Hemingway was involved in the war in Italy, but his *Farewell to Arms* has a sense of action and excitement that the trenches of Northern France could not provide. Frederic Henry has time for love, for privacy, and it is this rather than his experience of battle and the random confusions of the retreat from Caporetto that urge his farewell to arms. The retreat makes the farewell easier, for it makes it impossible for him to return to his duties—he does not even know if his duties still exist. But the panic and confusion do not seem to dismay him greatly. He recognises his opportunity. Neither *The Enormous Room* nor *A Farewell to Arms* is war literature in the sense that so much of the European reaction is an obsession, a grappling with the facts of the War. For Cummings, and particularly Hemingway, the War was an experience among many, which they used for their own literary purposes. They do not face the War directly and try to make sense of it.

In Britain the full extent of disenchantment was felt when it became clear that the hell of the trenches was bringing no reward. Returning soldiers were dismayed as peacetime society settled down with all the old inequalities and injustices. Men like Guy Chapman saw no place for the demobbed soldier who had been ruthlessly taught to deal with conditions of war as part of everyday life. They had been rendered unfit for a normal existence, particularly an existence of grim inactivity. War had brought full employment and higher wages. Peace brought unemployment and wage reductions. Worse, it brought cynicism and lack of direction.

The switch to peacetime production was neither properly planned nor adequately guided. Eight years after the peace, eight years of disintegration which the frustration and high-spirits of the twenties could not gloss over, industrial troubles came to a head with the General Strike in May, 1926. This was a portent of the ineffectuality of the hunger marches and demonstrations of the thirties. For nine days the country was paralysed as the unions came out in support of the miners' fight against the repressions that the War had held at bay. But the Union leaders failed even to consolidate, let alone exploit, labour's strong position, and J. H. Thomas, for the TUC, accepted with relief and without authority conditions less favourable than before. Strike leaders were victimised, in spite of promises to the contrary; many lost their jobs. The failure of the Union leaders was seen as the blackest betrayal. The miners themselves stayed out until the following November, when they had to admit defeat, and returned to longer hours and lower wages.

The middle classes felt that they had come face to face with the workers, and won. But for some intellectuals the General Strike was a significant moment in their political development. A few worried undergraduates, while their fellows were driving trains for the Government, found themselves in sympathy with the strikers and offered their services at local strike headquarters. It was the beginning of action, and although the strike failed it provided a stimulus for some that lasted through the thirties. The depression that followed the Wall Street crash of 1929 intensified and encroached on the lives of the comfortable. In Britain in the early thirties the figures for unemployement had reached three million, and amongst those who found jobs hard to come by and salaries barely adequate were the bourgeois and the university educated. In Germany the eyes of the discontented turned towards the Nationalist Socialist Party. Britain's Labour Government of 1929-31 retreated from the problem of unemployment. It was a fact that could be stated, not dealt with. The National Government that followed, still with Labour's Ramsay MacDonald as Prime Minister, introduced the Means Test, which drastically reduced the unemployment benefit of most families.

Social conditions and political facts began to intrude on the consciousness of the generation that had missed the war. The literary intelligentsia responded enthusiastically to books such as John Strachey's *The Coming Struggle for Power*, published in 1932, which illustrated the inevitable decay of monopoly capitalism and presented the future in terms of a choice between Fascism and Communism. Strachey was presenting a creed and a means of action that many found attractive. Julian Symons writes: "Strachey's lucid blend of popular Marxism and humanism had the force of a vision."[7] A year after the publication of Strachey's book Michael Roberts edited a collection of verse and prose called *New Country*, specifically geared to relating literature to politics and social conditions. It featured the poetry of Auden, Day Lewis and Spender, and also contained short stories and sketches that used documentary material. Its import- ance was enthusiastically recognised.

New Country reinforced writers' growing interest in society. Throughout the decade critical works appeared discussing the relationship between literature and society: Ralph Fox's *The Novel and the People* (1937), Christopher Caudwell's *Illusion and Reality* (1937), David Daiches's *Literature and Society* (1938), Philip Henderson's *The Poet and Society* (1937). But it was one thing to develop a meaningful theory of relationships, another to translate such a theory into revolutionary poetry and fiction. Many insisted that not only was it a socialist novelist's duty to produce revolutionary fiction; good fiction *had* to be revolutionary—and that meant Marxist. In his essay "A Marxist Interpretation of Literature" Edward Upward wrote: "A writer today who wishes to produce the best work that he is capable of producing, must first of all become a socialist . . . must go over to the progressive side of the class conflict. Having become a socialist, however, he will not necessarily become a good writer. The quality of his writing will depend upon his individual talent, his ability to observe the complex detail of the real world. But unless he has in his everyday life taken the side of the workers, he cannot, no matter how talented he may be, write a good book, cannot tell the truth about reality."[8]

Sentiments such as these led to a number of self-conscious attempts to produce Marxist fiction. They also encouraged the tendency to by-pass fiction altogether. The plain presentation of what were considered significant details of working-class life— a presentation that was often dull and shapeless—became an increasingly common mode of literary expression. This develop- ment of straightforward documentary reporting was further stimulated by the growing number of periodicals prepared, and eager, to publish short documentary sketches. *Left Review*, the *Adelphi*, *Tribune* were all born in the thirties and all published documentary material. They made fumbling attempts to make contact with 'proletarian' writers—miners, railwaymen, dockers—who produced plain, painstaking statements of fact. The editors were trying to hoist industrial workers into the world of the intellectuals, and their distant infatuation with the proletariat prevented them from applying either standards or understanding that might have been helpful to writer and reader alike.

Documentary found a more extensive outlet in John Lehmann's *New Writing* and in the Left Book Club. Both were initiated in 1936, a year which saw also the Jarrow hunger march, Fascist mob violence in the East End and the outbreak of civil war in Spain. Victor Gollancz was the originator and financial pillar of the Left Book Club. He conceived it as a means of left-wing propaganda (in fact the majority of his writers were Marxists, many Communists) and of uniting all shades of left and liberal opinion. It seemed to answer a need, for within six months there were 20,000 members, and by April 1939 57,000. It published commentaries, theoretical work, historical analyses and a large quantity of documentary material. Much of this was of a very different nature from the short proletarian sketch. Many of the books were written by left-wing gentleman adventurers who threw themselves into political situations abroad where greater intensity of action yielded dramatic detail that could not be found in the depressing and stagnant situation in Britain. Ellen Wilkinson's *The Town that was Murdered* (1939), an account of the depression in Jarrow, and Orwell's own *The Road to Wigan Pier* (1937) were two of the few Left Book Club documentaries inspired by conditions in Britain.

Germany and central Europe, Russia, China and Japan were the chief sources of material. One of the most distinguished of all the Left Book Club publications, Edgar Snow's *Red Star Over China* (1939), was a first-hand account of Mao Tse Tung's revolution. For the most part these books were undisguisedly autobiographical. The writer himself played an important role in them. He was an actor in events of historical importance and he interpreted his position through his writing. He was often the hero of his own documentary: Koestler himself deliberately wrote documentary as autobiography. His *Scum of the Earth* (1941) in which he described the early days of the Second World War in France and his detention in a camp for suspect aliens, was a Left Book Club publication.

Koestler calls the sections of this book "Agony", "Purgatory", "Apocalpyse" and "Aftermath". These titles indicate the kind of enlargement of frames of reference towards which Koestler in particular, with his self-dramatising description of events, tended. He writes with a consciousness of experience, and with a realisation that what he is describing is foreign to the experience of his readers. The people he describes in *Scum of the Earth* become almost an enlargment of his own personality; they are so much a part of his style of writing. But Koestler's writing occupied a special place amongst the documentation of politics: he was a Continental, he had come face to face with a climate of political activity that was only seen, sometimes envied, at a distance by Britons. His experiences had given him what seemed to be a challenging self-confidence, while the British intellectual left, though ready to state unhesitatingly the necessary doctrines, was confused by its anomalous class position and puzzled by the possibilities of action.

Documentary could become the adventurer's celebration of himself. George Orwell was a notable exception. Also, genuinely proletarian documentary usually avoided any kind of expression that smacked of egotistical rhetoric. *New Writing* was the chief sponsor of such writing. The project was originated by John Lehmann, with the help of Christopher Isherwood and Ralph Fox. It began as a bi-annual hard-back collection of verse, short stories and sketches, but with the start of the war it became first a monthly then a quarterly paperback. It published careful documentations, some of them by industrial workers, and, during the war, accounts of life in the Forces, air raids and civilian war conditions.

Lehmann himself says: "The aim of this kind of story was to arouse pity and indignation; and yet owing to a certain flatness and too monotonous an insistence on dejection and misery the examples that had come my way all too often failed to arouse any reaction except boredom. Not always; I had, I believed, made some real discoveries of writing talent whose natural material was working-class life, but the limitations of the genre had become gradually more obvious to me. . . ."[9] One of these discoveries was certainly B. L. Coombes, son of a Herefordshire farmer who had spent most of his working life in the Welsh mines. There was quiet confidence in his prose, a steady observation of detail, both in his short stories and in his autobiographical *These Poor Hands*, published by the LBC in 1939. *These Poor Hands* begins like this:

> I was fascinated by that light in the sky. Night after night I watched it reddening the shadows beyond the Brecknock Beacons, sometimes fading until it only showed faintly, then brightening until it seemed that all the country was ablaze.
>
> The winter wind that rushed across the Herefordshire fields where the swedes rotted in heaps, and carried that smell of decay into the small farmhouse which was my home, seemed to encourage the burning, until the night sky would redden still more. Sometimes I felt sure that I could see those flames and feel their warmth, but it could only have been fancy, for they were more than sixty miles away from us.[10]

Coombes places his life as farmer's son and miner in a context not only of the physical details of labour, but of cultural climate and aspiration. He brings together the details of his picture with an illuminating association—the red sky, the smell, the farm, his own longing become a part of one another. His imagination is not confined by material surroundings, for he is trying to present the quality of life. He tries, with some success, to stand half way between an audience beyond his working experience and friends remote from his writing experience. He avoids exploiting the natural drama of the work he describes, and the result is not flatness but an impressive frankness. He describes the distant glow of the South Wales' coalfields plainly, unpretentiously, yet

with a sense of their power and their strangeness. This is characteristic of his writing.

Coombes was an exception. Most of the sketches published in
New Writing, even those describing wartime conditions where
one might expect some excitement, were undistinguished and
dull. Orwell's pieces "Marrakech" and "Shooting an Elephant"
had a refreshing vitality. Behind this surge of documentation
there was clearly a propagandist intention. It was not, as it
seemed to be in the First World War, the facts themselves which
compelled expression so much as a political understanding of
social injustice. As Lehmann says, it was intended to "arouse
pity and indignation", and thus move to action. But the effects
seem to have been minimal. This kind of documentary could do
little more than satisfy the curiosity of the converted.

However, the short sketch and the first-hand report were not
the only forms that the setting down of social facts took. There
were a few novels by proletarian writers that drew on experiences of unemployment, prison, the criminal world, but these
were generally insignificant in number and in quality. Documentary material was more pointedly and more successfully
used by novelists moved by social conscience and political allegiance to dramatise the conditions of life which they observed.
Most of these writers shared the public school and university
background of so many of the spokesmen of the left.

These ranged from the novels of J. B. Priestley, based on a
lower middle-class environment and interweaving a drab hopelessness with cheerful homeliness, to the political allegories of
Rex Warner, directly influenced by Kafka. Priestley's fiction was
rooted in social reality, but he was not calling for reform so
specifically as for understanding. His manufacturing of drama
out of colourless and apathetic surroundings only served to
highlight the dull and deprived lives of most of his characters. A
preoccupation with the misery of certain kinds of life did not
seem to provide the energy necessary for revolutionary fiction,
or even for the radical and politically stimulating fiction of the
kind that was being written in the USA. During the decade John

Dos Passos produced the three volumes of his trilogy *U.S.A.* in which he tried to present the pre-war unrest and the post-war uncertainties of a wide spectrum of American society. The narrative is patterned with news reports and brief sketches of the careers of significant figures of the time. The result is an energetic, tense, kaleidoscopic criticism. John Steinbeck's *The Grapes of Wrath* (1939) was one of a number of books that focused attention on devastating social ills with some effect. The decade also saw the publication of James T. Farrell's three "Studs Lonigan" novels which give a violent picture of the malignant city of Chicago, where there is no space for decent feelings to breathe although they still somehow manage to survive. In Britain there was no work of socially conscious fiction which could compare with these ambitious and detailed pictures of society.

A considerable number of politically conscious novelists were trapped by the involutions of the middle-class consciousness faced with a threat to its security. There was a preoccupation with childhood and schooldays, memories of prep school horror and of scented, silk-clad mothers bending over small boys to kiss them goodnight. Few wrote with any real knowledge or understanding of industrial conditions. George Blake was one of these few, but even he reveals traces of sentimentality (although there is plenty of grim though warm realism). In *The Shipbuilders* he describes the Clyde-side shipyards with a non-partisan sympathy and an intimate knowledge. Perhaps the only genuinely revolutionary novel produced in the decade was Lewis Grassic Gibbon's *The Scots Quair*, although the political message, in spite of its inevitability, is qualified by the character of the heroine, who has been through such a variety of experience that she does not know on what to base her trust. In the three volumes that make up *The Scots Quair*, political activity, class exploitation and fierce commitment are directly related to the ordinary lives of ordinary people. The book has a powerful, basic rhythm—the sentences themselves have the rhythm of verse—that hammers in the conflicts of dreariness and catastrophe, of upper-class defence, middle-class nerves, and working-class defiance.

But again it was the situation in Europe that provided the most effective stimulus. Ralph Bates in Spain and Christopher Isherwood in Berlin used their observation of a particular European locality to furnish material for fiction. Isherwood evolved the happiest blend of fact and fiction. His stories of Berlin, in which he does not disguise his reportage and yet does not veer away from the telling of his story, were sharpened in focus and strengthened in substance by the author's political sympathies. Isherwood's stories are amongst the most successful products of the documentary habit of mind, but they were most definitely the products of an English response to Europe.

European writers were producing a very different kind of political novel. André Malraux wrote about the loneliness and torment of the intellectual plunged in the midst of violent action, in Spain or in China, forced to respond in a way that is both alien and exhilarating. At every point his heroes are trying to relate their minds to their actions, their motives to their minds, and their actions to political endeavour. If Malraux's characters are in their way as trapped as the Oxbridge products, there is a challenge to action in his novels which brought a welcome force to political writing.

Ignazio Silone wrote with a closer concern for ordinary humanity. With lucid simplicity he portrayed the life of Central Italy and gave politics a more intimate character. He showed the encroachment of machine-like Fascism, of life and death political conflict, on communities that were simple, crude, often petty but always solid, and weak through lack of knowledge, of contact and of solidarity. Revolution in terms of a village riddled with poverty meant something very specific, something very different in climate though perhaps not in kind from Malraux's volunteer revolutionaries. Silone never translated politics into watchwords, never lost sight of the individuals, the families and the communities that did the suffering, the thinking and the acting.

In England there were few such violent extremes to inject writers with a sense of urgency. But one event that did provoke an urgent response was the Spanish Civil War. Both Orwell and Koestler were in Spain at the time: Orwell fought, Koestler reported and propagandised. The Civil War excited the imaginations and consciences of a large section of the left wing in Britain. Even so inactive a supporter as Cyril Connolly wrote, in a description of revolutionary Barcelona: "The pervading sense of freedom, of intelligence, justice and companionship, the enormous upthrust in backward and penniless people of the desire of liberty and education, are things that have to be seen to be understood. It is as if the masses, the mob in fact, credited usually only with instincts of stupidity and persecution, should blossom into what is really a kind of flowering of humanity."[11]

But the total number of volunteers from Britain in the International Brigades was only about two thousand (and most of this number was working-class) although others joined ambulance and propaganda units. There were about 40,000 foreign volunteers altogether in the Brigades. Of the two thousand British over five hundred were killed and twelve hundred wounded. Spain brought together, suddenly and dramatically, the political experience of the working-class socialists and trade-unionists and the left-wing intellectuals. It also led the British socialists on to a European battlefield and thus for a brief time unified the socialist struggle while it introduced the British left to rifle fire. For the first time British socialists found themselves in a climate of violence, in the centre of the European arena.

What meeting place was there between poets like John Cornford and Julian Bell, scientists like Lorrimer Birch, writers like Hugh Slater, and miners from Durham, cotton workers from Lancashire? War melts away the barriers between classes, and also creates shared interests, bonds of knowledge and affection. Spain gave, then, a comradeship of class with class; but it gave more than this. For a few months at the start of the

Civil War, Spain seemed the image of a new world. For those who lived in Britain, what did "political activity" mean? Picketing a Fascist meeting, selling papers in the street, arguing at the local Left Book Club discussion group. To be transferred suddenly from this atmosphere to a country where political movements were taken with the deepest seriousness, where individual actions and beliefs no longer appeared trivialities beside the vast monolith of capitalist society, seemed like the realisation of a dream.[12]

Many, like John Cornford and Julian Bell, had longed for an opportunity for action and embraced it, even though with private doubts and miseries. The subsequent betrayal was all the more bitter for those who survived, and for those who did not owe absolute allegiance to the Communist Party. The Communists were soon in control of the government in Spain and took steps to eliminate their rivals and suspend the progress of the revolution until the war was won. Barcelona slipped back into the old ways. Rivals on the Republican side turned their rifles on each other. By May 1937 the Communists had demonstrated the strength of their control by getting rid of as many Trotskyists and Anarchists as they could lay hands on. Many were secretly disposed of. A few, like Orwell, were lucky enough to escape. Power became more important than winning the war.

By this time the first Moscow Trials had begun, and they directly influenced events in Spain. Stalin was more concerned with liquidating deviationists than with fighting Fascism. Help for the Spanish Republicans became an economic enterprise: all arms were handsomely paid for. Meanwhile troops, planes and arms came to Franco's aid from Germany and Italy. Britain and France remained strictly non-interventionist. Survivors of the war returned to Britain bitter at defeat, bitter at betrayal, and fearful at the signs of the efficiency and power of the Fascist war machine.

From Spanish experiences came a flood of documentary accounts. At last the chronicling instinct had some action to report. Propaganda has its natural origins in experience. While the participators described events, pessimistic with the experience of war and defeat and their witnessing of the sufferings of the Spanish people, many of those who stayed at home were provoked to condemn non-intervention policy and the air of aloofness with which British politicians refused to see that the war in Spain was the curtain-raiser to a full-scale European war. Left-wing propaganda had a vivid focal point.

Spain was quickly recognised as a symbol of socialist endeavour between the Wars, and was celebrated as such. The elimination of a promising section of the younger generation (our whole attitude to the culture of the thirties might have been different if more of those who had taken to action as well as to art had survived) had its parallel in the First World War. When, with the outbreak of the Second, it was asked where the poets were, it could have been answered that those who would not have shrunk from coming to grips with the conflict with Hitler were dead in Spain. But the Spanish experience marked the beginning of the end of an idealistic decade, not the first days of a social consciousness.

Spain did not, however, provide a stimulus for British fiction writers. The famous novels of Spain were André Malraux's *L'Espoir*, Ernest Hemingway's *For Whom the Bell Tolls* and Gustav Regler's *The Great Crusade*. Political and propagandist activity in the brief respite before the outbreak of world war slumped. Reportage and documentary on Britain were more adequately dealt with by Mass-Observation, founded in February 1937, than by amateur left wingers. This organisation, under the direction of Tom Harrisson, enlisted professional and voluntary observers to report on the activities, habits, likes and dislikes of the British people. In effect, it provided grist for the propagandist mill, for it poured out details, many trivial, some of central importance, of the conditions of life of the various sections of the population. Their reports were described as "social documents of real importance now and in the future" and it was felt that they encroached on the proper realm of fiction. "Is the realistic novelist to be taught to find his material not in life but in Mass-Observation?" asked Dilys Powell. William Plomer described the reports as "the raw materials of fiction".[13] There was certainly a widespread feeling that much of the substance of Mass-Observation reports were the ingredients of fiction: by the beginning of the war documentary reporting had become a widespread literary habit.

The Munich crisis of 1938, the Hitler–Stalin pact of 1939, shook the committed severely. When Britain finally declared war there was a deep sense of relief. The suspense was over. The issues suddenly became straightforward and there was renewed hope amongst the left. There was a general feeling that the war would necessitate radical social change. But by 1942 hope had dwindled again.

Those who saw active service were not inspired as Spain had inspired the defenders of the revolution. Evelyn Waugh's Guy Crouchback volunteers out of a sense of patriotic duty and eagerness for military experience, but finds that feelings such as these are irrelevant and misplaced. There is no sense either of defending one's country nor of confronting an enemy. Instead of the gallant cockney gritting his teeth through the Battle of Britain Waugh shows us the bewildered upper middle class admiring the pretty colours in the sky. Yet the war did provide new material for documentary, and a steady stream was published in, for instance, New Writing. The distinction between fiction and reportage was blurred. Snippets of personal experiences had the gloss of fiction, short stories the casualness of reality. But documentary no longer had a propagandising impulse behind it. It became part of an effort to make sense of the War not in terms of political creed but of the individual's identity. At the same time, as Orwell saw, the threat of totalitarianism grew even as Hitler was being defeated. A dominant feeling was that expressed by Keith Douglas: "To trust anyone or to admit to any hope of a better world is as criminally foolish as it is to stop working for it."[14] Acceptance was impossible but to put too much faith in the future was fatal.

It was much the same feeling that conditioned the responses of Orwell and Koestler at the end of the War. Koestler had been through the rigours of the Communist Party. He had been a Communist at a time and in a country when Communism really did seem to be the only alternative to Fascism. He had witnessed the disastrous collapse of the German Communist Party which heralded Hitler's success. Both he and Orwell had shared the left's optimism at the beginning of the War. They were both profoundly disappointed. When peace came Koestler took up the position of alert observer of events, trained to recognise opportunities for genuine progress. He did not reject his past mode of life but celebrated it as representative of his times. Orwell's position closely followed the stance he had taken during the War. He singled out totalitarianism as the chief enemy of democracy and attacked it. While Koestler offered himself as a representative example of a European middle-class intellectual Orwell remained solitary and unique. As the country was sliding towards the affluent fifties his writing was at its bitterest and most drastic.

2

FROM PARIS TO WIGAN

In 1947 Orwell wrote: "Every line of serious work that I have written since 1936 has been written, directly or indirectly, *against* totalitarianism and *for* democratic socialism."[1] Before 1936 the easier world situation and Orwell's own experience guided him along less specific lines. He had been born in India, where his father was a civil servant, in 1903. He was a scholarship boy through prep school and Eton, from where he went, curiously, straight out to Burma to join the Indian Imperial Police Force. His motives for doing this have never been made clear. In 1928 he left the Force, and spent two years with no prospects, no money and few contacts struggling to write in Paris. He continued the struggle in England, working as a teacher, in a bookshop and at a number of other jobs as he went through the long and painful process of establishing himself as a writer.

Orwell's service in Burma provided an intimate knowledge of the details of imperialism, and this was to have a profound influence on the direction his interests took. His time in Paris gave him the chance of quite a different kind of experience: he was at the receiving end of oppression. It is in *The Road to Wigan Pier* that Orwell gives his own explanation of this period in his life:

> I was conscious of an immense weight of guilt that I had got to expiate. . . . I had reduced everything to the simple theory that the oppressed are always right and the oppressors always wrong: a mistaken theory, but the natural result of being one of the oppressors yourself. I felt I had got to escape not only

from imperialism but from every form of man's dominion over man. I wanted to submerge myself, to get right down among the oppressed, to be one of them and on their side against the tyrants.[2]

Although Orwell wrote this in 1936 as if the impulse was no longer dominant, it remained of prime importance throughout his career and can be detected at every point. It was the beginning of his political consciousness. The impetus which transformed this consciousness into commitment was the urge to put thought into practice, joined with a compulsive curiosity. A phrase in this passage gives an important clue to Orwell's personality and approach. He talks of "the natural result of being one of the oppressors yourself" as if it were a reaction that everyone who had had this experience would ordinarily have. Of course, this was not true, and Orwell knew it was not true. He wrote in this way to make clear his own position, his own response to experience, and to suggest that it was a response that any average decent man would have.

Orwell's curiosity applied not only to an examination of his own motives at every stage in his life but to every aspect of the world in which he lived. It seems to have been curiosity, as much as anything, that drew him into uncomplaining acceptance of the poverty that he came to. There were elements of necessity, of chance and of perversity, but above all he wanted to learn about the lives of the people he observed, and wanted to confirm the truth of his observation by direct experience. Again in *Wigan Pier* he says:

What I profoundly wanted, at that time, was to find some way of getting out of the respectable world altogether. I meditated upon it a great deal, I even planned parts of it in detail; how one could sell everything, give everything away, change one's name and start out with no money and nothing but the clothes one stood up in. But in real life nobody does that kind of thing; apart from the relatives and friends who have to be considered, it is doubtful whether an educated man *could* do it if there were any other course open to him. But at least I could go among these people, see what their lives were like and feel myself temporarily part of their world. Once I had been among them and accepted by them, I should have touched bottom, and—this is what I felt: I was aware even then that it was irrational—part of my guilt would drop from me.[3]

This passage reveals and partly explains that mixture of self-effacement and self-enlightenment that is characteristic of much of Orwell's writing. He wanted to use experience simultaneously in a public and deeply private way. But the private impulse does not mar the tone of his writing—although personal obsessions sometimes do. He writes consistently as an observer. His efforts to preserve a balanced detachment often lead to a curious elimination of his personality. It is powerfully present in his writing; at the same time it is the nature of the experience itself, and its lessons, that interest Orwell. His own involvement as an individual is not important for its own sake, but as a means of enquiry and illumination.

Down and Out in Paris and London appeared in 1933 and was Orwell's first published writing except for one or two articles and reviews in the *Adelphi* and the *New Statesman*. He offered it as a record of experience, organised rather than fictionalised, and as a demonstration of how to destroy prejudice. This was all of a specifically social purpose that he saw in the book—it arose naturally from the facts he described. There is no gulf between fact, observation and message. Even at this early stage Orwell was able to eliminate the kind of loophole that allowed readers to disbelieve. No secondary or irrelevant interest interferes with the lucid presentation of detail, and the sustained tone of combined intellectual concern, emotional sympathy and unbiased detachment drives his words cleanly.

The first part of *Down and Out* is about Orwell's poverty, his jobs, the people he worked and lived with, in Paris. The second part describes his experiences as a tramp when he returned penniless to England and reluctant to apply to friends for help. *Down and Out* is perhaps the least passionate of Orwell's books. He was sure only of the facts he witnessed, not of their very wide implications. The tone is softer, uncomplicated by the paradoxes of solid political commitment. Although in the second half he manages to combine, almost unintentionally, a straightforward personal account with a detailed sociological investigation into the circumstances under which tramps and vagrants lived, he appeals to the warmth of common sense rather than the coldness of theory. Later he was to discover that a specifically socialist commitment involved him in tangled strands of allegiance and betrayal that he found exasperating, dishonest and tragically destructive. Here his social outlook is unclouded and attractively simple, although his view of human nature is acute and not optimistic, and later he was very reluctant to have to give up much of his socialism of simple alternatives.

It takes Orwell a single page to give the essence of "a representative Paris slum". Noise and smells predominate. Quarrels, fights and drunkenness were what gave colour to an otherwise drab level of life. Orwell makes us feel that anger and disgust are the only responses that it is worth making the effort to express, and so their expression becomes a daily necessity, taken for granted. Just because life is so confined, the details dull and unvaried, after the necessities of food, drink and sleep, little is worth noticing. And as the noise and filth increase the area of interest shrinks.

Orwell describes his hotel room:

The walls were as thin as matchwood, and to hide the cracks they were covered with layer after layer of pink paper, which had come loose and housed innumerable bugs. Near the ceiling long lines of bugs marched all day like columns of soldiers, and at night came down ravenously hungry, so that one had to get up every few hours and kill them in hecatombs. Sometimes when the bugs got too bad one used to burn

B

> sulphur and drive them into the next room; whereupon the
> lodger next door would retort by having *his* room sulphured,
> and drive the bugs back. It was a dirty place, but homelike, for
> Madame F. and her husband were good sorts. The rent of the
> room varied between thirty and fifty francs a week.[4]

Orwell deliberately avoids drawing attention to himself. He does
not intrude. He becomes "one", a generalised being whom he is
regarding along with the other details, a useful vehicle for describing how one tries to get rid of bugs. It is personal experience viewed with scrupulous detachment. The result of this
detachment is that when Orwell comes to make a subjective
statement we accept it without thought. We accept the statement that the hotel was "homelike" and Madame F. a "good
sort" in spite of what our own reactions might have been, as we
accept the fact that the rent "varied between thirty and fifty
francs a week". This is the most important achievement of the
documentary writer—to prevent his readers from accepting
some facts (those they wish to accept) while questioning others
(those it is convenient not to believe in). Orwell does this by not
emphasising the particularly shocking or the particularly unusual any more than he emphasises the trivial or the question-
able. Here it is not of fundamental importance in itself whether
the hotel was indeed "homelike", but the fact that Orwell does
not allow us to disbelieve it is at the very basis of his success as a
documentary writer.

Orwell shows how demoralising poverty is, and how subjectively damaging. It shrinks a man to "only a belly with a few
accessory organs" and the more limited the means of existence
the less able a man becomes to resist or fight against circumstances. This has two effects. It deprives one of the necessity of
being responsible, of paying attention to anything apart from
the avoidance of starvation, and it cuts one off from that vast
area of worry and concern that is a part of daily life, leaving
one with the single problem of pretending to have money when
one has none. This situation can be comforting:

You discover boredom and mean complications and the beginnings of hunger, but you also discover the great redeeming
feature of poverty : the fact that it annihilates the future.
Within certain limits it is actually true that the less money
you have, the less you worry. When you have a hundred
francs in the world you are liable to the most craven panics.
When you have only three francs you are quite indifferent;
for three francs will feed you till tomorrow, and you cannot
think further than that. You are bored, but you are not
afraid.[5]

Tramps are men in a permanent state of boredom and fear-
lessness. The tramp's predominant interest is the fact (not the
process) of getting from one spike to the next. Orwell says of
himself : "It is a feeling of relief, almost of pleasure, at knowing
yourself at last genuinely down and out." One feels that this
same sensation is experienced by many of the unemployed who
drift into confirmed tramping. (The impression is reinforced by
Philip O'Connor's *Vagrancy*.) They no longer have to pretend
that they want to be employed, that they relish the responsibility of looking after a wife and family. O'Connor says, "It is
by *not* seeing the world that the tramp is at home in it".[6] Relief
is experienced because it is no longer necessary to pay any
attention to the world.

Orwell is deliberately unromantic and unsophisticated in his
descriptions of tramping. (O'Connor mars his thesis by being
both romantic and sophisticated and sees the tramp as an almost
Christ-like figure.) There is nothing to disturb the coherence of
prose and fact; the style and method arise from Orwell's approach. His relaxed, flexible yet balanced prose allows him to
accommodate the constantly shifting points of interest. He
moves from generalised description of his own experiences to
detailed observation of a companion on the roads to moral and
social judgment. He describes Paddy, who, although he "had the
regular character of a tramp—abject, envious, a jackal's character" was "a good fellow, generous by nature and capable of shar-

ing his last crust with a friend; indeed he did literally share his last crust with me more than once. He was probably capable of work too, if he had been well fed for a few months. But two years of bread and margarine had lowered his standards hopelessly. He had lived on this filthy imitation of food till his own mind and body were compounded of inferior stuff. It was malnutrition and not any native vice that had destroyed his manhood."[7]

The prose has a confidence that is the result partly of sureness of observation, partly of the precision of every word. If Orwell uses a well-worn phrase, such as "sharing his last crust", he uses it literally, and does not allow it to become a means of short-circuiting communication. Here Orwell reveals significantly his attitude to many of the people with whom he came into contact. It is an attitude of combined sympathy and disgust. He cannot pretend that he likes Paddy, although he appreciates his personality, yet the more he experiences of the details of Paddy's life the greater is the warmth—it is warmth and understanding rather than pity—he feels for him. This attitude contributes to the quality of Orwell's prose, to the subjective detachment and the human commitment, to the vigorous yet unromantic way in which he uses ordinary words. This inevitably gives a profoundly moral tone to his work, and makes us want to use the word "honest" to describe his writing. The moral tone and purpose, and in this case the social purpose, is as clear as the prose itself. Orwell wrote with a combined sense of the self-evidence of what he was describing and of the likelihood that his readers would be only too ready to disbelieve it. The reviewers of *Down and Out* regarded it as an interesting book about a member of the middle classes behaving oddly rather than as an important social document.

An author Orwell much admired was Jack London, who, in a far more conscious and deliberate way than Orwell, decided to get to know London's East End at the turn of the century. At this time London already had a reputation as a writer, but this was his first planned muckraking assignment, and one of the first of what was to become a significant genre of radical writing

in the United States. In 1902 London acquired a disguise and
passed himself off as a native East Ender. He wrote, in a letter to
his friends George and Carrie Sterling: "I've read of misery and
seen a bit; but this beats anything I could even have imagined.
Actually, I have seen things and looked the second time in order
to convince myself that it was really so. This I know, the stuff
I'm turning out will have to be expurgated or it will never see
magazine publication. . . . I think I should die if I had to live
two years in the East End of London."[8] This is an emotional and
dramatic response to social horror. The facts London describes
are in themselves no worse than those Orwell handles thirty
years later, but Orwell's literary phrasing of them is far different. His tone is subdued, underplayed, straightforward. In *The
People of the Abyss* (1903), London's chronicle of the East End,
he is impressionistic, almost melodramatic. He does not attempt
to disguise his own subjective involvement:

> . . . as far as I could see were the solid walls of brick, the
> slimy pavements, and the screaming streets; and for the first
> time in my life the fear of the crowd smote me. It was like the
> fear of the sea; and the miserable multitudes, street upon
> street, seemed so many waves of a vast malodorous sea, lap-
> ping about me and threatening to well up and over me.[9]

London could be precise and detailed, but here he writes in
generalities. We are given an impressionistic picture composed
of plurals—"walls", "streets", "multitudes", not "the street",
"these particular people". Never would Orwell use such a phrase
as "miserable multitudes" where the very fact of the allitera-
tion and the unspecified misery produces a blurred picture rather
than a clear focus. Orwell would not rely on the largeness of
metaphor to convey the power of an impression. Here, London's
response is dispersed by "it was like" and "seemed", introduc-
tions to simile. His comparisons are so striking in themselves
that we forget for a moment that London is describing the experience of walking through the crowds of ill-clad, filthy, starv-

ing slum-dwellers. London's imagination has taken him right away from its initial impulse. Orwell never allowed his imagination to function in this way, an asset in his documentary writing, though perhaps a liability in his fiction.

Orwell was concerned to produce a reaction in his readers rather than to describe a reaction in himself. London was after the same thing but in a less direct way. He approached his readers through his own subjective response, and acknowledged, and made no attempt to eliminate, the gulf between himself and the people he described. "That's all they are—beasts . . . beasts, shot through with flashes of divinity",[10] he wrote, before he had encountered the London slums. There is romanticism and superiority in that phrase, both qualities that Orwell tried to destroy. There is no such extravagance in his painstaking attempts to come to terms with strange modes of existence, and although there is, inevitably, self-consciousness, it is very different from Jack London's. It is a self-deprecating, self-eliminating self-consciousness.

Yet Orwell found the down-and-out's London of the 1930s shockingly similar to that of 1902. Many of the facts of existence were the same. Orwell and London saw much the same destruction of human potential, much the same attitudes amongst the very poor. The material conditions had barely improved and the scope of life was just as limited. The photographs in the first edition of The People of the Abyss and those in Orwell's next documentary, The Road to Wigan Pier, are disturbingly similar. The clothes, the expressions, the stances, as well as the details of living, bear a horrifying resemblance. The thirty years had made very little difference.

In Down and Out Orwell uses no devices. When it is necessary he explains what he is doing without artifice. Because of this there is a minimum of substance between experience and language. Jack London's similes create layers of extraneous matter between the facts and his readers. Orwell's carefully employed prosaic vocabulary eliminates interference. His balanced and colloquial sentences grow out of his common sense and his attempt to identify with a happy, decent medium. London appealed to his readers' instinct for drama, Orwell to their sense of decency. He does not have to add a message to his descriptions; the message is present in the language itself. At the end of *Down and Out* he gives us a brief, matter-of-fact chapter consolidating his material and offering some suggestions as to what could be done to help vagrants. He moves out of his role of observer with no change of tone. Far from our being disturbed by his blunt "I want to set down some general remarks about tramps" it adds force to what he has to say, for he has already established his credibility.

Honesty of presentation was for Orwell the fusion of an acute and unprejudiced eye with a language that was simple and exact and with only natural decoration. He was no puritan in the sense that he was against the decorative and elaborate, but he deplored the forcing of elaboration into spaces too small for it, and any kind of confusing, irrelevant artificiality. He had a deep suspicion of any form of expression that disguised facts rather than illuminating them. Later he was to discuss at some length the relationship between language, honesty of purpose and political commitment. At this stage the morality of his writing is almost instinctive. It seems to belong to the facts themselves as much as to his own response. In a discussion of Orwell's honesty Richard Hoggart says: "We also mean by Orwell's 'honesty' his training himself to get rid as far as possible of the expected, the social-class, response. . . . He tests on himself, bites on his teeth, the kind of socially conventional coinage which most of us merely accept: he tests it by talking flat out about the smell of working-class people or about assumed differences in status and the misery they cause."[11]

Orwell certainly did train himself. Being down-and-out was the first step. Part of this shedding of conventional response was that the honesty did not get lost in transit, somewhere between the initial purpose and the final expression. In Orwell's case the quality is held in the quality of his language. He rid himself of phoney and facile vocabulary at the same time as he avoided conventionality. But in *Wigar Pier* this process becomes a little strained, a little over-deliberate, so that the balance between honesty and conviction is disturbed. The intention to be honest interferes with the honesty itself, and deflects the reader's attention from fact to tone of voice. In *Down and Out* the intention is more relaxed; in *Homage to Catalonia* it is more finely handled.

Orwell had made a deliberate step out of the middle class into the no man's land of strays and vagrants where the traditions were bred of necessity and the habits of hopelessness. But he was not able to shake off the fog of decaying middle-class values that clung round him. He wrote three novels in quick succession which worried at the problems of the rebellious member of the middle classes, trying to disentangle himself from what had become empty standards and sordid snobberies. Yet he himself rejected the modes of escape that his heroes attempted. He felt that both escape and attack were necessary. To step deliberately into working-class life provided opportunities for both. The aspects of working-class life that attracted him were part of a nostalgia for the Britain of before the First War, memories of a simple and comfortable life without the necessity, or the wish, for ill-constructed artificiality. In spite of the grim facts of *The People of the Abyss* the picture he had in his mind of the contented working-class family sitting around a roaring fire was not entirely fictional. We get glimpses of it—admittedly they are not frequent—in some of the autobiographical works of the period, for instance in Jennie Lee's *This Great Journey*, in which she describes life in a Fife mining village. But the relative prosperity of the period during and just after the First World War, the time that Jennie Lee describes, did not last long. The years of growing unrest and the General Strike were the years of Orwell's absence from England. His urge for an experience of oppression coincided with the aftermath of the 1926 betrayal and the increase of widespread unemployment.

When, in 1936, Orwell was contracted by Victor Gollancz to carry out a survey of conditions amongst the unemployed in the North of England for the Left Book Club, it was consistent with

Orwell's previous experiments that he should go straight to the homes of the worst stricken families in the worst stricken areas. He was much criticised for not giving a balanced picture, but now his purpose was uncompromisingly propagandist. He came to know some shocking facts and meant to shock the public with them.

The first part of *The Road to Wigan Pier* (1937), the book that resulted from his investigations, maintains the even tone of *Down and Out*. There is vitality but not emotionalism in the prose, precision but not dullness in the presentation of fact. Orwell's attitude towards the people he is describing is sometimes gentle and affectionate, sometimes savagely critical—the savagery lies in the relentless accumulation of detail, as in the picture of the Brooker household. But his reactions are unexpected by any conventional standard, and this becomes almost a technique of illumination. Because Orwell does not react according to a conventional pattern his words take on an altogether more vivid meaning; we cannot escape their significance as they are not lost in clouds of preconception.

The book begins with a description of the Brookers' lodging house. Orwell spares us nothing of the dirt and discomfort, but ultimately what appals him most is the same quality that condemns the middle class in his eyes—the sterility of life.

On the day when there was a full chamber-pot under the breakfast table I decided to leave. The place was beginning to depress me. It was not only the dirt, the smells and the vile food, but the feeling of stagnant meaningless decay, of having got down into some subterranean place where people go creeping round and round, just like blackbeetles, in an endless muddle of slovened jobs and mean grievances. The most dreadful thing about people like the Brookers is the way they say the same thing over and over again. It gives you the feeling that they are not real people at all, but a kind of ghost for ever rehearsing the same futile rigmarole.[12]

Here Orwell emphasises as "the most dreadful thing" not the dirt, which is what most of us would notice, but the repetition of conversation. It is the effect of sordid surroundings on human beings that primarily concerns him, not the surroundings themselves, although he weaves the details of both into an inseparable pattern. He uses metaphor, but metaphor that is a natural part of the scene—we can see the black-beetles crawling around the chamber-pot. They do not introduce a new note, they do not disperse the quality of the response.

It was the evidence of apathy and decay that horrified Orwell. And as it became clear to him that a socialist system would be necessary to right the material wrongs of the working class he began to see socialism as a cure for this kind of stagnation. An essential part of his pre-First War vision was vitality. He was often to feel that revitalisation was of predominant importance, and found it hard to accept any kind of regimentation or discipline for this reason, even though he could understand their political necessity. Political necessity used in terms of party politics was a phrase he condemned.

In *Wigan Pier* Orwell never suggests that his knowledge and intimacy are more than the details he presents clearly reveal. He writes at a distance. Although the chamber-pot clearly disgusts him he is not involved with it, he does not connect himself with it by an emotional response. His directness avoids the paternalism that his position as outsider and intellectual superior might otherwise encourage. He admires in almost the same tone as he deplores. The physical strength and stamina of the miners is a fact just as the rottenness of the houses they live in is a fact. This method of presentation, as we have seen in *Down and Out*, is an essential part of his value as witness.

It is clear why the working class, living in conditions far different from the comfortable nostalgic vision (perhaps essentially a *middle*-class vision) that appealed to Orwell so strongly, still attracted him. He talks of the "deadening, debilitating effect of unemployment upon everybody" but then says "A working man does not disintegrate under the strain of poverty as a middle-class person does . . . they realise that losing your job does not mean that you cease to be a human being. . . . Families are impoverished but the family-system has not broken up. The people are in fact living a reduced version of their former lives. Instead of raging against their destiny they have made things tolerable by lowering their standards."[13] Orwell saw a courage and dignity amongst the unemployed that he found entirely absent in the case of the depressed middle class. The working-class unemployed retained their sense of human decency as long as the family remained the centre of life. Their standards were functional, not hollow. Orwell found a more decent, vital and attractive kind of humanity amongst working-class people than he ever did amongst the class to which he belonged. This was an important element in his socialism.

Orwell's picture of the working class has been criticised, not for inaccuracy, but for a failure to come to life. Richard Hoggart writes:

Orwell's picture of working-class life, even of that good side typified in a working-class interior, is too static, is set like a picture caught at a certain moment. So it becomes in part a nostalgic looking back (and for Orwell himself probably also suggested an un-anxious calm, free of status-striving, which was a balm to him). In general his portrayal of the working classes in *Wigan Pier* has not sufficient perkiness and resilience, is a bit dispirited. One can see why, given the kinds of people he chose to describe. Still, he did offer it as a picture of "the working class".[14]

The difficulty here is the problem of disentangling what is static in the facts and what in their expression. It is clear that Orwell's nostalgia, which *was* static because it was composed of a series of remembered pictures, did infect his approach to the contemporary situation. He was continually comparing the grim reality with the happy image. The result was that it was hard to be optimistic, yet he convinced himself that the happy image could have some reality, and also convinces us that the grimness of his facts lies in the facts themselves, not in his approach.

He had an eye for the devastatingly symbolic image as well as the tiny, contributory details. An example is his description of a woman seen from a train.

> The train bore me away, through the monstrous scenery of slag-heaps, chimneys, piled scrap-iron, foul canals, paths of cindery mud criss-crossed by the prints of clogs. This was March, but the weather had been horribly cold and every-where there were mounds of blackened snow. As we moved slowly through the outskirts of the town we passed row after row of little grey slum houses running at right angles to the embankment. At the back of one of the houses a young woman was kneeling on the stones, poking a stick up the leaden waste-pipe which ran from the sink inside and which I suppose was blocked. I had time to see everything about her— her sacking apron, her clumsy clogs, her arms reddened by the cold. She looked up as the train passed, and I was almost near enough to catch her eye. She had a round pale face, the usual exhausted face of the slum girl who is twenty-five and looks forty, thanks to miscarriages and drudgery; and it wore, for the second in which I saw it, the most desolate, hopeless ex-pression I have ever seen.[15]

There is certainly no resilience in this nightmarish picture, no impression of humanity carrying on cheerfully in the face of hardship, and the hopelessness colours Orwell's own feelings as he writes. He is at pains to show how this woman, surrounded by the sordid details of her life, becomes nearly as lifeless as they are. The language is hard, yet it catches the weariness of the scene. There is a kind of death in the hyphenated words—"Slag-heaps", "scrap-iron", "waste-pipes". The heavy monosyllables and the prosaic phrases underline a feeling of pessimism, of in-evitability. The blunt rhythm of the prose contains a savage condemnation. Yet at the same time there are hints of the falling

back on generalisation which Orwell has resort to in the second
half of the book and which damages his case: "thanks to miscarriages and drudgery", he writes. He, and we, can accept the
drudgery as a certainty, but the miscarriages are a detail that
Orwell himself cannot verify, cannot observe in the same way as
he can observe the girl's sacking apron and clumsy clogs. He is
thrusting an assumption into a description that otherwise relies
solely on the perception of external detail.

Here Orwell uses grim flat language to match a desolate scene.
But at the same time, in *Wigan Pier*, Orwell is very much concerned with impressing us with the fundamental energy of the
working class, even though he would like this energy to be
geared to a return to a previous quality of life rather than to a
development into a new one. He responds most readily to those
hints of warmth and family solidarity that he found. But he was
remembering all the time the ignorance and preconceptions of
his readers, intellectuals of the left with a tendency towards
theoretical romanticising at a safe distance.

Richard Wollheim sums up Orwell's technique in this way :

What he does is to pick out from the material at his disposal a
number of details all of them as startling, as shocking, as
arresting as possible, and then to set them down in a style that
is very deliberately and self-consciously none of these things
. . . the accumulation of these sharp, stabbing pictures
doesn't seem to add up to a vision of the whole : what we are
left with is a series of stills, mostly "close-ups", which no one
has animated.[16]

It is important to add that along with the shocking details are
the plain, everyday details, and it is partly the association of
both that produces Orwell's effect, and gives a quiet, interacting
energy to the "stills". As Orwell accumulates the plain statements of shocking facts he is also gathering together the elements of a solid background. In the sense that he cannot hope to
be totally comprehensive he is as impressionistic as London.

The significant difference is that Orwell's information and details bite into each other. It is not simply that they are intimately related. They are knotted together to form a tough, almost savage construction that becomes a symbol of a whole climate of living. Both Hoggart and Wollheim find that the total effect lacks vitality. But there is certainly power in the language, and a subdued sense of power also that comes from the movements of, for instance, the miners. If by vitality we mean evidence of rapid movement it is not there in *Wigan Pier*. If we mean energy, then that energy is present. And part of the force of Orwell's writing lies precisely in his embodiment of that dispiritedness that Hoggart condemns. There is no sense of drama in Orwell's descriptions. But there is an urgency that pulses through his writing.

Orwell's indictment is straightforward, but his purpose in this first section was twofold. He set out to expose the condition of the unemployed, to describe their houses, the way they spent their money, the way they spent their time, and also the working conditions of the miners in particular. But, almost more important, he was also trying to explain working-class people in a precise and sympathetic manner. He wished not only to put before the public facts that were not being faced, but to put before members of the Left Book Club details of working-class life which they generally failed to include in their appreciation of the proletariat. For Orwell working people could never be explained and dismissed as the "proletariat". He was more interested in why they spent their dole money on chips and ice cream than in their theoretical economic function, or even their economic rights. For this reason Orwell addressed *Wigan Pier* to the left wingers of the bourgeoisie and wrote a second section.

Almost half the book comprises an autobiographical sketch explaining the development of Orwell's own attitudes and a bitter attack on the intellectuals of the left, the men who condemned capitalist exploitation at an ignorant distance from its effects. This attack caused some embarrassment to the Left Book Club, and Victor Gollancz felt compelled to write a foreword. It is an attempt at self-defence larded with slightly patronising praise of the awkwardly honest and politically innocent Orwell. Gollancz attacks Orwell for being naïvely enthusiastic, for using vague general terms, but does not answer any of Orwell's particular criticisms. He dismisses Orwell's "elemental appeal of 'liberty' and 'justice' ", condemns what he sees as a lack of realism, but ignores Orwell's crucial points about the meaninglessness of Marxist jargon in the face of real facts. Gollancz moved from theory to practice; he saw political realism in terms of ideology and manoeuvring for power. Orwell moved from practice to a theory that he was deeply suspicious of. He drew back both from an ideology that demanded obedience to its dogma and to its habits, and from what seemed to him to be a phoney, and therefore misleading, sense of comradeship. In his attempt to invalidate Orwell's criticisms Gollancz talks of his being "still a victim of that early atmosphere, in his home and public school, which he himself has so eloquently exposed. His conscience, his sense of decency, his understanding of realities tell him to declare himself a socialist: but fighting against this compulsion there is in him all the time a compulsion far less conscious but almost—though fortunately not quite—as strong: the compulsion to conform to the mental habits of his ideas."[17] Orwell is an "extreme intellectual" and a "snob", and Gollancz also implies that he is far too simple-minded to understand what socialism is about.

Criticism of this kind arose from Orwell's frankness in acknowledging the nature of his class background and the aspects of working-class life that repelled him. To say that the working-class smell was, to the Left Book Club mind, a sign of Orwell's snobbery. For Gollancz a genuine commitment, a genuine understanding of what was involved in being a socialist propagandist would have meant that Orwell would have instinctively avoided the kind of tactless remark that both compromised himself as far as class loyalties were concerned and compromised his creed in the eyes of those who were theoretically at its centre.

Orwell's main contention is that socialism is prevented from being a genuinely popular movement because middle-class socialists are exclusive. They can only communicate with each other, and cannot make contact with those who do not speak their own jargon and are not prepared to undertake the same blind commitments. Orwell himself was one of these. Throughout his life he rejected committing himself to a single political party or organisation. He may have felt that the organisations should have made the effort to accommodate him, rather than the other way round, and in some respects he was right. No socialist party could afford not to make efforts to recruit followers. Orwell's hatred of the odd habits of some socialists is what finally destroys the balance of this section of *Wigan Pier*. He takes these as representatively discouraging. There was clearly—and there still is—a wide basis of truth in Orwell's attack. There was personal bitterness in it, but it was a bitterness that grew out of the self-destruction of a movement in which Orwell believed. This was an intensely personal involvement.

Characteristic of the very mode of thought Orwell was attacking, Gollancz does not reply by pointing out that Orwell was speaking only of a very small section of the socialist movement and is almost entirely ignorant of the Unions and of the Labour Party as a whole. He can only suggest that Orwell attacks his own side from a compulsion to support the enemy, not from a passionate desire to strengthen the forces of socialism. Gollancz's remarks are important, for they typify the ambivalent attitude towards Orwell's writing of many of the left-wing intellectuals of the time. They could not fit Orwell into their system. Orwell himself clearly expressed the love–hate relationship that was reciprocal:

Sometimes I look at a Socialist—the intellectual, tract-writing type of Socialist . . . and wonder what the devil his motive really *is*. It is often difficult to believe that it is a love of anybody, especially of the working class, from whom he is of all people furthest removed. The underlying motive of many

Socialists, I believe, is simply a hypertrophied sense of order. The present state of affairs offends them not because it causes misery, still less because it makes freedom impossible, but because it is untidy; what they desire, basically, is to reduce the world to something resembling a chessboard.[18]

Orwell is here following the implications of behaviour and phraseology backwards to suspected motive. He is confusing the certainty of his observation with supposition, and it inevitably hampers the points he is trying to make. This aspect of socialist belief troubled Orwell deeply and he deals with it most drastically in *Nineteen Eighty-Four*. Orwell offended socialists because he would not fit into the familiar pattern of factionalism and party-lining; he exacerbates this offence by hitting out at those who did, and in *Wigan Pier* he hits out wildly and loses his balance. He would not commit himself to any particular group of ideas. He had to be admired because he was a first-rate reporter, a reliable witness and an excellent writer. But socialists on the whole were unhappy and embarrassed at his presence in their midst. Life was much easier for socialists and non-socialists alike if they ignored Orwell. *The Road to Wigan Pier* had a guaranteed sale to Left Book Club members, but his next book, *Homage to Catalonia*, published a year later, sold only a few hundred copies.

The general response to *Wigan Pier*, to be seen at its most understanding and detailed in Harold Laski's review in *Left News*, the organ of the Left Book Club, consisted of dismissing Orwell's attack on the grounds that its basis was emotional simple-mindedness, that because his kind of socialism was based on an appeal to "better feelings" it was invalid. Certainly, although Orwell was pessimistic about events he was optimistic about people. He did believe in the existence of better feelings. He also believed that a solely materialistic and disciplinarian appeal was both unattractive and destructive. But his own understanding of the techniques of propaganda was never on so simple a level. He geared his attempts to communicate to the public's refusal to believe. He included a sketch of his own political education in *Wigan Pier* as a means of breaking down resistance by relating his own development to socialist belief.

Laski says that Orwell's attitude "refuses to confront the grave problem of the State. It has no sense of the historic movement of the economic process. At bottom, in fact, it is an emotional plea for socialism addressed to comfortable people."[19] Orwell did not claim to be a social theorist. His political beliefs were based on common sense rather than on an understanding of economic processes. But although he did not have great understanding of movements or determinism he had a very real understanding of the past, and the past was an aspect of history that many socialists ironically forgot. If Orwell was addressing comfortable people (and certainly most members of the LBC were comfortable) it was in order to make them feel less comfortable, to make them aware of the discomforts of others and the hypocrisy of their own position. He was trying to illuminate precisely those details that the economic processes tended to overlook.

Orwell was always subjectively involved in his material although he maintained a precise detachment and his personality does not intrude. In *Wigan Pier* many of the particularities of his anger are petty even when the roots of his anger are not. He did not, for example, pause to make a case against the crankiness he condemns, and it was both unjust and unwise of him to dismiss as insincere individuals with odd habits. But, significantly, it was not the particularities that his critics attacked; it was his entire case against the left-wing intellectuals. While it can be said that many of his remarks irritate rather than convince, and mar the tenor of his more important argument, it is clear that he caught those he criticised on a sensitive spot. They were put in the position of having to justify their existence as socialists. They were put on the defensive, and angered that this was so.

Orwell's tendency to become preoccupied with inessentials, to give them weight out of all proportion, recurs in his writing, but never so blatantly as in *Wigan Pier*. It has the effect of dissipating the acuteness and honesty of his prose, and generating, by its own irrelevance and lack of proportion, an irrelevant response. Orwell's critics were sidetracked by his own wavering from the point. But Orwell's experience of 1937 was to alter his perspective and the quality of his conviction, and he never again indulged in that kind of muddled encounter. As the threat to his beliefs increased urgency forced him to develop a more acute sense of priorities.

Orwell confused his approach in *Wigan Pier* by his ambivalent relationship with political organisations. But his confrontation with the depression confirmed his commitment to socialism. Another writer, born thirty-odd years before Orwell in another country, arrived at his socialist convictions through his own observation and experience. Upton Sinclair, a writer at the very heart of the American muckraking movement, published in 1906 his devastating exposure of that part of industrial Chicago centred on the meat-packing industry. Jurgis, the Lithuanian immigrant hero of *The Jungle*, comes to understand the meaning of capitalist exploitation via experiences of the utmost horror and degradation. He is cheated and harried at every turn, loses his wife and child in the most horrible of circumstances, and is forced to beg to avoid starvation. The blood and filth of the stockyards impregnate every paragraph, but Jurgis rises above all this, embraces socialism, and prepares to dedicate himself with new hope and energy to the cause. Sinclair's book is not pessimistic. Although the incredible grimness of the facts he is handling far outweigh anything that Orwell faced, Sinclair has an ever-present belief that in spite of the savage accumulation of human tragedy an appeal to humanity's good nature will have some effect. He seems to be assuming that it is only ignorance that allows the conditions he is exposing to be tolerated by anyone other than the stockyard bosses and the workers.

Sinclair does not make one conscious, as Orwell continually does, that he is pitting his strength against immense forces of opposition, although he understands perfectly the vast and

intricate network of graft and influence that is working against
him. The half-ironic jauntiness of his tone reveals an almost con-
fidential amazement that this kind of injustice could be allowed
to occur. It is a calculated tone, aimed at gaining the ear of his
audience, and it is far different from Orwell's matter-of-fact,
almost incidental, mentioning of evils:

> But let no one suppose that this superfluity of employees
> meant easier work for anyone! On the contrary, the speeding-
> up seemed to be growing more savage all the time; they were
> continually inventing new devices to crowd the work on—it
> was for all the world like the thumbscrew of the medieval
> torture chamber. They would get new pace-makers and pay
> them more; they would drive the men on with new machin-
> ery—it was said that in the hog-killing rooms the speed at
> which the hogs moved was determined by clockwork, and
> that it was increased a little every day. In piece-work they
> would reduce the time, requiring the same work in a shorter
> time, and paying the same wages; and then, after the workers
> accustomed themselves to this new speed, they would reduce
> the rate of payment to correspond with the reduction in
> time![20]

Sinclair's language is cluttered, his sentences often ponderous, a
curious mixture of the colloquial and the stylised. The use of
exclamation marks, phrases such as "let no one suppose" and
"for all the world" go some way towards creating a climate of
familiarity, at times an almost embarrassing familiarity, between writer and reader. It gives the impression that the writer
is equally knowledgeable about the packing houses and his
readers. Orwell presents background facts and figures and individual workers in the same tone of voice. Sinclair's plain, jerkily
cantering prose breaks into stark details of death and mutilation
or extravagantly romantic images. His tone and style veer and
swerve: "So he went on, tearing up all the flowers from the
garden of his soul, and setting his heel upon them." The result of
this kind of metaphor is that Jurgis's suffering acquires a gran-

deur, a significance, that Orwell's families struggling on the dole are far away from.

Perhaps both Sinclair's language and his approach are classless in the sense that he is not continually self-conscious about the gulf between his own class background and that of the people he writes of. He himself came from decayed American gentry but spent most of the years of his adolescent life living in poverty. His experience of hard times was more needful than Orwell's. But, like Orwell, he certainly is not writing for a working-class audience. The sales of many of his novels were enormous and *The Jungle* at least had a concrete effect. It influenced the passing of the Pure Food and Drug Act of 1906. Orwell was never able to claim such success for his writing.

Sinclair investigated and wrote in the midst of what was already an established tradition of radical writing in America. Liberal opinion had, in some cases at least, moved away from armchair disapproval to a closer contact with the sources of social evils. In the first six years of the century a dozen or so radical documentary novels had appeared, some, like Frank Norris's *The Octopus* (1901) written through the eyes of a middle-class observer, some, like Jack London's, plunging more directly into the social ferment. The amount of socially concerned and politically committed fiction increased as the century wore on until conviction dwindled with the disillusion of the late thirties. Orwell's *Down and Out*, while not being the first book of its kind, was something of a phenomenon. Even when documentary writing was at its height in Britain there was little that was genuinely muckraking in the sense that the author decided to investigate and write up a situation by becoming involved in it. Those who did joined armies and causes. They did not, usually, join miners and factory workers, still less those on the dole. Orwell, by gritting his teeth—and it is fairly clear that he did not *enjoy* living on bread and margarine or his stay at the Brookers'—battered his way, inevitably a little blindly, into foreign situations. While some admired him for it, others resented the fact that he had courage as well as conviction.

3

THE EXTREME EXPERIENCE

A writer who did go down the mines, from choice rather than from necessity, was J. B. Pick. He described his experiences autobiographically in *Under the Crust* (1946) and fictionally in *Out of the Pit* (1951). Pick was an educated member of the middle class. He intended to become a writer, but he did not become a miner solely in order to write it up, although this seems to have been part of his motive. Chiefly, he seems simply to have wanted the experience. Pick never worked at the coal face but he became thoroughly familiar with the men and the workings of the mine and the mining village in wartime. He had time to evolve a relationship with the mine and his work which Orwell did not have. Orwell's descriptions of the pits in *Wigan Pier* are based on observant but immediate reactions. In *Under the Crust* we follow Pick from his initial bewildered response when faced with the overwhelming noise and dirt of the screens to the ambiguous relationship he describes here: "At one time when I went into Nottingham after a day in the pit I would feel an almost physical hatred of everyone who did not work there also, loathing their respectability, complacency, and anything else about them which I could possibly regard as offensive. At other times I tried to avoid thinking about the pit at all, or seeing the coal, coal-trucks even, or miners who might remind me of it."[1] The hero of *Out of the Pit* is a young miner who is thoroughly used to his job, although he does not completely accept it. We see the work of the pit through the eyes of one who takes the horrors of the pit for granted, but behind him there lurks the middle-class writer with a middle-class reader in mind, who marshals significant details that the practised miner would barely register. Dave, the hero, is uneasy about his job not because of its dangers or its appalling conditions but because it is a dead end. Once you are a collier you can rarely go further. Only a tiny proportion of miners who had the time and energy for study became pit managers.

In *Under the Crust* Pick makes his own position and attitudes clear. He is even-toned and modest, so much so that it almost constitutes a fault and gives rise to a sense of near embarrassment when he writes of personal affairs. His descriptions of the pit seemed to be tempered by a refusal to be a shocked innocent, and therefore to lack some vitality. They are perhaps a little too studied. But the early part of the book, in which Pick cautiously feels his way into the work and comradeship, is impressive. It tails off into a personal interlude concerned with details and emotions that do not belong to the major part of the book. Like Orwell, Pick finds it necessary to place his life and motives in some kind of context. He is not concerned to make any particular political point. If he is writing propaganda it is propaganda implicit in the facts he brings to light. And as he never works at hewing the coal or filling the tubs, except when they are accidentally overturned, and does not go through the terrible experience of "travelling" that Orwell describes so unforgettably, he does not present the worst aspects of coal mining. An added factor is that conditions in the midlands coal fields, where Pick worked, were better than those in South Wales and the northeast. Pick was not seeing the worst of the pits.

Orwell's concern with context and relationship is of a different nature from Pick's. Orwell describes the miners in general; he does not describe the particular individuals with whom he was involved or how he got on with them. He gives very little idea of the kinds of conversations they had or of the miners' reactions to his visits and investigations. When he supplies the background details of context and uses these details to establish precisely the nature of his relationship to what he is seeing and doing, he concentrates almost entirely on class. He is dominated by class barriers and the effort both to recognise their existence and to overcome them. Pick, also, is unable to move away from class differences, but he is much more concerned with describing his personal relationships with his fellow workers, whom he got on with and why, who accepted him and who ignored him. He had a particular eye for those who were, like himself, outsiders, and of course wartime brought many more outsiders into the pits. On the whole he gives us a picture of comradeship, and we cannot help feeling that this is the point the whole book is straining after. Orwell leans in the opposite direction. He suggests that he cannot begin to pretend that he was accepted in any way by the miners: of course, he did not work with them. In *Down and Out* there had been no material difference between himself and his fellow tramps. In *Wigan Pier* he was an observer on the sidelines, however many mines he went down. It was not a role he liked, and perhaps it was partly responsible for the disproportionate emphases in the second section.

Pick is precise, conscientious, in the manner of his descriptions:

> The pit bottom was electrically lighted and had brick walls. It was ten feet high near to the cage, but gradually lowered so that a hundred yards away you had to bend your head and the lights disappeared. Through a hole in one wall was the office where the under-manager, the foreman, and Jabez, spent most of their day. Passages led away on either side. A group of black-faced, weary miners would be waiting to ascend. The foreman tried your lamp, you hooked it to your belt and walked into the dark.[2]

We are given a picture that is in no way impressionistic. It gives no suggestion about what the writer feels at confronting these details, and there is something slightly disjointed in the string of facts. It might almost be a meticulous description of a photograph of the scene moving competently through the significant points. "The pit bottom was electrically lighted and had brick walls." The facts are there but there is a certain blankness about their presentation. We are not convinced that these two facts should be contained in the same sentence. The straightforward statement does not bring the effect of the electric light on the brick walls into our vision.

Although Pick makes it quite clear, in his description of the partly psychological illnesses he developed after he had been working in the pit for some time, that his reactions were very profound, we do not get many hints of it when we are watching the writer confronting the pit. The result of this kind of description is that when Pick is explaining mechanical processes, the hooking up of the tubs, for instance, which involve a lot of intricate detail, his meticulousness works helpfully. At the same time, in spite of the clarity, it is difficult to follow the details of these processes in our own imagination. We can follow Pick from point to point intellectually, but we cannot picture the whole process. We do not feel that the *writer's* imagination has interpreted and organised it for us.

Orwell's description of descending in the cage provided a strong contrast:

> You get into the cage, which is a steel box about as wide as a telephone box and two or three times as long. It holds ten men, but they pack like pilchards in a tin, and a tall man cannot stand upright in it. The steel door shuts upon you, and somebody working the winding gear above drops you into the void. You have the usual momentary qualm in your belly and a bursting sensation in the ears, but not much sensation of movement till you get near the bottom, when the cage slows down so abruptly that you could swear it is going upwards again. In the middle of the run the cage probably touches sixty miles an hour; in some of the deeper mines it touches even more.[3]

While Pick's intention is not to describe what it is like to descend into the pit for the first time—he is describing something that he himself has done over and over again—Orwell's purpose is to do just that. He continually relates the experience to phenomena his readers are likely to be acquainted with. He describes feelings—the qualm in the belly—which in retrospect are perhaps not important but at the time were momentarily dominant. The tone is casual; the conscientiousness is overwhelmingly evident. Some of the facts are qualified or slightly imprecise : "two or three times as long", and later "perhaps four hundred yards under ground". But these qualifications do not disturb the authenticity or real nature of the facts. It is not necessary to know the exact dimensions of the cage; the point is that we are left with a vivid understanding of what it is like to descend.

> When you crawl out at the bottom you are perhaps four hundred yards under ground. That is to say you have a tolerable-sized mountain on top of you; hundreds of yards of solid rock, bones of extinct beasts, subsoil, flints, roots of growing things, green grass, and cows grazing on it—all this suspended over your head and held back only by wooden props as thick as the calf of your leg. But because of the speed at which the cage has brought you down, and the complete blackness through which you have travelled, you hardly feel yourself deeper down than you would at the bottom of the Piccadilly tube.[4]

Orwell's description is a tapestry of the new and the familiar, of imagination and observation. He blends these elements; the result is that we feel the descent, we feel the weight of earth above us and at the same time we see the slightly comic structure Orwell has erected above us, including the bones of extinct beasts and the cows grazing on top. The significance lies in the fact that we are *with* Orwell. We share the relationship Orwell has established with his facts. We make the connection with the Piccadilly tube because Orwell makes it seem an obvious and helpful one. We are rarely with Pick; we are reading about his experiences at some distance.

There is another barrier to our involvement in Pick's writing. Although he explains mining processes with such care he does not explain their relationship to the entire system. We are never sure how his particular job fits into the whole picture. Orwell works explanation into his description. Pick, whose knowledge of the workings of the pit was probably considerably greater than Orwell's, does not provide the background detail that he was well qualified to give. The remoteness of the jobs he does from the process as a whole makes them more difficult to grasp. And one cannot believe that the miners, who did a job that entered so intimately into their entire lives, felt this remoteness. In fact Pick focuses most attention not on the job itself, or on the conditions of the mines, but on certain individuals with whom he worked. Their family backgrounds, the way they speak, become more important than what they are doing and why, so that whenever there is any kind of crisis in the job, and these occur frequently, we lose track of their movements and the causes of crisis. In *Down and Out* Orwell is able to handle simultaneously details of action, purpose and personality. In *Wigan Pier* the nature of the book's intention shifts interest away from personality, but the important thing is that we are never confused by his descriptions.

B. L. Coombes was no amateur miner. He went down the pits at the age of eighteen. In his books *These Poor Hands* and *Miner's Day* (1945) as well as in a number of short stories and sketches he communicates the intimate feel as well as the facts of a miner's life and work. His prose is relaxed and accomplished. He describes, not with a consciousness of producing a descriptive passage, but in a tone of quiet appropriateness:

We cannot travel many yards in any direction without having to push our way past the brattice cloth which is placed to turn the air current. Heavy, clinging stuff it is, reeking of tar, and our skin burns if it rubs against this cloth. The airways spread about like the veins in a man's body, and we can find our way by throwing up a handful of dust and watching

which way it blows. Back on the roadways we follow the
narrow tramlines.[5]

Coombes is writing, as Orwell and Pick are, in order to communicate a strange world to those who know nothing of it. But he is
so deeply involved in the experiences he writes of that there is
no sense of him writing with a self-conscious effort at communication. The "we" here is natural and genuine, and obviously much more direct than "you" or "one" and much more
meaningful than "I". Coombes writes of things as he finds them.
His own sensibility and his style, that is as honest as Orwell's but
much gentler, point out the relevance and importance of these
facts. He conveys an impression of the human mind and phy-
sique exploring, in conflict, at odds with the world underground, at the same time in sympathy and understanding with
it. The men know how to make the best of their surroundings,
yet there is always the danger that they will be taken unawares.
There is a pleasant, insistent lilt in the prose—"heavy, clinging
stuff it is, reeking of tar, and our skin burns if it rubs against
this cloth"—that emphasises the closeness of the relationship
between the men and the unnatural kind of nature that lurks in
the pits. The verb at the end of the phrase, the repetition of
"clinging", "reeking", the string of monosyllables controlling
the pace of the sentence—the rhythm here, with its echoes of
the Welsh tongue, is an important quality of the prose.

Neither Pick nor Orwell can match the quiet authority of
Coombes's prose. He describes disaster, unemployment, the
General Strike, wartime mining, all with a profound sense of the
miner's way of living, thinking and talking, and with an understanding of the relationship between the pits, the coal itself, and
the men. Perhaps no one but a miner can understand this relationship. Certainly the inevitable self-consciousness of the
middle-class amateur intrudes and dissipates the necessary experience and sensitivity. Coombes wrote about the South Wales
coalfield. Mark Benney, yet another outsider, investigated the
mines of the north-east, and presented the results of his investi-

gations in his book *Charity Main* (1946). *Charity Main* is a semi-fictionalised documentary and it possibly succeeds better than either *Wigan Pier* or *Under the Crust* in eliminating this self-consciousness. Or rather, the self-consciousness is made an important factor in the book, an important starting point for finding out about mining and its people.

Mark Benney had spent the first part of the Second War as a skilled worker in the engineering industry. Later he became an official in the Coal Control, and it was in this capacity that he visited the mines of north-east England. In *Charity Main* he becomes "Johnson", an official visiting the coal field concerned with the problems of wartime mining and miners. Benney's descriptive method ranks with Orwell's in its natural absorption of detail and relevant focus. In creating a fictional persona through whom to observe the miners' lives Benney to some extent solves the problem Pick cannot move away from—the problem of stance and of the personality of the writer. Johnson is not an intrusive personality. He is kindly, thoughtful, has some knowledge of the coal industry but little about the actual conditions of mining. He is neither a completely ignorant outsider nor familiar with his surroundings. He avoids Pick's tendency to suggest both the role of objective observer and knowledgeable worker. Johnson is prepared to go some way towards embracing the life of the pit as a whole; Pick only seems to make moves towards individuals. He remains wary and, we feel, unhappy, about the coal-dominated community. Johnson is not uncritical, but he enters into pit life with a warm-heartedness which Pick lacks, and a knowledge that his position might give him the opportunity to help, an opportunity which Pick knows he cannot have. Here Benney describes Johnson's digs:

The cottage, the village, the slag heap behind the village, all insisted on a harsh raw elemental scheme of life, where the cardinal virtues might flourish but refinements and comforts were never intended to have a place. And here was a bedroom suite of degenerate "modernistic" design, and a china cabinet containing a twenty one piece tea set coloured black with silver spots, and framed mirrors on the wall, and a revolving bookcase, and satin runners on the sideboard and table, and a cubistic hearthrug.[6]

Orwell could not have attempted a description of this kind without letting a certain bitterness of comment trickle through. Benney allows the comment to arise from the contrast between the landscape and the interior. The final irony lay in the fact that this was a room that had hardly been used by the young married couple who had furnished it. The rather sad artificiality of its contents is increased. At first glance Benney's prose is not as impressive as Orwell's. Orwell, at the same time as maintaining his stance, varies the tone and speed of his writing. In fact, he deliberately contrasts them, or, more often, does not vary the tone when the sense conventionally asks for this. Benney's writing is consistent and without any startling effects, but continually warmed by plain humanity. One can detect behind it the acute eye of the sociologist—he was in fact a trained sociologist—an eye which emotion cannot waver.

Although there are these obvious differences between their writing Orwell and Benney are very similar in their effect. They both have a curiosity which is not so apparent in Pick and not so important in Coombes. The fact that they are trying to find out how things really are is what stands out, and the fact that they are communicating with precision and honesty what they observe is the result of the quality of their writing. In the following descriptions by the two writers of the same process at the coal face the difference in styles is very evident, the pictures of this particular activity very similar:

Norman, his black muscular body glistening in the olive-coloured light of his lamp, worked easily and quickly, crawling about with the agility of a mole. There was, too, an urgency behind his work that seemed almost unnatural. His shovel drove forwards and cast back not only in a steady rhythm, but a fast rhythm. When he had to hack away a bulge on the face where the shots had broken the coal off cleanly, his pick bit into the mineral with a flail-like rapidity and the full weight of the powerful shoulders behind it. It was full-blooded, unrelenting and unflagging effort, that would have seemed wholly admirable in a man working in the full light of day; down here, in the darkness of a two foot seam, it was almost unbelievable. And yet, Johnson could obscurely sense, it was the appropriate, probably the necessary rhythm of work here. Where bodily comfort was out of the question, there could be no half-way effort; one either worked in a sustained, tearing fury, or not at all.[7]

Here Benney allows the fictional Johnson to disappear almost entirely. He does not intrude or colour the description in any way. Nor does Norman's activity belong particularly to Norman; he is transformed into an example of the filler at work. When a thought is put into Johnson's head it is not important that it is Johnson's thought, it is important simply that the thought be expressed. In describing one particular named figure, whose identity is not important and in eliminating the describer Benney focuses all attention on the job itself. Benney's prose is energetic, matching the energy of the activity. It is also slightly careless—the word "full" repeated three times in a single sentence—but curiously the carelessness adds to the vigour of the language. "Full weight" and "full-blooded" together would have seemed like artifice. The addition of "full light" gives the impression that the writer is seeking the best words to convey an impression regardless of the slight clumsiness. The result is that the expression overrides the clumsiness.

Orwell describes the same activity:

There is the heat—it varies, but in some mines it is suffocating —and the coal dust that stuffs up your throat and nostrils and collects along your eyelids, and the unending rattle of the conveyor belt, which in that confined space is rather like the rattle of a machine-gun. But the fillers look and work as though they were made of iron. They really do look like iron —hammered iron statues—under the smooth coat of coal dust which clings to them from head to foot. . . . You can never forget that spectacle once you have seen it—the line of bowed, kneeling figures, sooty black all over, driving their huge shovels under the coal with stupendous force and speed.[8]

Orwell's personality is strongly alive in this description, but far from detracting from the picture he describes it transmits its vividness. It is through him and his awareness that we see what is going on. In Benney's description the neutrality of tone results in a depersonalised exactness bolstered by the energetic sturdiness of his language. Orwell threads personal reaction through objective reporting and makes the scene throb with life and effect. He brings us into it. "Your throat", "your eyelids", "you can never forget"—this is not just another way of saying "one"; we are present alongside him.

They are on the job for seven and a half hours, theoretically without a break, for there is not time "off". Actually they snatch a quarter of an hour or so at some time during the shift to eat the food they have brought with them, usually a hunk of bread and dripping and a bottle of cold tea. The first time I was watching the "fillers" at work I put my hand upon some dreadful slimy thing among the coal dust. It was a chewed quid of tobacco. Nearly all the miners chew tobacco, which is said to be good against thirst.[9]

Orwell rarely says "I". When he does, it is to relate a tiny, completely personal experience to which he instantly gives a relevant focus—"I put my hand upon some dreadful slimy thing". The point here is not just that he makes a comment about chewing tobacco, but that he is illustrating how experience can never be separated out and sectioned off in the way that many documentary writers find it hard to avoid. Part of his experience of watching the fillers was putting his hand on "some dreadful slimy thing". The fact that Orwell's description is not continuous, but built up through a page and a half of detail and comment is important. Orwell moves from the appearance of the fillers to their actions, to their hours of work, to what they eat in their break. His own responses and his own emphases break through—"as though they were made of iron. They really do look like iron . . ." The repetition here is plain and convincing. The spontaneous insistence on a fact carries all the necessary weight.

Looking back at Benney's passage we can see that he puts all his effort into describing Norman's activity. He does not allow himself to be distracted. The quick succession of verbs, adjectives and adverbs builds up a rapid intensity, but our eyes are focused on a tiny area of action, while Orwell manages to re-create the atmosphere of the pit as a whole. Orwell does not describe a single individual figure, yet we can see the row of men working as vividly as we can see Norman. A single word makes a good point of comparison between the two writers. Benney uses the word "unbelievable". Certainly it is virtually impossible for the reader to grasp the full significance of what it must be like to work on one's knees in a two-foot seam shovelling coal, but the word "unbelievable" itself bears no particular significance. It seems to lie rather innocently and ineffectually in Benney's sentence. Orwell has a way of making what is essentially a commonplace word take on a startling aspect. In his hands a phrase like "almost unbelievable" would mean precisely and literally what it said. Benney does not try to make it have anything more than the toned-down meaning we have come to expect from what was an originally uncompromising word.

In comparing the writing of four men who described the same area of experience the central problem of documentary is inevitably raised, the problem of personality versus the facts. Except in the case of Benney who is writing something that is neither a first-person account nor fiction but fact cast in a fictional framework, these writers present themselves directly as

C

vehicles of perception. They observe, they record, they interpret. The relationship they establish with the facts they handle is clearly the clue to the tone and the success of their documentary. How can we measure the success of documentary? We have to sort out whether it is complete, whether it convinces as being the truth, whether it is in fact the truth, whether the truth commands our attention. As readers our own response determines how convincing and how commanding the writing is. Our assessment of truth and completeness depend to some extent on our own experience and understanding of the facts involved. It is an assessment that is not always possible, and so we rely more and more on whether we are interested and convinced. We can extract from this, first of all, that the good documentary writer must be a good writer. He must be able to handle language not just convincingly but with an understanding of the way it works. He must be able to translate observation and perception into words. If Pick is the least good of these four writers it is because he is not always able to carry out this translation adequately. The language he uses does not relate himself to the facts. Many of his attempts at precision and objectivity are clumsy although they seem to be accurate.

If Coombes is perhaps the best of the four, although he does not have the power of Orwell, it is because the problem of the relationship between language, fact and personality is totally wiped out. Coombes's personality is important because he is a miner, not because he is a writer describing a miner's job. Language, persona and environment are so intimate that we question none of them. Benney to some extent sidesteps the problem with his creation of Johnson, but this itself could have brought fresh difficulties which do not in fact arise. Johnson has his function in the mining community, even if it does not include mining itself. He is not a volunteer, he does not have behind him motives of curiosity for its own, or his own, sake. Benney handles Johnson with a natural ease. Orwell himself barges through the problem. In fact, he refuses to acknowledge its existence for he refuses to accept that there should be anything

artificial in his dual role of witness and writer, of experiencing
and translating fact. Inevitably this brings some mistakes, but it
also works with a more startling and memorable effect than the
other three. He relinquishes nothing either to conventions of
response or conventions of style. He is simultaneously casual,
coldly objective, shockingly personal, and above all determined
to force his readers to absorb everything he says.

Orwell handles the problem of personality by entirely remov-
ing it most of the time, then suddenly reintroducing it, either as
a means of interpretation or as a detail to be examined along
with other details. He does this most successfully in a later book,
Homage to Catalonia. But in *Wigan Pier* he strongly maintains
the stance of being both observer and actor. Because he makes it
quite clear that he is ready to enter into the worst of things—
while Pick on the other hand cannot disguise a certain hesitancy
—he links us with the most savage of the details he presents. He
himself is the linkman. He transmits his experience in the most
intimate way, and his language almost has the force of physical
touch.

Orwell's tone is deceptively relaxed and unemotional, yet we
know, because of the way in which his honesty burns through,
because of tiny details like the "dreadful slimy thing", that his
reactions are full-blooded and uncompromising. His prose is
both these things too; its ease and restraint, its understatement,
reinforce its refusal to compromise. But in all this there is a
challenging tension, something like an electrical charge that
leaps through the writing and makes its readers almost breath-
less. Moving right away from the mines to a documentary account of a different kind of extreme situation, the Second World
War, we find a writer who has solved, with no apparent trouble,
the problem of fact and personality, a writer who is often as
impressive as Orwell but has none of Orwell's faults and few of
Orwell's characteristics. Keith Douglas, who died in Normandy
at the age of twenty-four, described in notebooks kept at the
time of the tank battle at Alamein and its aftermath, in which
he served as a tank commander. The notebooks were first pub-

lished in 1946 as *Alamein to Zem Zem*. Douglas seems to be almost unconscious that there should be any difficulties in the relationship between his stance as writer and what he describes. He is neither hesitant nor self-conscious about his own persona —he uses "I" continually, but completely naturally. There is never any separation between what he was doing and what he was observing:

> Six days after I had heard rumbling on the western skyline, that famous barrage that began it, I moved up from the rear to the front of the British attack. Through areas as full of organisation as a city of ants—it happened that two days before I had been reading Maeterlinck's descriptions of ant communities—I drove up the sign-posted tracks until, when I reached my own place in all this activity, I had seen the whole arrangement of the Army, almost too large to appreciate, as a body would look to a germ riding in its bloodstream.[10]

Douglas himself becomes a part of the operation he describes. He is neither impersonal nor without subjectivity, but his reference to completely private activity, his reading of Maeterlinck, does not jar with sudden inappropriate emphasis on the personal. A detail like that is not particularly significant, but it is relevant. It shows us how his mind was working, and in the context of the whole description Douglas's mind working is a functioning part of the battle, like the working of the tank he commands. He maps out the behind-the-scenes of the battle for us with a superb economy and lack of strain, yet he is neither sparse nor casual. We see and understand as much as he does. In other words we are both as clear and confused as he is. We ride along with the germ in the body's bloodstream.

> First the various headquarters of the higher formations, huge conglomerations of large and small vehicles facing in all directions, flags, signposts, and numbers standing among their dust. On the main tracks, marked with crude replicas of a hat, a bottle, and a boat, cut out of petrol tins, lorries ap-

peared like ships, plunging their bows into drifts of dust and rearing up suddenly over crests like waves. Their wheels were continually hidden in dustclouds: the ordinary sand being pulverised by so much traffic into a substance almost liquid, sticky to the touch, into which the feet of men walking sank to the knee. Every man had a white mask of dust in which, if he wore no goggles, his eyes showed like a clown's eyes. Some did wear goggles, many more the celluloid eyeshields from their anti-gas equipments. Trucks and their loads became a uniform dust colour before they had travelled twenty yards: even with a handkerchief tied like a cowboy's over nose and mouth, it was difficult to breathe.[11]

In the first quotation "I" is repeated five times in two sentences. In the second it is not used at all. Yet there is no change of tone or emphasis. The focus is not swerved from Douglas himself to a collection of objectively observed details. Everything is presented on the same level of writing. In some respects this is also what Orwell does. Although his tone and emphasis do shift continually they do not shift according to how much Orwell features in his own descriptions—he himself is treated exactly as any other detail in the book. In Douglas's description we see him as part of this sea of traffic. We see him both in goggles and without goggles. It does not matter that he neglects to tell us whether or not he was in fact wearing goggles, because he himself is neither more nor less important than those who figure in his general description. Here it is appropriate that he should be a part of the general description. Earlier it was appropriate that he include a private detail about his activities. But at the very end of the passage he shifts again to show us, indirectly, himself: "even with a handkerchief tied like a cowboy's over nose and mouth, it was difficult to breathe." There is no mention of "I" but it is quite clear that "it was difficult" means "I found it difficult" as well as having a more general meaning. Douglas is not presenting himself as a detached outsider witnessing events. He is fusing the "I" into "we" without mentioning either. He is merging the personal detail into the general picture, and thus merging the witness and the actor.

Much of Douglas's clarity and precision lies in the way in which he puts the details of his description together. He moves from headquarters to lorries to men, linking them by revealing the closeness of their relationship with the same set of difficulties. "Their wheels were continually hidden in dustclouds: the ordinary sand being pulverised by so much traffic into a substance almost liquid, sticky to the touch, into which the feet of men walking sank to the knee." Each point is presented both separately and in association with others without which a single point would be meaningless. The extraordinary progression of the final phrase of this sentence illustrates this. We move from the idea of touch to the picture of feet, to which we immediately relate the substance and its stickiness. From feel we move to men, from men to walking. It is as if a slow-motion film of this action was being shown. We begin with the contact of the feet with the pulverised sand and go through the entire motion of walking and sinking to the knee. The resulting picture is breathtaking in its completeness and its simplicity.

Throughout *Alamein to Zem Zem* Douglas manages to maintain this unerring instinct for the appropriate detail positioned in this uncannily vital way. Orwell has no such instinct, which is precisely the strength of his writing. The quality of his writing is such that he can slam together in a single sentence details that jar with one another. The tact and judgment with which Douglas moves from the particular to the general are at the root of his stance as a chronicler. He does not in fact use the real names either of himself or of the characters who feature in the notebooks but this itself is a result of tact, not a deliberate creation of fictional personalities. Perhaps the crucial test of Douglas's method is that he can write of his most personal relationships, his affairs with women, in a totally unembarrassed and unembarrassing manner. Orwell refrains almost entirely from mentioning personal relationships, even when they would be relevant. Pick does mention them, and becomes irrelevant. Douglas

THE EXTREME EXPERIENCE 71

is both revealing and unexhibitionist in what he says. Again, it is his selection of appropriate detail that allows this. He tells nothing about his background, nothing about any events that occurred before he began the notebooks except for brief references to his training period in Palestine. All that we know about the friends he mentions, about the two women in Alexandria with whom he was involved, is what actually occurs at the time of writing. We become curious about these people as we become curious about people whom we have met and like and lose touch with. In other words both their existence and their relationships with Douglas are totally convincing.

Of the four mining writers the one closest to Douglas's style is B. L. Coombes. His lack of self-consciousness, his position in the midst of the situations he describes are much the same. He has the same lack of solemnity and the same seriousness of intention. But there is a significant difference in the fact that Coombes writes with familiarity about the mines, while Douglas writes with ignorance yet a refusal to be balked about the desert battle. He writes with a belief that there is no fact which he encounters, whether he is able to conceive of it beforehand or not, which language cannot handle. His descriptions of the dead, presented with an artist's care and curiosity and with a man's ability to be stunned and sickened, reveal this:

> He seemed to move and writhe. But he was stiff. The dust which powdered his face like an actor's lay on his wide open eyes, whose stare held my gaze like the Ancient Mariner's. He had tried to cover his wounds with towels against the flies. His haversack lay open, from which he had taken towels and dressings. His water-bottle lay tilted with the cork out. Towels and haversack were dark with dried blood, darker still with a great concourse of flies. This picture, as they say, told a story. It filled me with useless pity.[12]

Here Douglas continually emphasises the fact that this man was once alive. His expression, the paraphernalia that lie around

him, the haversack, the water-bottle, all draw attention to the
final actions of his life. At the same time they confirm his death.
It is this suggestion of paradox that "tells a story", a story that
is in some way more meaningful than an individual's feeble
struggle for life. The short plain sentences and the irony at the
end express the intensity of Douglas's reaction. We feel that it
is in fact the pity that is directing his words—there *seems* to be
no calculation in his writing. It is this apparent lack of calculation, so very different from the almost inevitable poses, although
genuine in their own way, of many First World War writers,
that allows Douglas to approach unswervingly any kind of fact.

These five writers were all English, and revealed in a general
way a characteristic of the English documentary writer. They
were neither self-dramatic nor did they dramatise the facts that
they handled. If they wrote with a propagandist purpose in their
minds their purpose was regulated by a serious intention to tell
the truth, by a conviction that the truth ought to be publicised.
Orwell included a section of autobiography in *Wigan Pier* because he wanted to relate his own development to the situation
on the left; Coombes wrote an autobiographical documentary
because his own life revealed the facts that he wanted to set
down. In both *Charity Main* and *Alamein to Zem Zem* the autobiographical element is important as a vehicle rather than as a
subject. Pick, as we have seen, confused his position as auto-
biographer and chronicler, but it is not difficult to detect how
and why he did so.

When we turn to the writing of Arthur Koestler it becomes
much more difficult to sort out the strands of personality and
documentary. The appropriate private detail and the significant
objective description become so blended, so juggled about by
the language and stance of the writer, that it becomes almost as
treacherously easy to condemn as to praise. The reader's approach is further confused by the fact that Koestler wrote about
himself and his experiences as an example, a typical illustration,
of the fate of the Central European middle-class intellectual.
Scum of the Earth, published by the Left Book Club in 1941,

cannot strictly be called either autobiography or objective documentary. At the end of the book Koestler says: "The 'I' of this narrative, his thoughts and fears and hopes, and even his incongruencies and contradictions, stand for the thoughts and fears and hopes, but above all for the burning despair of a considerable portion of the Continent's population."[13] In fact Koestler's personality is so present that he does not come through as a representative figure. This confuses still further the level of the autobiography. Koestler ends his tale of his life in France from the outbreak of war to the collapse by rather abruptly stating that the details of his escape from Marseilles to Britain were personal and accidental and therefore not a relevant part of his example. Yet even here the book overflows with his individualism. The very nature of the details he selects for his descriptions are stamped with his personality, his moral and political outlook, and his experience of political suffering.

The main part of *Scum of the Earth* is concerned with Koestler's stay in the internment camp of Le Vernet. He was interned as a suspect alien, in spite of, or because of, the fact that he had spent many years engaged in anti-Fascist agitation. The massive, confused and bigoted bureaucracy that sent him to Le Vernet varies little from the First World War bureaucracy that imprisoned E. E. Cummings. Le Vernet contained a vast assortment of political refugees, most of them, like Koestler, with a long history of anti-Fascist activities behind them. At this time France was at war with Hitler. The remnants of the International Brigades, professional people from all parts of Central Europe, various waifs and strays who had been picked up without identity cards, men who had spent the greater part of their adult lives in Fascist prisons, were gathered together in a camp that compared unfavourably with Dachau and the death cells in Seville prison, where Koestler himself had spent some months.

There are perhaps two striking features of Koestler's attitude to the subjects of his descriptions. We feel that he is describing what he *expected* to find, that his experience of Europe in the thirties had conditioned him to consider Le Vernet as a consequence of his kind of life. Behind this we sense that this conditioning has given him some kind of superiority, not so much over his fellow internees as over his readers. Also, Koestler had at this stage already come to his own conclusions about what was happening in Europe and the fate of his particular class and of socialist and communist agitators. His language is underlined with finality. We feel that he has examined and judged the case, and it is the judgment rather than the examination that informs his writing.

A third feature of Koestler's writing is that we are always conscious of his separation from the people and things he describes. It is not only that he was at that time quite a well-known writer with all kinds of useful contacts, not only that he managed to get himself exempted from manual labour, not only that he was one of the very few who were actually released. The separation is contained in the writing itself. He suggests that he got to know well the four men who shared his section of the barrack in which they were housed. Yet his descriptions of these men are almost entirely composed of their past histories. Their pasts are presented as a means of presenting personality—or rather, they are a substitute for personality. In fact our grasp of the kind of men these are is very slight. The result is that our conception of Koestler's relationship with them is similar to that of the interviewer with the interviewee. Koestler gets down all the facts, but we look for something more.

This kind of writing can be legitimately defended, especially when we remember that Koestler was not presenting *Scum of the Earth* as autobiography in the ordinary sense. But it makes the whole question of the writer's stance, and of his relationship with his facts, very complex, almost artificial. We cannot get away from Koestler's personality or from the distinctive style of his writing. Yet none of the tests that have been applied to the other writers discussed seem to work here. Koestler, for instance, uses "you", as Orwell does, as a more colloquial "one". "The good thing about Kuryatchuk was that you could not argue with him—he just looked at you silently with his little elephant eyes and gave no answer, being unable to think of one; and the solemn silence ensuing ended the argument."[14] Here, we do not automatically translate "you" into "one" but into "I"; we feel that it is a device for eliminating the constant repetition of "I" and the consequent emphasis upon individuality—an emphasis which Douglas can avoid. This is because it is associated with observations and interpretations that are Koestler's own, without there being anything to suggest that they were general— "his little elephant eyes", "being unable to think of one". Koestler continually articulates apparently general feelings in a way that stems directly from the interaction of his particular observations and his particular conclusions about past experience.

Koestler's descriptive method is, not surprisingly, scientific: he was trained as a scientist:

> On each row slept fifty men, feet toward the passage. The rows were divided into ten compartments by the wooded poles supporting the roof. Each compartment contained five men and was 105 inches wide; thus each man disposed of a space 21 inches wide to sleep on. This meant that all five had to sleep on their sides, facing the same way, and if one turned over, all had to turn over.[15]

Koestler's precision here is not the precision of the sensitive observer missing nothing, but of the scientist measuring and calculating. The effect is quite powerful (although it is interesting to note the slightly odd use of "disposed of"; this was the first book that Koestler wrote in English). At this point we might expect some detail of personal discomfort to underline the communication of suffering, but no such detail appears. All the necessary emphasis is contained in the final sentence, even in the final phrase—"if one turned over, all had to turn over". Koestler's calculations combined with his short sentences and short phrases and very emphatic punctuation carries the force of his writing. Behind this force is a very strongly marked didactic intention, revealed in the kind of phrase he uses here:

These, roughly, were—and doubtless still are—the material conditions in the camp of Le Vernet. It has to be remembered, however, that it was notoriously the worst in France. But it must also be mentioned that as regards food, accommodation, and hygiene, Vernet was even below the level of Nazi concentration camps.[16]

Koestler's grasp of experience and the beliefs that went with it were so powerfully in control of his mind and his writing that he was rarely able to move away from propaganda, using the word in its most general sense. Of course, in the most general sense, all four writers about the pits were also propagandists. But they did not have Koestler's particular syndrome of experience driving them on from behind. They were, in fact, more modest both in their understanding and in their pretensions. Koestler's experience and the urgency of what he had to communicate made modesty irrelevant. The miners' case was urgent too, but only Orwell attempted to challenge seriously the traditional apathy and ignorance of the British public.

Scum of the Earth, like Wigan Pier, was published for a particular and limited audience. At its height the Left Book Club membership did not exceed 60,000. Scum of the Earth was in fact no more communicative or persuasive than Wigan Pier. It is not possible to assess the effects of documentary except in one or two extreme cases. Upton Sinclair's The Jungle was such a case, but it is impossible to trace any particular effect to any of the books discussed in this chapter. We can only say that Wigan Pier stirred up a great deal of controversy, but even that was limited to a small section of the population. So we are left with the original problem of how we should approach documentary.

It is clear that tone is of great importance, and that tone itself is the result of the writer's relationship with his evidence and his style of writing. To a great extent style is, again, determined by the writer's approach to fact and the part his personality plays in interpretation and expression of fact. We saw in the case of Pick's Under the Crust that his descriptions of mechanical processes, although amongst the best of his writing, did not quite come off because of the lack of contact between the operations and the men who carried them out. Coombes made this relationship very intimate, so intimate in fact that his persona as writer and his function as miner were inseparable. This eliminated the problem of tone. Orwell and Mark Benney both wrote with a full consciousness of the distance between themselves as writers and the facts they were witnessing. Both overcame incipient difficulties by the strength of their observation, their honesty, and by simply making no attempt to disguise the distance. Benney by his creation of a fictional persona avoided the complications of an intrusive first person. Orwell by simultaneously using the first person as a balanced interpretative vehicle and seeing himself as objectively as he saw any other fact worked out a valid relationship. Keith Douglas eliminates the problem in a way that is similar both to Coombes and to Orwell. His relationship with facts *is* his experience. He is a witness, yet he is a part of the battle and in this respect no different from any other soldier. The fact that he is a witness is inseparable from the fact that he is a soldier.

Koestler's writing seems to break all the rules that these comments suggest. He *is* separate, he *is* different, and his writing, suffused with his own personality, emphasises this. Yet as a documentary writer and a propagandist he is here powerfully convincing. His experience had crucial lessons to communicate. We could say the same of the others, but the fact remains that Koestler convinces us that the lessons he has to teach are more crucial and more immediate than any others. It is the urgency and the insurgent self-dramatisation that throw the relationship between writer and experience on another level. *Scum of the Earth* was one of Koestler's earliest attempts at documentary writing. Later we shall have the opportunity to assess more precisely Koestler's relationship with his evidence.

4

ORWELL AND THE MIDDLE CLASS

In *Wigan Pier* Orwell's revolt against his own class was savagely expressed in terms of a condemnation of left-wing middle-class intellectuals. While articulating their allegiance with the working-class they continued to relax protected by bourgeois padding—this was his allegation. And certainly the position of many of the left-wing intellectuals of the thirties does not stand up well to hindsight. The phrases of the committed poets were too frequently made flabby by romanticism or injected with an artificial toughness that is remote from reality. C. Day Lewis's "You That Love England", for instance, moves with such a loose rhythm that the eye glides over the occasional tough line, such as "refugees from cursed towns and devastated areas". There is too much that is general, too little of the particular, and the soft "w's" of the final line lose it all its force—"wielders of power and welders of a new world". It was this kind of soft generalisation that Orwell, who forced himself into the worst of things, could not take.

Edgell Rickword, in an essay on "Culture, Progress and English Tradition", demands the identification of culture with the interests of the working class. He sees this identification in terms of the intellectual's self-discipline, his "participation in the constructive work of society", his dedication to the needs and education of the working class. He makes no mention of the fact that the working class might have a thriving, or at least distinctive, culture of their own. Rickword says, "Wherever the working class is strong and unified it attracts the intellectuals to it";[1] Orwell pointed out that intellectuals were not likely to be attracted by overflowing chamber pots and bed bugs. If, in *Wigan*

Pier, he tended to dwell on some of the more appalling details of working-class living it was because he could not tolerate the enthusiastic unawareness of what "working class" meant. Orwell himself took pains to find out, although this did not mean that it was any easier for him than for any other middle-class intellectual to identify himself with the working class. The aspects of the working-class home that appealed to him so strongly, the warmth, the cosiness, the family life, were not necessarily confined to that class—although it is certainly true that the larger the house the thinner the vision becomes.

Orwell felt that an essential part of the movement towards the working class was the rejection of sterile middle-class values. It was just this which did not happen, that, perhaps, could not happen. The public school and university background which produced so many of the writers of the thirties—Michael Roberts, C. Day Lewis, Rex Warner, Louis Macneice, John Lehmann, Auden, Spender and Isherwood were all at Oxford or Cambridge—dominated their lives and inevitably brought along with it a great deal of social and cultural dead wood. They had important traditions behind them which facilitated the release from commitment that the forties brought to many of them. Orwell, while not, except in some details, rejecting tradition had cut himself an essentially traditionless way forward. It was this that made his position so difficult and so isolated.

From a very early stage Orwell's revolt against the middle class seems to have been encouraged. His own background gave him an understanding of the tyranny of money; his time at Eton made the minor tyrannies of class acutely clear to him. His experiences in Burma gave him a first-hand acquaintance with major oppression. His struggles in the last years of the twenties and the early thirties put him on the receiving end of oppression. Few English writers of the period had such a variety of class experience within such a short time. But in Europe the situation was rather different. The course of Koestler's life, for instance, although it seems so traumatic, was in accordance with the Continental tradition of the responsibility of the intelligentsia. The intelligentsia were almost a class in themselves; they had a recognised function : didactic, interpretative, a function that was on the whole liberal. Between the Wars, if not before, the intelligentsia became for the most part Socialist or Communist. The left-wing intellectual of Vienna, of Berlin, of Paris, felt himself to be in a politically more effective position than his English counterpart, and less tied by virtue of background and education to the bourgeoisie. He had channels of action open for him which in Britain had to be sought for.

In Britain the whole concept of direct action had a challenging ring for the middle class—threatening or romantic, depending on one's political position. But on the Continent it was accepted. This did not necessarily mean that there was a closer association between the intelligentsia and the working class; Koestler's hero in *Arrival and Departure* is an example of middle-class guilt and unease in the face of his proletarian comrades. But it did mean that the intelligentsia's involvement with working-class issues and its identification with what Edward Upward called "the progressive side of the class struggle" was much more natural, and not hedged about with all kinds of embarrassments and misunderstandings.

Clearly Orwell would have been happier amongst such a tradition, although perhaps as a part of it his nature would have demanded revolt. As things were, revolt was essential. It is clearly enough implied in *Down and Out*, but it was in the novels written between this first book and *Wigan Pier* that it achieved its bitterest, most concentrated expression. At this time Orwell's own lack of money and success must have affected his attitude. There must have been a temptation to become like one of his own heroes, Gordon Comstock. But in fact what Orwell condemned during this period were those aspects of modern life that he attacked until his death, that he attacked most forcefully in *Nineteen Eighty-Four*. In the thirties the bourgeoisie came to represent all that Orwell most loathed. They in their negative acquiescence in capitalism, their apathy, their narrowness, seemed to Orwell to be the greatest barrier to political progress. He could tolerate full-blooded capitalists, tyrants of authority and the genuinely upper-class with greater ease than the gutlessness and pretension of the class where he had his own roots. There were self-evident ways of explaining and attacking Hitler. There seemed to be no answer to the vague and pernicious self-centredness which the middle class perpetuated.

He saw its members both as oppressors and as feeble and pitiable underdogs, brought to subjection by their own clinging to the formulae of the ruling class. For the rigid Marxist there was no problem—the bourgeoisie was to be hated and destroyed almost with more fervour than the upper layers of society. This was what the Marxist intellectual implied and turned away from. For Orwell as for most of the contemporary left-wing middle class this was a dilemma that was never solved and rarely faced. There was much that was valuable in bourgeois culture—even Lenin said so. But it was the bourgeois sub-culture, which Orwell crudely symbolised by the aspidistra, which revolted him and which most intellectuals ignored. It is the death of all human brightness represented by George Bowling's wife in *Coming Up for Air* that Orwell wants to destroy. His suggestion, in *Wigan Pier*, that the middle class should put itself into voluntary liquidation, was as much a defiant and disgusted gesture as a logical proposal. But in the novels Orwell is still in the process of coming to grips with the problem, and it is the recoil rather than anything more positive that we grasp.

These early novels are without exception charged with the bleak, sterile atmosphere which was very much a part of his own experience. He transmits the intensity of his own reaction to it, but although this intensity gives his novels something of their power, it also explains one of their failings. In *Keep the Aspidistra Flying*, the blackness, the impossibility of anything going right, becomes almost obsessive and its dramatic usefulness is hampered. At times Orwell's own reaction envelops the action of the novel, lying like a heavy fog preventing movement and development. Neither incident nor personality can puncture the uniform greyness. It was not until *Nineteen Eighty-Four* that Orwell was able to use this drabness to its best effect. There the lack of colour, the dismal streets and the flat existence of London's inhabitants contributes to the sense of the state's power and humanity's dread. But in the early novels Orwell was making much more particular statements, and his detail did not always do what was required of it.

Colonialism had first revealed to Orwell the extent of what social injustice could mean, and it also provided the subject of his first novel, *Burmese Days* (1935). This is the most vigorous and colourful of his pre-war novels. The stagnation of a group of white colonialists in the township of Kyauktada, given a little artificial colouring by the powers of imperialism, does not overwhelm the novel. The lively squalor of native life and the magnificent jungle scenes provide a necessary balance. In his picture of the whites in Burma Orwell presents the situation of a part of the English middle class wherever they are. Gordon Comstock's sister and George Bowling's wife are in essentially the same situation. The whites wield the power of the oppressor, but always to inflict mere indignity, never to achieve real triumph. They themselves sink into the dejection of the oppressed—the tenor of their lives is really more squalid than that of the poorest natives, and it is much more limited—but refuse to admit it. In *Wigan Pier* Orwell was to approve of the unemployed family relinquishing standards when they are no longer able to live up to them. In *Coming Up for Air* George Bowling bitterly and mockingly attacks his wife for clinging to standards that can only be ludicrous in the circumstances in which they live.

The perspective of the lives of the white community of Kyauktada and the perspective of Mrs. Bowling's life are no greater than that of the *plongeur* or the tramp. In this kind of situation sensitivity is an embarrassment because it implies a recognition of inadequacy. Bowling, because of his discontent, is a hideous failure in the eyes of his wife. Flory, the rather half-hearted hero of *Burmese Days*, is acutely conscious of the con-

striction and falsity of colonialist life and is therefore a liability
to the community and an object of suspicion. The unhappiness
of the community's other members is quite apparent, but they
spend their days trying not to recognise it in each other. Drinking at the club is an essential part of this non-recognition. Flory
tries to move out of the tight circle, but the fact that he tries to
fraternise with the natives and to extend the daily actions of his
life beyond the community's narrow frontiers only isolates
him : and isolation increases his unhappiness. The vicious circle
was to become a characteristic of Orwell's fiction.

The novel is relentless : from the beginning Flory has no real
chance of changing the circumstances of his life, and the very
fact that he makes the attempt reduces his chances of survival.
The more he fights the more powerful becomes the European
influence. He cannot escape, and his actions are confined so
savagely that he almost inevitably disintegrates. This is a situation that recurs in Orwell's writing : the trapped hero thinks he
sees a way out, then fails to achieve what in fact is finally revealed to have been a delusion from the start. Flory, and later
Gordon Comstock, put a vast amount of effort into what turn
out to be meaningless revolts. They are meaningless not so much
because of the nature of the opposition, but because the pro-
tagonists do not really understand what they are revolting
against—and because they are not full-blooded enough.

Flory pins his hopes on Elizabeth Lackersteen. It is in her that
his revolt becomes confused. He is trying to fight against the
sterility of the white community. Yet he sees in marriage a
means of escape from what would otherwise be inevitable deterioration, marriage within the community meaning an embracing of its values, or non-values. To Flory Elizabeth is a
symbol of the outside world, of unspoilt youth. She is in fact
conventional, selfish and insensitive, and represents nothing that
Flory craves. It is quite clear that she does not have the potential
to become anything other than eminently acceptable to the
Europeans. Neither does she really exist for Flory as a person, in
spite of his dreams of companionship, but rather as a kind of

ornament which he wants to cheer up his life. He does not see that such a marriage would be corrupting, would be the final nail in the coffin of his sensibilities. Elizabeth would clearly become a copy of the other European wives: petty, narrow-minded and vicious. But she rejects him in favour of a more eligible suitor—who in his turn rejects her—and Flory commits suicide before he has time to test his isolation further.

Orwell emphasises Flory's self-hatred and his lack of self-confidence. He has a birth-mark on his face, of which he is acutely self-conscious. The birth-mark becomes the focus of all his hesitations. In fact Orwell forces Flory's disfiguration into a symbol, and the result is that we become too conscious of its artificial function. It becomes almost a substitute for character-isation. Orwell's tendency to force too much out of a symbol of this kind is seen again in *Keep the Aspidistra Flying* and in *Nineteen Eighty-Four*. Gordon's aspidistra is a symbol that only he takes seriously. Winston Smith's varicose ulcer works more successfully because it is a genuine part of Winston's physical inadequacy. But it is on the verge of becoming over-burdened.

In all his novels, except in the superbly simple *Animal Farm*, Orwell's characterisation is extraordinarily uneven, almost jerky. He seems at times unable to take his characters right through all the stages in their development, or their downfall, even though he himself is quite clear what these stages are. Flory sometimes has a relentless and depressing authority which is completely convincing. At other times Orwell's focus becomes blurred. Flory with his dog in the jungle, surrounded by natural colour and natural noise, is real. Flory in the club surrounded by unattractive men drinking lukewarm gin is not. The explanation partly lies in the nature of the conversation. It is intended to illustrate rather than express, so that we begin to lose touch with the personalities behind it. The speech of the frequenters of the club helps to fill in the picture we have of them. Once they have spoken we learn nothing more about their characters from further conversation.

One result of this is the tendency of Orwell's minor characters to disintegrate when they are alone. It is as if they are needed to prop each other up. Gathered in one room they stick together amorphously; this is part of the threat to Flory. But the threat is so great that Flory as a character withers in the face of it. In theory this could successfully represent a genuine confrontation. In fact Flory's reality dwindles. Neither his personality within the book nor his character as manipulated by Orwell can stand up to it.

In the portrayal of the Burman community there is a sympathy that is entirely absent from the presentation of the Europeans. And yet ostensibly it is a Burman, U Po Kyin, who is the villain of the piece, almost directly responsible for Flory's suicide. He contrives the humiliation that Flory cannot live through. The Burman community is present with a solid reality. There is a sharp edged clarity and an unsentimental understanding in Orwell's presentation of his Burmese characters and their curious mixture of abject humility and tough pride, of contempt for the whites and intense envy and admiration. This gives the novel some depth and draws attention away from some of the weaknesses. There is another source of energy in the natural descriptions. The best of the writing in *Burmese Days* is contained in the descriptions of Flory's walks, the leopard hunt, in the constant awareness of a very powerful and strange natural world. It is a world with which Flory is in alliance. It provides his escape from the civilised savagery of his fellow colonialists, and it is in the jungle that his relationship with Elizabeth comes most alive.

Their relationship is illuminated as they enter the natural and animal world. Their first encounter, which seems so promising, is filled with light by the shambling presence of the innocuous water buffalo, and Elizabeth responds at once to those aspects of Flory's character which later she despises—the more genuine aspects, in fact. Flory himself becomes a richer personality amongst natural beauty. When they return to the world of the club and petty controversy all this is lost. Again during the hunting expedition the relationship is transformed. There is real joy of experience. But this, too, has its ironic riposte when Flory presents Elizabeth with the foully cured leopard skin.

Again and again Orwell presents trapped humanity, and the resulting situations usually contain elements of tragedy suffocatingly wrapped round with hopelessness. In some cases the determination of his characters to embrace more than the immediate consequences of their actions, to be uncompromisingly either black or white, forces any tragic sense out of their individual predicaments. Flory's awareness of his position does not put a break on his disintegration but increases his responsibility for it. Because he understands the facts he understands the difficulty of combating them. But we do feel something tragic in the general situation, in the slow but automatic crumbling of humanity that takes place in the restricted, isolated community, so conscious of its superiority yet always on the defensive. We find these people pathetic, feeble and unforgivable. Flory is sensitive and sympathetic. He has principles and a conscience. The fact that none of these qualities can function properly is partly a result of his weakness and self-delusion. We do not feel moved by his death. And yet we are left with a blistering indictment of colonialism that focuses not so much on the effects of oppression on the oppressed as on the oppressors. It is as debilitating, Orwell is saying, to wield the whip as it is to feel the lash. Worst of all Flory, momentarily at the centre of a drama, becomes merely a fragment of the past. His friend Dr. Veraswami is ruined. U Po Kyin is elected first Burmese member of the club. And the threats to the tiny insignificant society, in the shape of Flory, the white outsider, and Veraswami, the native intruder, sink without a trace. Life goes on exactly as before. If there is any tragedy, it lies precisely in that fact.

Nineteen Eight-Four is Orwell's most extreme statement of the ineffectuality of individual action: Flory kills himself, Winston Smith becomes a radically different personality—in fact has his personality destroyed. In the two novels that followed *Burmese Days* Orwell continued his offensive against the middle class, but it remains an attack that is mounted at the expense of the individuals concerned. Dorothy, the clergyman's daughter, and Gordon Comstock are both trapped by environment and circumstance. They each make an attempt, Dorothy's partly involuntary, to break out. They each fail. They fail partly through their own weakness, partly through the insidious and pernicious nature of the environment and the class that grip them. And as class has made them what they are, they can almost be excused all responsibility for failure. It is perhaps this lack, or confusion, of responsibility that Orwell most bitterly attacks.

Dorothy, the chief character of *A Clergyman's Daughter* (1935), is the least successful of Orwell's fictional rebels. He is just not able to get far enough inside an unfamiliar consciousness. There was natural drama in the background details of *Burmese Days*. In *A Clergyman's Daughter* Orwell's own experience did not provide such a solid basis. The details of Dorothy's world are pallid, fluctuating and inconsistent. Dorothy herself is a pale, actionless creature who does little through her own initiative. The novel is essentially picaresque, but Dorothy does not direct her own footsteps.

It is not enough for Orwell to convey a precise sense of what it feels like to struggle with inadequate resources to make the Sunday joint last four days. This tells us what it is like not to have money; it does not illuminate Dorothy's personality. And although it is important for us to understand what Dorothy's struggle means in everyday domestic terms, we need this understanding as a support to Dorothy's character, not as a substitute for it. Orwell adds to his difficulties by deliberately selecting a watery personality as his centre. Dorothy is not only pale in appearance, she is pale in her responses. There are no extremes in her personality, no energy in her actions. At times she seems to fade into the detailed background. The hop-picking passages, for example, do not bolster her personality, as the jungle scenes bolster Flory's, but render it inconspicuous. She becomes no more important than the hop-picking itself.

The theme of the novel is hardly important. Dorothy's loss of memory, her subsequent wanderings and loss of faith, her return to her father's vicarage resigned to her fate as permanent slave to her environment, are the bones of an almost accidental plot. We are not so much interested in Dorothy's struggle with her faith as in the pictures of contemporary Britain for which this is a vehicle. In fact there are a number of aspects of the plot which it is difficult to take seriously—the cause of Dorothy's loss of memory for example. It seems that Orwell deliberately removed from her actions all sense of motive. In this she is the precise opposite of Gordon Comstock, who is throughout very conscious of the reactions between himself and his environment and the pressures that motivate him. It is difficult to grasp why Orwell should have made Dorothy motiveless. It removes what could have been an important cohesive factor in the plot. Its only dramatic purpose lies in the fact that Dorothy's awareness at the end of the novel is given a certain ironic force. It leads her back to the fold rather than into the world to act on her new convictions.

Dorothy's wanderings from quiet village to squalid London lodgings, from hop-picking in Kent to private school teaching, enable Orwell to bring together a series of detailed observations of the contemporary scene. The observations themselves are acute and energetic—they are in fact straightforward documentary and really should be looked at alongside *Down and Out* and *Wigan Pier*—but they lie in rather an actionless way in the construction of the novel. Although Dorothy is constantly on the move, there is no real movement in the novel. She is the essential link, and yet she is not purposeful enough to act as such. We look for a tightness of construction, a more deliberate and directed movement, a more dramatically prepared climax. We do not find these, and this contributes to the failure of Dorothy's predicament to convince.

The documentary passages are the real source of life in the novel, although they are presented in a series of static tableaux. The description of the night spent in Trafalgar Square is particularly memorable, and could stand on its own as a documentary sketch. Orwell's stance becomes that of witness rather than of fiction writer—in fact it has verged on this right through the novel, and this has caused some of Orwell's difficulties. In this passage we have no feeling at all of Dorothy's presence or her eyes watching what is going on :

> The people wriggle their wind-nipped faces into the heap like sucking pigs struggling for their mother's teats. One's inter-ludes of sleep shrink to a few seconds, and one's dreams grow more monstrous, troubling and undreamlike. There are times when nine people are talking almost normally, times when they can even laugh at their situation, and times when they press themselves together with a kind of frenzy, with deep groans of pain.[2]

Here it is Orwell himself that we are conscious of. We realise at once that he is describing something that he himself has ex-perienced, and he is describing it as if he himself were there. Dorothy becomes one small part of a mass of suffering. The details overwhelm her. In itself it does not matter. But it does not have any particular significance in Dorothy's development, and the scene which should be—and could be—the climactic point of the novel is allowed to dwindle in dramatic intensity as Dorothy moves off into further phases of her wanderings.

A Clergyman's Daughter is the least successful of Orwell's novels. He himself acknowledged this. Most of the reasons for its failure stem directly from Orwell's own uncertain position as a member of the middle class. At this time, before his political commitment had become specific, Orwell emotionally and intel-lectually rejected the middle class, but he himself being a pro-duct of respectability it was hard for him to find a secure posi-tion in society without some kind of compromise. He under-stood the mentality of those who, having ventured beyond the bounds of their social environment, were driven back within them. Perhaps in writing A Clergyman's Daughter he was try-ing to demonstrate to himself just how difficult it was to cast off conventional ties. Orwell's problem was Gordon Comstock's, but his attitude to reality was so utterly uncompromising that he could not begin to let himself try and escape in the way Gordon attempted. His attack on the middle-class environment was very personal. It could not be disentangled from his own experiences, and neither can *A Clergyman's Daughter*.

Not only did Orwell feel obliged to write about the contemporary scene, he enjoyed writing about England. His sense of obligation flattened Dorothy into an instrument of observation —not her own, but Orwell's. He was not able to look at society through her personality. His enjoyment gave his observations their vitality. He concentrated on the conditions and circumstances of life rather than on the individuals involved in them. This works perfectly in documentary, but in fiction it makes the writer's task a great deal more difficult. Orwell's documentary intentions swamp the other aspects of the novel. He is not really interested in Dorothy's loss of faith—it is after all the major development in her character—and cannot make it real for us in the way that he can make the facts that influenced her real. What is missing is Dorothy's own consciousness. Orwell let his own do all the work.

We can learn something of the bitterness of Orwell's position from his next novel, *Keep the Aspidistra Flying*. This novel is not without faults, but it is much richer, tougher and more relentless than *A Clergyman's Daughter*, and nearer home than *Burmese Days*. It is savagely and deliberately confined. The pressures on its hero, Gordon Comstock, are so great because he is restricted not only by his own attitudes and circumstances, but by the drabness of London life without money. Gordon thinks that by his decision to reject money, to earn as little of it as possible, he can break away from its tyranny and the tyranny of the classes who have money. But in fact the less money he has the more conscious he is of every penny, the more of a slave to money he becomes. London closes in on him. The meagre bookshop in which he works and the meagre lodgings which are all he can afford are his only territory of existence. He cannot afford to escape, to take a bus to a different locality, even to find solace in making love to Rosemary, because he cannot afford contraceptives.

The result of this confinement is the aggravating awareness of the futility of Gordon's uncompromising position. When he realises he is achieving nothing he decides that it is his ambition to achieve nothing. We suspect continually that it is not anger at monopoly capitalism that urges him to opt out from the rat race, but boredom and self-resentment. There is no political consciousness in his actions at all. When he loses his job and has to take another at a lower wage he embraces the opportunity to sink—it means, as it means for the tramps of *Down and Out*, that he no longer has to feel responsibility. He gives up trying to organise his life, to make any effort on his own behalf, and to respond to human beings on even the most undemanding level. Gordon allows his sordid surroundings to dictate his responses to other individuals, especially to Rosemary. For this reason we condemn him, and cannot sympathise as we sympathise with Flory or with Dorothy.

Gordon is a son of the depressed middle class who has been disgusted by the attempt to cling to meaningless standards of gentility. Orwell offered this as an explanation of the attraction of Communism to middle-class intellectuals: "why did these young men turn towards anything so alien as Russian Communism? Why should *writers* be attracted by a form of socialism that makes mental honesty impossible? The explanation really lies in something that had already made itself felt before the slump and before Hitler: middle-class unemployment."[3] Gordon does not turn to Communism, but middle-class unemployment, the fear of unemployment, the cuts in wages— teachers' wages, for instance, had been reduced in 1931—were an important part both of Gordon's background and his own situation. Gordon shares the predicament of those who were leaving university at the end of the twenties and the beginning of the thirties—the time when Orwell himself returned from Burma to try and make a new career for himself. It is not insignificant that so many of the thirties writers went into school teaching : it was one of the few professions a man with a degree could get into without difficulty. Gordon himself goes from school to an advertising office, but his longing for a more creative and less enslaved existence persuades him to leave it.

He at first feels that because he is fighting against all that he considers poisonous and degrading his own life will in some way become vigorous and creative. But because it is such a personal and essentially selfish revolt it is bound to be limited. The fact that his actions bring no satisfaction he blames on his lack of money, and the vicious circle utterly demoralises him. He loathes middle-class values, yet he will not allow Rosemary to share the expenses of an outing together, although he knows she can afford it. Rosemary and Gordon's monied friend Ravelston are the only two genuinely energetic and warm characters in the book. Both are generous and frank, yet Rosemary comes from the same sterile middle-class background as Gordon, and Ravelston, according to Gordon's logic, ought to be hateful on account of his wealth. Rosemary has the courage to ignore both Gordon's surroundings and their perversion of him. Gordon resents this courage.

Advertisements become the focal point of Gordon's hatred. They feature almost with the energy of a character. As Gordon moves around London they are always present, and are a continual reminder of Gordon's enemies. We come to know the faces and the slogans on the posters as well as we come to know Gordon. They seem to be continually jeering at him in their picture of a bright, non-existent world, and it is just this mockery that angers Gordon most. But it is significant that Gordon sees the objects of his hatred in terms of symbols—the posters, the aspidistra—for he never really gets his picture of society into perspective.

There is a similarity, in the kind of sub-existence that Gordon sinks into, between *Keep the Aspidistra Flying* and some of J. B. Priestley's novels. Orwell himself had no respect for Priestley. In a review in the *New English Weekly* Orwell spoke of the

"Priestleyan assumption that 'real' life means lower-middle-class life in a large town and that if you can pack into your novel, say, fifty-three descriptions of tea in a Lyons Corner House, you have done the trick."[4] *Keep the Aspidistra Flying* is a novel of depressed, if not lower, middle-class life in a large town, though it never has the scope of most of Priestley's novels. In *Angel Pavement* the collection of faded personalities in the disintegrating office of Twigg and Dersingham and the drabness of their lives matches the mood of much of Orwell's writing. Priestley is concerned with very much the same kind of minutiae of daily living that fascinates Orwell. He tells us exactly where and what his characters eat, he details their bus journeys, tells us how they spend their money down to the last penny. And for most of them life is as unrelieved and sterile as it is for Gordon Comstock.

But there is something near to cheerfulness in the way Priestley presents these details and describes this dreary life. Many of the characters in *Angel Pavement* are totally pathetic, but their creator obviously has a great affection for them, partly, it seems, through the belief that they are real, that they could be seen walking down any street. Reality works in quite a different way on Orwell. It reinforces his bitterness rather than encouraging tolerance. Priestley describes Turgis, a clerk with Twigg and Dersingham, returning to his Camden Town lodgings:

Number Nine, like all the other houses in Nathaniel Street. was small and dark, and its gloomy little hall was haunted by a mixed smell of cabbage, camphor, and old newspapers. Turgis never noticed this smell, but on the very rare occasions when he visited some other and less odorous house, then he noticed the absence of it, his nose declaring at once that it had found itself in an unfamiliar atmosphere.[5]

There is a hint of Dickensian comedy in this passage—as there is in the name Twigg and Dersingham. Priestley understands the unpleasantness of what he describes, yet he does not allow Turgis himself to feel it. Priestley's own attitude of slightly

patronising superiority is revealed in affectionate humour—
"his nose declaring at once that it had found itself in an unfamiliar atmosphere". These are features entirely absent when
Orwell describes a similar scene—Gordon returning to the respectable lodgings he has before losing his job:

> Willowbed Road, N.W., was not definitely slummy, only
> dingy and depressing. There were real slums hardly five
> minutes' walk away. Tenement houses where families slept
> five in a bed, and, when one of them died, slept every night
> with the corpse until it was buried; alley-ways where girls of
> fifteen were deflowered by boys of sixteen against leprous
> plaster walls. But Willowbed Road itself contrived to keep up
> a kind of mingy, lower-middle-class decency. There was even
> a dentist's brass plate on one of the houses. In quite two-thirds
> of them, amid the lace curtains of the parlour window, there
> was a green card with "Apartments" on it in silver lettering,
> above the peeping foliage of an aspidistra. . . .
>   Gordon took out his key and fished about in the keyhole—
> in that kind of house the key never quite fits the lock. The
> darkish little hallway—in reality it was only a passage—smelt
> of dishwater, cabbage, rag mats and bedroom slops. Gordon
> glanced at the japanned tray on the hall-stand. No letters, of
> course.[6]

The significant difference between the two passages is that
Turgis is indifferent to his surroundings while Gordon is rawly
sensitive to his. Turgis has never had any other experience of
life, while Gordon was brought up amongst pretensions to good
living that were rather higher than the pretensions of Willow-
bed Road. While Priestley can suggest that there is nothing particularly obnoxious about the smell of cabbage, Orwell implies
that it is the most ghastly smell imaginable. They are each describing much the same area of London. Priestley is content to
ignore the slums around the corner, Orwell emphasises them
with a few choice details, although they bear no important rela-

tion to the plot. While Priestley generalises only to the extent of saying that Number Nine was like all the other houses in the street Orwell makes sweeping statements such as "in that kind of house the key never quite fits the lock". It is the pretension that Gordon has no tolerance for, the pretensions to a cramped decency which is undermined by the smell of cabbage, while Turgis would not be aware, and would not care, if the "mingy decency" were contrived or genuine. He has always lived with it and feels strange without it.

Priestley's characters, like Orwell's, are not able to break out of their surroundings. They are occasionally allowed brief escapes, but these tend to be unhappy interludes from which they return with something like relief. There is sometimes the moralistic suggestion that they are much better off not adventuring outside the familiar confines of their lives. The high point of Turgis' life is his weekly Saturday evening out. He always follows the same routine : a bus to the West End, tea in a Lyons Corner House, then the pictures. Always he is dreaming of an encounter with "a wonderful girl" which never happens. It never occurs to him to do anything else, but he is always very conscious of the fact that his life is rigidly bound by the amount of money he has to spend. Orwell dwells on similar details of London life when he describes Gordon's wanderings. He is forced to walk everywhere, and we always know precisely where he is, geographically, though Gordon himself does not know where life is taking him. There is a shaded irony in this, an irony that is never present in Priestley's writing. As Gordon appears to walk in ever decreasing circles the city grows more oppressive. Turgis's life may be limited by the bus routes from Camden Town to Angel Pavement and to the West End, but it does not grow more limited. Gordon allows life to bring him to a standstill; finally he does not even move from his room.

When Gordon makes the attempt to break out he fails dismally. His night out with Ravelston ends in drunkenness and the loss of his job. The trip to the country with Rosemary, at first deceptively warm and carefree, ends in humiliation and anger.

As the material world intrudes, as they emerge from the fields to the pseudo-tudor villas, Gordon is utterly defeated by a cowardice that does not match his principles. When faced with having to choose whether to spend more money than he can afford or admit to a hotel waiter that he has very little, Gordon has not the courage to do the latter. He has created rules for himself that are as rigid as the class conventions he so much despises, and this scene is a relentless expression of his failure. From this point his revolt no longer has any substance.

The lesson is reinforced when he tries to make love to Rosemary, significantly *after* his humiliation in the hotel. The crudity of his advances outweighs the tenderness, and finally it is not so much Rosemary's rejection of him that is so devastating as Gordon's selfishness and vicious detachment. As Rosemary lies naked in the sun Gordon is fully clothed feeling his eightpence clink in his pocket, and thinking, "Get on with it, that's the great thing, get on with it and damn the future!"[7]

Rosemary's rejection magnifies humiliation into squalid and grotesque failure. Gordon's anger and sulkiness show that while he is cursing money he is in reality resenting his own lack of it. "Even in the most secret action of your life you don't escape it; you've still got to spoil everything with filthy cold-blooded precautions for money's sake."[8]

The day in the country, the only day that promises some kind of fulfilment, marks the point at which Gordon becomes completely incapable of halting his deterioration. He has a preconceived vision of the consequences of all his actions, and grows perversely determined to fulfil the details of this vision. When he has to move into the slums he is determined to make the most of his downfall:

To spend your days in meaningless mechanical work, work that could be slovened through in a sort of coma; . . . to sit over a squalid meal of bacon, bread-and-marge and tea, cooked over the gas-ring; to lie on the frowzy bed, reading a thriller or doing the Brain Brighteners in *Tit Bits* until the small hours;

it was the kind of life he wanted. . . . Without regret, almost intentionally, he was letting himself go to pieces. . . . Life had beaten him; but you can still beat life by turning your face away. Better to sink than rise.[9]

The important point here is that Gordon is still fatally class-conscious. It offends him to have to live in a slum; there is no inherent reason why his meal should be squalid or his bed frowzy. He makes no effort to make his slum more habitable.

The final confrontation of Rosemary's energetic warmth and Gordon's depravity, the unenjoyed consummation of their love in Gordon's squalid room, has, inevitably, comfortless results. It is the climax of Gordon's unresisted demoralisation, not of love, an essentially irresponsible act although Rosemary proposes it, but it does ironically provide the means of shocking Gordon into the realisation that even conventional life is serious. Rosemary's pregnancy leads him back to the middle-class fold; it also generates real warmth of response in him. He resents the principle but enjoys the fact of having a wife and home, of impending fatherhood. His ridiculous gesture of insisting on providing their flat with an aspidistra is in fact outweighed by his pride and excitement. The aspidistra is an overloaded symbol, but it finally comes to represent Gordon's uncompromising attempts to keep light and colour out of his life just at the time when his prospects are brightest. It reminds us that Gordon's character has not been transformed, and, most important, that although he has been forced to reject the amorality of his old life, he has found no vigorous way of replacing it. He remains fundamentally complacent.

Gordon's revolt fails because there is no constructive purpose behind it. The novel was written before Orwell himself had given any positive indication that he would embrace the principles of socialism. In none of these three novels does disgust with middle-class values link up with political belief. As Orwell himself admitted it was not until his experiences in Spain that his commitment became solid. The suspicion of politics, which Gordon to

D

some extent reflects, stayed with Orwell right through his career. He did not trust men who made politics their career rather than a part of their moral outlook, and part of their daily life, as Orwell did. Both Gordon and Dorothy might have made sense out of their revolt if they had had a genuine political belief. It seems fairly clear that Orwell, although he maintained his independence, found a very necessary guide in his commitment.

We cannot read these novels as political novels. They are novels about class, and they are documentaries. In many respects their picture of contemporary Britain is devastatingly accurate, and although politics do not feature in them the tone of Orwell's descriptions is as fiercely committed as the tone of the documentary in *Down and Out* or *Wigan Pier*. The more casual tone of Priestley's writing emphasises this. Priestley, from a rather different standpoint, was concerned with many of the same areas of life that Orwell handled. He, too, was a man of the left, but his commitment does not inject itself into the language he uses in the same way that Orwell's does. He was, perhaps, too fond of much of what he described. It can be said of most of the left-wing fiction and documentary of the period that, however explicitly socialist the ideas expressed, the language rarely contains the challenging hatred that runs through these novels of Orwell's. In *Wigan Pier* this electrifying quality becomes something of an embarrassment, but fictional characters and fictional situations on the whole tone it into something more meaningful. Even if Orwell's characters cannot make their revolt as creative as his was they express with bitter clarity Orwell's own harried and isolated class position.

5
THE NECESSITY OF ACTION

In July 1936 the generals' revolt against the government of Spain began. Orwell went to Spain towards the end of that year. He went as a journalist sponsored by the Independent Labour Party and with a contract from Secker and Warburg to produce a book about his experiences. Like almost everyone else he had little idea of what was going on. He did not understand the complexities of the war, or its origins, and went to Spain out of curiosity and interest rather than from any passionate conviction. But his experience of revolutionary Barcelona impressed him deeply, and he at once felt compelled to fight. By December the spirit of revolution, which Cyril Connolly had described so enthusiastically, was already beginning to decline, but enough remained to move Orwell to say "There was much in it that I did not understand, in some ways I did not even like it, but I recognised it immediately as a state of affairs worth fighting for".[1] Typically, although Orwell at once set about investigating the situation with his usual thoroughness, his first response is instinctive. But he followed the logic of that response and joined the POUM (Partido Obrero de Unificacion Marxista) militia. POUM, though very much isolated and a party with which Orwell was not fully sympathetic, was the party in Spain most closely associated with the ILP. Orwell's combination of logic and instinct led him further in the direction of transforming words into actions than many of his fellow socialists were prepared to go. It would have been easy and justifiable for him to carry on with the job he went to do, but to enlist was consistent with his way of life as his way of life was consistent with what he wrote. It was part of his attempt to eliminate the disparity between intention and action, between words and deeds.

Homage to Catalonia, the record of his experiences, is perhaps Orwell's most important work politically. It is also the most finely written of his documentaries. He did not present an impressionistic image of war, nor did he celebrate his own actions. His purpose, as always, was to tell the truth as far as it was possible, whether the truth about the ordinary details of life in the trenches or about large-scale political conspiracy. The Civil War had more than a symbolic meaning for Orwell, and even in retrospect, in his essay "Looking Back on the Spanish War", it was an indication of life he wanted to give. It came to mean more than the classic representation of the defeat of socialist revolution, although it contained all the classic levels of betrayal and Orwell had closely observed them.

This observation brought him an intense and personal understanding of betrayal. It confirmed his distrust of Communism and extended the basis of his pessimism. But it was also Orwell's first experience of fighting in the trenches, his first chance of carrying revolutionary activity to its most logical and extreme lengths, and this was bound to be important to him. Even more significant, the war confirmed and clarified his belief in socialism, and gave it a solid centre that he had never found in England.

Most of the volunteers from Britain joined the predominately Communist International Brigades. Orwell was unusual in fighting with POUM, but there were other ILP members with him. He viewed his time at the front with an almost quizzical detachment. It is clear that at times he enjoyed his first experience of war. When it was not enjoyable it was often extremely tedious. There was little fighting: the worst Orwell had to endure was perpetual and extreme discomfort. He had plenty of time to absorb the details of the situation and the people around him. The Republican army was a tattered and pathetic mob, many of the soldiers were boys in their teens, ill-armed largely because the Communist Government was afraid that the Anarchists and

POUM would turn against it if they obtained efficient weapons. The atmosphere was dominated by pathos and clumsiness. At that time on the Aragon front there was little opportunity for displays of courage. But the most significant feature of the militia was the equality of rank:

> The essential point of the system was social equality between officers and men. Everyone from general to private drew the same pay, ate the same food, wore the same clothes, and mingled on terms of complete equality. . . . In theory at any rate each militia was a democracy not a hierarchy. It was understood that when you gave an order you gave it as comrade to comrade, not as superior to inferior.[2]

This, like the classlessness of Barcelona, was what appealed to Orwell so profoundly and helped to confirm his socialist beliefs. The Republicans lost the war, but for a brief space of time men lived happily and constructively under a socialist system. In explaining the way in which this kind of discipline worked— " 'Revolutionary' discipline depends on political consciousness —on an understanding of *why* orders must be obeyed"—Orwell explains how socialism should work.

It is helpful to compare Orwell's account of war with those of other writers. There were many books and essays produced describing experiences in Spain, but most of these are coloured by the consciousness of fighting an ideological war and being on the losing side, a self-consciousness, in fact, which is inevitably shaped by the bitterness of defeat and betrayal. As impressions of the individual struggling with the facts and objects of war, descriptions of the First World War are more impressive and more interesting. In these we are more conscious of the individual's handling of life and death and of the likelihood of death eating into their normality. Descriptions of the Spanish War inevitably fix our attention on Spain's peculiar tragedy, and the helplessness of outsiders who come to her aid.

Robert Graves's *Goodbye to All That* displays a mixture of

horror and jolliness, of objectivity and egotism, which focuses
attention on himself rather than on events. The intention is not
so much to record details as to present an individual hemmed in
by details, but dominating them with a certain ease. Graves discusses his fear in a tone of relaxed enquiry. Beside *Goodbye to
All That* the prose of *Homage to Catalonia* is uncluttered, the
language precisely articulate and the tone vital and unequivocal.
There are no contortions of personality. *Homage to Catalonia* is
a dramatic but undramatised document; *Goodbye to All That* a
deliberate *tour de force*. Where Graves is flamboyant Siegfried
Sassoon is good natured, the bitterness of his poetry controlled
by his easeful response to nature and his penetrating understanding of the facts of war.

Neither *Goodbye to All that* nor *Memoirs of an Infantry
Officer* can rival the intensity of the work of the German writers,
Renn, Toller and Regler. Their reaction, like Wilfred Owen's, is
a constant conflict between being entirely overwhelmed by the
situation's horror and the compulsion to communicate it, to
find some kind of articulate meaning. They attempted to bring
physical chaos under intellectual control, and they had a much
deeper and more complex vision of chaos than had the English
writers. Gustav Regler's reaction was the most tortured, his
prose the most expressive :

> We lived in a lunar landscape, quite inhuman, carved up in
> the fear-inspired geography of the trenches, strewn with the
> rotting fragments of corpses; a neutral territory with which
> no divine spirit could wish to have further dealings. But then,
> did any such spirit wish to have dealings with us? I doubted
> it; there was too little sense in the things we did. At night we
> crept out between the lines, scarcely knowing one from the
> other, and flung grenades at random into shell-holes. We sat
> in dug-outs shored up with timber and killed rats.[3]

Because Regler concentrates on expressing the oppressive feeling of uselessness as much as physical suffering his picture is

more disturbing than that of Graves who can dwell on death with something like passive irony. (Regler's writing does bring Paul Nash to mind, but on the whole there is a marked difference between the German and the English writers of the First World War. The English writers seemed to be able to preserve their sense of humour—perhaps damagingly—which shone through the shock.) The random flinging of grenades into shell-holes represents an abyss of senseless action. It is this more than the rotting corpses that horrifies. The passage emphasises a crucial difference between the two wars: the First War meaningless, the Spanish War with almost too much meaning crowded into it. Yet a comparison with *Homage to Catalonia* illuminates the quality of the documentary, and of personal response, in both books.

Orwell puts his picture together out of the facts of sight, sound and smell that he experiences. He is not after an image or an expressive symbol. When he uses a simile it is precise, and usually drawn from common experience. He is constantly making use of the commonplace to throw light on the unusual and shocking. He describes his *centuria* approaching the front line:

> As we neared the line the boys round the red flag in front began to utter shouts of "Visca POUM!" "Fascistas—maricones!" and so forth—shouts which were meant to be war-like and menacing, but which, from those childish throats, sounded as pathetic as the cries of kittens. It seemed dreadful that the defenders of the Republic should be this mob of ragged children carrying worn-out rifles which they did not know how to use. I remember wondering what would happen if a Fascist aeroplane passed our way—whether the airman would even bother to dive down and give us a burst from his machine-gun. Surely even from the air he could see that we were not real soldiers.[4]

As always Orwell is relying on ordinary language to convey intense feelings and an out of the ordinary situation. "It seemed

dreadful", he writes, and proceeds to show just how meaningful
the word "dreadful" is. He does not achieve this by creating any
kind of drama or tension, by using language as a means of inflat-
ing incident. He is simple and exact, and achieves his full effect
by a very delicate irony: the Fascist airman, would not, of
course, have hesitated to shoot down "the mob of ragged children". The apposition of the shouts and "the cries of kittens",
"the defenders of the Republic" and the children with their
worn-out rifles is not dramatically exploited, but leads gently
to our full recognition of the horror.

Regler describes a fellow soldier:

> He looked, in his uniform, like a child in fancy-dress. The
> whole thing was such an evil joke. The churned-up, rat-grey
> earth around us, where for years nothing would grow, was
> like an indictment. The child in fancy-dress had hand-grenades
> slung round his waist which he would detach to fling in the
> faces of strangers. Back in the wood Gabens had always been
> full of poetry; he was like an aeolian harp amid the trees,
> moved to song by every puff of wind. Now, however, he was
> like a damned soul, with lice in his shirt, gasses in his entrails,
> sores on his toes, a strayed eighteen-year-old Job.[5]

Regler's prose is packed with irony, regret, horror, a whole range
of emotions that he is trying to force his language to accommodate. He moves rapidly from the precise detail to the vague,
impressionistic phrase, and his tone swerves from pathos to
melodrama to tragi-comedy. It is a deliberate inconsistency. He
is trying to force a reaction by using precisely the opposite
method of Orwell, through powerful contrasts and dramatic
similes. Regler sees Gabens not merely in a physical landscape
but in a tapestry of his own emotions and moral feelings.

It is not only that each writer uses vocabulary of a different
quality. Regler is interpreting what he has witnessed as he describes it. The interpretation is violent, intense, subjective and
profoundly moral. It is not necessarily logical nor does it obvi-

ously grow directly from the facts that Regler marshals. The interpretation interferes with the prose, although it does not interrupt it, and sets up a constant process of change, back and forth, between physical detail and an appeal to other layers of existence. Orwell, though so eminently direct in his writing, is more oblique in his interpretation. He does not interfere, he merely guides. He indicates unequivocally how his readers should respond by convincing them of his authenticity, his accuracy and his good faith. He does not lay down the law about what ought to be believed, but tells what seems to be the truth in such a way that it has to be believed.

It is this paradoxical obliqueness of Orwell that contributes to the frequently observed Swiftian element in his writing. It leads him to arrive at entirely unexpected comments, or to twist a casual observation so violently out of proportion that it becomes shocking, or to describe suffering and death in such a brief and unmoved tone of voice that its conventional inappropriateness again shocks, as in the following passage:

My strength was coming back, and one day, by going slowly, I managed to walk down as far as the beach. It was queer to see the seaside life going on almost as usual; the smart cafés along the promenade and the plump local bourgeoisie bathing and sunning themselves in deckchairs as though there had not been a war within a thousand miles. Nevertheless, as it happened, I saw a bather drowned, which one would have thought impossible in that shallow and tepid sea.[6]

The curious bathos of the final sentence, and particularly of the final phrase, which should not have been in any sense anticlimactic, is very similar to the technique Swift uses, and matches it rhythmically also, although in Swift's case the juxtaposition usually works within larger units. Orwell makes no attempt to prepare us for death; he deliberately places the fact of drowning casually in a calm and quiet scene. It is parallel to a sentence like Swift's "Last week I saw a woman flayed, and you will hardly believe how it altered her person for the worst". And yet Orwell's purpose was rather different from Swift's. He was not predominantly a satirist. He was not trying, as Swift was, to arrive at exposure through savage ridicule. He was combining a technique of exposure through understatement and exposure through the unexpected association of the commonplace and the startling.

Orwell describes deaths at the front in much the same fashion. He does not attempt an impression of "death", nor an analysis of his own reaction, but produces a plain picture of what men look like when they are wounded and dying, or, in his own case, what he felt when he thought he was dying. Graves witnesses the deaths of friends with a similar detachment, but there is a buoyancy, a feeling, almost, of self-congratulation that he himself is alive, that colours the descriptions, and detracts from the power of understatement. It is difficult at this point not to return to Keith Douglas, whose calm yet agonised description of the man dead beside his haversack challenges all others. Both Graves and Orwell avoid the emotional intensity which Douglas expresses in such a controlled fashion. Douglas wrote without irony, while the deliberate underplaying of conventionally emotional situations, which both Graves and Orwell use, lends itself to irony. Graves's description of the sergeant who blows himself up when he is explaining how not to handle a grenade, Orwell's description of the continual accidental going off of guns and the mule driver who was "accidentally shot by a political delegate who was playing the fool with an automatic pistol and had put five bullets in the mule driver's lungs"[7] are both on the same unexpressive level. The element of shocking comedy is similar to that of Swift's Modest Proposal.

Orwell was inadvertently involved in the street fighting in Barcelona of May 1937. Trouble between the Anarchists and the Communists had been expected, and when the fighting began Orwell found himself defending POUM, although he was not committed to their beliefs and was in fact trying to get a transfer to the International Brigades. At that time Orwell considered the

Communist policy of concentrating on winning the war and meanwhile suspending revolutionary activities the most sensible position. He writes:

> The Communists had a definite practical policy, an obviously better policy from the point of view of the common sense which looks only a few months ahead. . . . What clinched everything was that the Communists—so it seemed to me— were getting on with the war while we and the Anarchists were standing still. This was the general feeling at the time. . . . The revolutionary purism of the POUM, though I saw its logic, seemed to me rather futile. After all, the one thing that mattered was to win the war.[8]

But when it became clear that part of government policy was the systematic liquidation of Anarchist and Trotskyist factions (particularly Trotskyist—this was the time of the Moscow Purges) Orwell's natural reaction was to defend the persecuted. Also, of course, he was in a good position to have knowledge of POUM's activities.

Orwell apologises for devoting two chapters to an explanation of the political situation in Spain and the book has been much criticised on the grounds that these chapters interrupt the narrative. Clearly Orwell's attempt to establish the truth about the street fighting would be of little value without a broader perspective of the various parties and factions involved. Just as clearly, Orwell could not simply ignore the street fighting, for he was intimately concerned with it. In wider terms, he could not attempt to describe an essentially political war without discussing politics. The political chapters are a very proper part of the narrative and of Orwell's "homage to Catalonia". It is now fairly well established that the feud became violent as a direct result of an attempt by the Communists to take over entire control of Barcelona. The government Civil and Assault Guards were well armed (with arms that the men at the front desperately needed) while the Trotskyists and Anarchists had very little in the way of weapons. However, the fighting itself did not settle very much. It was after it subsided that serious steps were taken to quell opposition to the Communists.

Orwell sets out to give a clear and accurate picture of the precise facts of the fighting itself and of the subsequent outlawing of POUM. Being a small party, Trotskyist and the least strong it was singled out as scapegoat. The Communists laid total blame for the fighting on POUM. The party was outlawed, its leaders and many of its followers hunted down, imprisoned and done away with. Orwell himself narrowly missed a similar fate. The Communist characterisation of POUM was widely accepted in Britain, and Orwell spends some time in illustrating the inaccuracy of many of the newspaper reports that followed the Communist line.

Typically, Orwell begins by eliminating all pretensions and pointing out the limits of his usefulness and the limitations of his method :

> It will never be possible to get a completely accurate and unbiassed account of the Barcelona fighting, because the necessary records do not exist. Future historians will have nothing to go upon except a mass of accusations and party propaganda. I myself have little data beyond what I saw with my own eyes and what I have learnt from other eye-witnesses whom I believe to be reliable. I can, however, contradict some of the more flagrant lies and help to get the affair into some kind of perspective.[9]

He takes a chance, for there can be two reactions to declaration of fallibility, one a conviction of the writer's honesty and therefore reliability, the other a dismissal of anything unpalatable he might say. It is a risk Orwell continually takes, in an almost defiant manner, but it is to some extent cancelled out by his technique of persuasion—the devotion to detail, the balance, the self-effacement, the avoidance of any kind of clouded expression. All this combines to make us believe that when Orwell says

POUM had only eighty rifles he is correct, and the reports that spoke of them manning captured tanks are wrong. Orwell's emphasis on his own bias and the impossibility of complete objectivity is also counteracted by his systematic exposure of the inaccuracies and deliberate lies of the press. He does this by revealing, as well as their lack of correspondence with the facts as he observed them, their inconsistencies, illogicalities, contradictions and vagueness, particularly over the accusations they were heaping on POUM. It is imprecision above all that Orwell attacks. Precision should be the journalist's major weapon; too often it was considered to be too risky a quality for anyone who was not genuinely independent to handle.

Homage to Catalonia was not a popular book. It did not coincide with the mood on the left that responded to Spain as the battlefield of idealistic socialism. Of its first edition it sold barely nine hundred copies of the fifteen hundred printed. It was scantily reviewed, and those reviews it received were patronising in tone and countered Orwell's exposure with precisely those arguments he had been at such pains to destroy. V. S. Pritchett represents a typical reaction to Orwell's embarrassing concern with the truth :

> . . . being constitutionally "agin the government" he undertakes POUM's defence. There seems to be no doubt that the wretched POUM got a raw deal. But though he writes with honest indignation about the lies that were spread about men who were fighting the common enemy and has the idealist's attractive and understandable loathing for the grey arguments of expediency, Mr. Orwell is, I am afraid, wrongheaded when he carries the defence into the field of high politics and strategy.[10]

This represents what had by this time become a standard response to Orwell's writing—a superior toned praise of his honesty joined with disparagement of his political judgment. In V. S. Pritchett's review we are not told *how* Orwell is "wrongheaded", and, of course, Orwell was deliberately not carrying his defence into "the field of high politics and strategy"—he limited it to his own experience. He described the facts, exposed the lies and suggested that the Republican military position was endangered because of the waste of men and arms in Barcelona. The implication of Pritchett's comment is that because Orwell is "honest", "an idealist", and loathes "the grey arguments of expediency" he is not to be taken seriously. The words are used as disparaging criticism. This was the kind of mental reaction that provided a basis for the apologists of Stalin.

On his return from Spain Orwell discovered that he had to face this reaction continually. Kingsley Martin refused to publish his articles on Spain in the *New Statesman*. A large part of the left in Britain dismissed Orwell as it accepted the Moscow Purges and the Nazi/Soviet Pact. It was almost impossible to penetrate the barriers against fact and the refusal to believe in anything but the innocence of Communism. The consequences of doubt meant facing up to the full impact of betrayal and defeat and for many the reaction was much delayed. Orwell returned to England a convinced, if embittered, socialist only to find that no one wanted to listen to him. His experience of action had come from his understanding of its necessity, but had inevitably given birth to a hatred of war. The growth of Fascism, the evident nearness of war on a much vaster scale, the antics of the left-wing factions and the general refusal to face facts generated an intensely depressed response. Munich, the Nazi–Soviet Pact and the inevitability of a Fascist victory in Spain fertilised Orwell's growing pessimism. Paradoxically, and characteristically, they also reinforced his socialism.

In the summer of 1936 Koestler was working in Paris with the Comintern Propaganda Department. His career before this had been erratic and varied. Koestler was two years younger than Orwell and had spent his early days in Budapest and Vienna. He left the university at Vienna in 1925, before completing his degree, to go to Palestine. Fired with Zionism, and inspired by personal contact with Vladimir Jabotinsky, the Zionist leader, he spent some time on a *kibbutz*, a communal settlement, but, significantly, was not found suitable for acceptance on a permanent basis. It was in Palestine that he began his journalistic career. He worked briefly in a tiny news agency and began to write articles which he sent back to Europe. By 1932 he was foreign editor and assistant editor-in-chief of Berlin's *B.Z. am Mittag*. It was in this year also that he joined the German Communist Party.

Koestler's political experiences were both more varied and more extreme than those of Orwell. Koestler came to grips with politics in the disturbed climate of the Europe of between the Wars. Orwell's only experience of action (apart, of course, from his police work) was in the Spanish Civil War. In England he had been sheltered from both the danger and the drama of European politics. In such a context it was natural that Koestler, having a passionate sympathy for the underdog and a powerful vision of utopia, should join the Communist Party, especially the German Communist Party, at this time the most thriving and active force on the left. It was less natural that Orwell, fiercely pledged to an ideal, should reject commitment to any party, creed or authority other than his own conviction.

Koestler went to Paris after the Reichstag fire of 1934, when he was no longer able to live in Germany. The Party in Germany was disastrously in ruins. Koestler himself says that it prepared for its own defeat by carefully working out detailed and elaborate systems of going underground if the occasion arose. There was no effective opposition to Hitler. Koestler, like Orwell, went to Spain as a journalist, a professional and experienced journalist. He went officially as a correspondent of Hungary's *Pester Lloyd* and of England's *News Chronicle*, but in fact as a Communist propagandist working for Willi Meunzenberg, head of the Propaganda Department.

The war in Spain brought together for the first time the European and the English left-wing experience. Koestler's own political career had to some extent prepared him for a conflict of this kind. He had lived in a number of centres of activity, in Palestine, Berlin and Paris. He had had a number of political functions to fulfil. He had spent a year in Russia refusing to believe the implications of what he saw, he was well versed in Marxism, he was well acquainted with the more sordid and mundane facts of political life. Idealism had long since ceased to play a dominant part in his political thinking and activity. His actions were dictated by what he saw to be the logic of commit-ment. For Orwell and many British socialists Spain represented the climax of idealism. Koestler was both hardened and uneasy.

The majority of Englishmen who volunteered in Spain were politically unsophisticated, and what experience they had was on the level of Labour Party and Trade Union politics which was far removed from the struggle for survival against Hitlerism in which Koestler had taken part in Germany and France. He was familiar with conspiracy and danger, schooled to it, to an extent that made left wingers in England appear to be playing at politics. And yet he had never fired a gun for his cause. He was as innocent, in these terms, of revolutionary action as any Englishman. And while so many other innocents were under-going their baptism by fire Koestler remained an observer. His two visits to Spain were both made as a journalist. He could not obey any instinct to fight that he may have had for he was bound by the demands of the Party. He had a function to fulfil which did not include entering into combat. For many English-men the experience and the failure in Spain proved to be over-whelming. Their political understanding did not have the neces-sary resilience to accommodate the bitterness of Spain, and then to face later a retreat from Communism while retaining their socialism. For Koestler Spain rubbed salt into wounds that had before them barely manifested themselves. The reaction to the strain of his visits to Russia, where he was forced to find the intellectual means to deny the facts that his eyes witnessed, was much delayed. Spain triggered it off. The fact that he went from Spain to England, after three months in a death cell, and found himself in an entirely different political atmosphere encouraged the deterioration of his Communism and the growth of his pessimism.

When Koestler went to Spain he was already aware that there existed differences between his own inclinations and the Party. He had already felt the strain in Paris. In spite of this he set out, as he had been instructed, to produce a piece of deliberate propaganda which he knew to contain half-truths, if not lies, and distortions. *Spanish Testament* was his first and last attempt at Party propaganda. It was published in France on Koestler's return from his first visit to Spain. An edition including *Dialogue with Death*, an account of his prison experiences in Seville, was published by the Left Book Club. Gollancz published the book without knowing that Koestler was a Party member. But it was in fact as a result of this, and of lecturing to Left Book Club audiences whose ignorant fellow-travelling appalled him, that Koestler found himself making his first public utterance of a divergence from the Party line, in refusing to condemn POUM outright.

Koestler's official status as the correspondent of a London newspaper enabled him to enter Fascist territory and to obtain an interview with General Quiepo de Llano, one of the chief Fascist propagandists whose savage and fanatical broadcasts were put out every evening. But Koestler had to depart in haste, as he was recognised, and the remainder of this visit was spent in Republican Spain. In his accounts of the fighting Koestler is chiefly concerned with emphasising Fascist lies and savagery, and one cannot legitimately approach his descriptive writing as straightforward documentary. He devotes a chapter specifically to the discussion of propaganda and its techniques—ironically, for he used some of those techniques himself. He quotes extensively from Fascist journals. But his exposure is geared to a defence of the Communist position. He discusses atrocity propaganda, and claims that the Fascists regarded the application of terror to the civilian population as an integral part of their insurrectionist policy, and that, for the most part, the atrocities attributed to the Republicans had little basis of truth. Later historians seem to have established that, whereas Fascist atrocities were organised and systematic, Republican acts of brutality were spontaneous and angry outbursts. The Communist liquidation of defective elements was another matter, and, needless to say, Koestler does not touch on this.

Koestler gives an indication of the pressures under which he had to work and the way in which he felt propaganda ought to be tackled when he relates how Meunzenberg urged him on :

> He would pick up a few sheets of the typescript, scan through them, and shout at me : "Too weak. Too objective. Hit them ! Hit them hard ! Tell the world how they run over their prisoners with tanks, how they pour petrol over them and burn them alive. Make the world gasp with horror. Hammer it into their heads. Make them *wake up* !"[11]

Writing that was geared to making the world gasp with horror was clearly going to produce something very different from Orwell's frank methods of persuasion. Any hint of the fallibility of the writer would be fatal, any open discussion of the limitations of a particular approach would destroy the argument before it was begun. The success of this kind of writing lies in its absolute and supreme self-confidence. Koesler's style is clipped, almost bullying. He states his case with a brisk and truculent authority :

> How much truth is there, then, in the atrocity stories disseminated without restraint by rebel propagandists and their foreign supporters ?
>
> It is true that in the first undisciplined days after the revolt the embittered masses set fire to churches, burned palaces, went in for lynch law.
>
> It is untrue that after this period acts of cruelty were perpetrated to any great extent, or systematically, against the civilian population or prisoners of war.
>
> And what of the execution of the hostages of Irun ?

And the torturing of the prisoners of war, the crucifixion of officers, the burning alive, castrating and crippling of true patriots?

Lies—all of it.[12]

Koestler is not concerned with establishing a climate of honesty through the tone of his writing. The brief paragraphs, the crescendo of questions, the bare statements of fact, add up to a rather hit or miss method of communication—the barrage can either be utterly destructive or miss its mark entirely. The brief impatience of words like "then" inserted in a phrase, the clipped authority of "it is true" and "it is untrue", the sudden lapse from particularity into generality—the churches and palaces, buildings, not people, are mentioned, while the implications of "lynch law", the killing of human beings, are not gone into— these are the characteristics of this kind of propagandist writing. Koestler merely asserts, as any propagandist on any side could. The long list of crimes attributed to the Republicans and the angry and impatient dismissal—"Lies—all of it"—contains no more genuinely convincing quality than any other piece of similar writing. Koestler's handling of facts is no more persuasive. He is not, in fact, employing a method of persuasion, as is Orwell, but a method of assertion.

There is a lack of ease in Koestler's writing (this might be due to translation difficulties), an awkwardness which the business-like tone cannot override, which is uncharacteristic of his later writing. He made no attempt to impress with simile and antithesis, as he does later, no real attempt to construct a developing argument. Much of this was clearly due to the terms on which he was writing. He was not writing for any purpose of his own— in fact, he seems to have felt considerable distaste for what he was doing—but carrying out an exercise. The book had to be vetted by the appropriate Party authorities at every stage. Koestler was not himself concerned with whether his words were effective in the way that Orwell was intimately involved with every word he wrote. Koestler wrote later about the Spanish

War with no particular sense of devastation, but it is likely that this experience of containment had an intensely profound effect on his subsequent development. Perhaps, though, it cannot be detached from his experience of Communism as a whole.

As if to reinforce the constraint of *Spanish Testament* the tone and the scope of *Dialogue with Death* are very different. Koestler is concerned with his own reactions to events and builds his account around this. He does not, as he does in *Scum of the Earth*, confuse his own personality with what he is witnessing, for he himself is the point of his objectivity. He presents descriptions, not statements. and his language is illuminated by a genuine curiosity in events, himself, and the people with whom he comes into contact. And, finding himself in the centre of an intrinsically dramatic situation, he finds the means legitimately to exploit it.

Koestler was arrested by the rebels in Malaga when he stayed to witness the town's fall into Fascist hands. For three months he was in prison in Seville, constantly expecting to be taken out and shot. He describes his feelings as he listened to the firing squad and wondered when it was going to be his turn. His account is uncluttered, straightforward and, in spite of the extreme situation, less decorated with patterns of metaphor and contrast than later autobiographical writings. The authority that makes *Spanish Testament* seem impatient is impressive in *Dialogue with Death*. One senses that the book was written primarily as a private organisation of thought rather than as a deliberate self-dramatisation. Perhaps it is because of this that the detached look at personal thoughts and feelings is more convincing than it often is elsewhere. He achieves a combination of an almost matter-of-fact tone and dramatic articulation—a dramatic articulation that produced rather different results in *Spanish Testament*.

On the night of Tuesday seventeen were shot.
On Thursday night eight.
On Friday night nine.

On Saturday night thirteen.

I tore strips off my shirt and stuffed my ears with them so
as not to hear anything during the night. It was no good. I cut
my gums with a splinter of glass, and said they were bleeding,
so as to obtain some iodised cotton wool. I stuffed the cotton
wool in my ears. This was no good either.[13]

The association with the bare facts of the numbers shot with
the torment of listening to the firing squad has a power which is
increased by the expression of the torment through the means
taken to prevent it rather than by direct statement. It is this
concern with small details in association with large issues and
profound emotions that gives *Dialogue with Death* its distinction. Koestler reveals with intense precision how, when one is
living in daily expectation of death, the most minute details, the
most irrelevant factors in relationships with other human
beings, become of vast importance. The tone of voice in which
the warder addresses him can radically change his mood. The
confinement and the oppression force him to respond desperately to every tremor of change.

Koestler was eventually released after a long campaign had
been waged by the press and public figures in England. When
war broke out two years later he was back in France. He had
broken with the CP and was writing *Darkness at Noon. Spanish
Testament* had presented an immediate and forced reaction
to events. It was artificial both in its distortion of truth and in its
relation to Koestler's real feelings. He had a great deal to catch
up on, and his subsequent novels seem to have involved the
working out of a backlog of reaction. It was a process that was
constantly interrupted and Koestler never achieved the immediacy and the tense sensitivity of response that was Orwell's. His
relationship with his past acted as a weight on his writing rather
than as an impulse.

The process of arriving at a definite break with the CP coincided, significantly and influentially, with the writing of Koestler's first novel *The Gladiators* (1939). He found it increasingly

difficult to reconcile private inclination with Party demands. His reaction, the reaction to years of self-deception, was to embark on the analysis of the movement of revolution that he continued to conduct for many years. Koestler considers that his membership of the CP was in the circumstances natural and justifiable. The circumstances are those he describes in his picture of the European "laboratory" which was his training ground.

> . . . the laboratory in question was Central Europe in the second quarter of this century; and the stimuli to which I reacted were first the financial, then the physical destruction of the cultural stratum from which I came. At a conservative estimate, three out of every four people I knew before I was thirty were subsequently killed in Spain, or hounded to death at Dachau, or gassed at Belsen, or deported to Russia, or liquidated in Russia; some jumped from windows in Vienna or Budapest, others were wrecked by the misery and aimlessness of permanent exile. My reaction to these stimuli was, on the other hand, the state I have described as Chronic Indignation; each new shock made detachment appear a crime, restraint a shameful escape. On the other hand, I knew that detachment and restraint are essential values in art. Thus the conflict between action and contemplation logically led into the conflict between art and propaganda. I have spoilt most of my novels out of a sense of duty to some "cause"; I knew that the artist should not exhort or preach, and I kept on exhorting and preaching.[14]

Koestler's sense of duty led him into the Communist Party, led him to write propaganda in the full consciousness that he was distorting the truth, and finally led him to reject wholeheartedly both the CP and Marxism at the stage when the events he describes were reaching their climax. But it did not lead him to write propagandist fiction in the sense that Upton Sinclair, or even Orwell, wrote it.

Koestler's novels can only be approached and understood in the light of the state near to schizophrenia that his relationship with the Party produced. To be politically committed was almost a necessity.

> In the nineteen-thirties conversion to the Communist faith was not a fashion or a craze—it was a sincere and spontaneous expression of our optimism born of despair : an abortive revolution of the spirit, a misfired Renaissance, a false dawn of history. To be attracted to the new faith was, I still believe, an honourable error. We were wrong for the right reasons.[15]

The antithetical pattern of his novels is contained in these sentences. Koestler was continually conscious of being pulled in two directions at once. His novels are an attempt, if not to reconcile, to make sense of this duality. His passion for analysis in some ways made the task more difficult for it eliminated shortcuts and emphasised the irreconcilable. The duality is again present here, where Koestler explains the two forces that drove him to Communism :

> To the psychiatrist, both the craving for Utopia and the rebellion against the status quo are symptoms of social maladjustment. To the social reformer, both are symptoms of a healthy rational attitude. The psychiatrist is apt to forget that smooth adjustment to a deformed society creates deformed individuals. The reformer is apt to forget that hatred, even of the objectively hateful, does not produce that charity and justice on which a utopian society must be based.[16]

Most of Koestler's novels are, in some way, an examination of this formula of conflict. He did not begin to write until after the experience of Spain when he was moving away from the Party. He does not concern himself with putting over a certain doctrine; his purpose is to examine the process of revolution itself. He is interested in theories and their demonstration. His novels are constructed out of arguments and debates rather than from characters and their activities. Environment is important as the "laboratory" was important to Koestler—as the source of impulses and motivations. If "contemplation" is sacrificed in his novels, it is sacrificed to intellectual debate, not to the limitations of propaganda.

6

THE REVOLUTIONARY HERO

The "European laboratory" nourished Koestler's analysis, provided him with fresh evidence, and confirmed the tendency of his conclusions. But as the conclusions hardened the area of interest and of action (with the exception of *Thieves in the Night*) narrowed. *The Gladiators* is on a larger scale than any of his subsequent novels, simply in terms of the number of characters, the sweep of movement, the historical and topographical background. It is the most vigorous of Koestler's novels.

The emphasis lies on the problem of a man who commits with others a collective and spontaneous act of rebellion and finds himself, partly through will, partly through compulsion, the acclaimed leader of a revolution. It is the problem of the progress from destructive act to constructive activity. The commonest criticism levelled against the political novelist, the novelist who is primarily concerned with demonstrating theories, with moving from hypothesis to proof, is that character becomes secondary to formulae. At the centre of all Koestler's political writing is the dilemma of the individual embroiled in the conflict between collective necessity and individual morality. The battle of ends and means is the battle that rages through Koestler's writing. It is a battle that would have no meaning without the individual consciousness. History is about people, both as individuals and as mass. *The Gladiators* demonstrates the failure of revolution as a failure of both the individual and the mass. The question that remains, the question that haunts first Spartacus, then Rubashov in *Darkness At Noon*, is whether the failure is inevitable. Koestler cannot provide the complete answer. He can only show that people themselves seem to be acting out the answer "yes".

Spartacus is not the prototype of the people's dictator : he is not a Stalin-figure. His fate is not the result of the disintegration of self-willed authority. He emerges as leader naturally and instinctively. He has a quality that is appealing, confidence combined with an uncertainty that is first endearing and later fatal. But he is a precarious leader and therefore a precarious hero. It is the fact that he is the creation of the collective will that makes him so vulnerable, and makes it inevitable that the protection of his symbolic value reveals the most positive signs of the revolution's disintegration.

Spartacus's ability as leader is revealed in moments of choice. At first choice consists in symbolising the collective will. When the first major challenge comes, when the rebels are surrounded on Vesuvius by Roman soldiery, defections occur, and Spartacus has to make the effort to create and guide the collective will. Here his hesitation to assume absolute authority is as fatal as his authoritarian actions are later. His responsibility, his hesitations, and the mere fact that he is leader, isolate. Spartacus's isolation is almost complete from this point. He makes little personal contact with his followers. He sometimes seeks help, but there is no give and take. He gives no sign that he accepts the advice that is offered. He can only in fact respond to essentially emotional ideas, and even this is a veiled response, translated into surging, metaphorical language. "He who receives [prophecies] . . . will have to run, on and on, until he foams at the mouth and until he has destroyed everything in his way with his great wrath."[1] Spartacus is gripped by a vision of the revolutionary leader, the receiver of prophecies, being forced to destroy. He recoils from the picture but cannot shake it off. It haunts him, and although he continually asks himself "is it necessary to destroy the individual for the sake of the collective good ?" the power of the vision is such that he can seek no other answer but that of necessity.

Of course, Koestler is demonstrating that Spartacus had no

alternative. It is the vision itself that is necessary. The Essene, an outsider with experience of idealism, feeds him with idealistic generalisations which he eagerly grasps hold of—but they are the only relevant generalisations. They provide the opportunity to make sense of leadership, to transform rebellion into revolution. But the Essene is taking his examples from past idealistic failures, and is teaching Spartacus the facts of revolution rather than hope. Spartacus precipitates his movement into the flow of historical inevitability by embracing the tradition of failed revolt. Outside such a tradition he would be purposeless. Within it he is not able to become an active historical agent; he is bound by its laws.

Koestler suggests that the laws of revolution dominate those details of background that provided its inspiration. Yet background is of more importance in *The Gladiators* than in most of Koestler's novels. Through the conservative and status-seeking eyes of Apronius, the clerk, are introduced the many years of unrest that have intruded upon bourgeois lives. The history of dictatorship and rebellion, of a starving populace and Rome filled with cheap corn, of political intrigue and military hysteria, is sketched in. Amidst these details is presented the mass of slaves and peasants who join Spartacus out of a confusion of motives of hunger and revenge. The people themselves *are* the background. They are the product of all that has happened. But this only reinforces the isolation of Spartacus. He is different. The fact that he is leader puts him into the category of individual rather than mass, and this is what he cannot really understand. He understands hunger and oppression, but not what happens to the desire for freedom when it is multiplied by thousands. When, as he finds it more difficult to control events, indecision and inactivity confirm his isolation they encourage the random expense of energy on the part of his followers. It is not the result of conscious brutality so much as of the restless nervousness that comes when the leader's grip cannot be felt.

The climate of unrest that the flashbacks on history introduce is sharpened not only by the fact of revolt but by the general disintegration that the revolt highlights. Koestler shows how initial rebellion, in the attempt to grow into genuine constructive revolution, brings disintegration and conflict, both within the revolt and outside it. The efforts at positive action emphasise the differences between the rebels themselves and further the crumbling of the once ordered society of Italy. It is not simply the fact that slaves leave their masters and Roman legions are defeated. The whole of the populace of Italy has felt the ground trembling beneath its feet. The final defeat of Spartacus has only restored the equilibrium temporarily. At the end of the novel we are back where we started from—Apronius does not get his promotion. There has been no change, but it is just as likely as it ever was that order will be seriously disturbed. And if rebellion achieves nothing concrete it can at least do this—disturb the *status quo*, shake up the populace, make those in authority tremble, reverse, if even for a short space of time, the established order of things.

In terms of the psychological health of the state this is probably a useful activity. In terms of the movement of history it leaves few ripples and the surface remains tediously calm. The revolt of the gladiators is consigned, if not to oblivion, to that heap of revolutionary failures where the historically curious poke about Spartacus himself has little historical awareness. The Essene is the only character whose experience allows this, although Fulvius tries to make sense of revolution with the help of his learning. What he writes is a chronicle, a commentary rather than a placing of events in historical perspective.

Rubashov in *Darkness At Noon* finds consolation in his meditations on historical perspective. The long debate he carries on with himself right through the book is an attempt to justify not so much a particular theory of history as the individual's role in history. It is the individual, above all, that Koestler is concerned with. The individual is examined under the shock and strain of extreme circumstance. Koestler had left the Party in the spring of 1938. *Darkness At Noon* represents his final repudiation of

Communism. The repudiation was made absolute by the events surrounding the Moscow Trials.

Between 1936 and 1938 there were about eight million political arrests in Russia. The victims ranged from leaders in the Party to peasants who had unwittingly committed acts of sabotage by not learning with sufficient rapidity how to handle machinery. In his book *Conspiracy of Silence* Alex Weissberg says: "After periods of examination which rarely exceeded three months, all these men, with very few exceptions, pleaded guilty, and where they were actually brought before the courts they confirmed their confessions in public."[2] Weissberg says that they were all innocent. It is certainly impossible to believe that they were all guilty, if only on the grounds that eight million conspirators would surely have achieved more than they in fact did. These are the facts behind *Darkness At Noon*, which precipitate Rubashov's debate. The book was published in England in 1940, but Koestler had been writing it during the days when Europe was moving towards war and the strain of disillusion was strong. A sense of urgency infected his writing as it had not done in *The Gladiators*.

Alex Weissberg was a personal friend of Koestler's. He was arrested in Kharkhov in 1936; his wife had already been arrested but was soon released. Many of the details of methods of interrogation were communicated to Koestler by Weissberg's wife. But Koestler drew largely on his own experience and perceptions—his experiences of prison in Spain, his work with the German Communist Party, his observation of Russian life during his long trip there in 1932. Koestler's involvement with Communism had been intense and personal, not only because of his private motives, but because the times demanded intensity and the way in which the Party moulded his life and outlook made it personal. But Koestler escaped its grip; many of his friends did not. Some were arrested in Russia. Most of them were trapped, in one way or another, between the two monumental threats of Fascism and Communism. Koestler's personal involvement sharpened his reaction to the Moscow Trials.

Rubashov, a character who grew out of real and intimate experience, is also a symbolic figure. Companion to the scenes of mass arrest, imprisonment, baseless accusation and exhausting interrogation described by Weissberg were the experiences of some of the major figures of the Bolshevik Revolution, of Trotsky himself, arch-scapegoat, exiled from Russia in 1929, murdered in Mexico by a Stalinist agent in 1940. Less well known was Victor Serge, a classic wanderer through the "European laboratory", who chronicled the growth of his antipathy to Stalin and the Thermidorian reaction in *Memoirs of a Revolutionary* (1963). He also suffered imprisonment, then exile. By 1938 the pattern was a familiar one. As Koestler drew away from Communism he was able to respond with knowledge and sympathy to the victims of events in Russia.

Koestler's intentions in writing *Darkness At Noon* were to reveal some of the facts of the Purges, to present an assessment of the mentality of those concerned, and to offer an explanation of why so vast a proportion of the victims confessed to incredible charges. The reaction to the Purges of the European public in general, and of Communists and fellow-travellers in particular, had been incredible to a man who understood the logic of Stalinism. There was, particularly in England, cut off from the full impact of events in Europe, an unquestioning acceptance of the guilt of millions of men—it was harder to believe that the Trials could have been entirely manufactured than to accept the confessions that came from the mouths of the "guilty". David Caute writes:

At the time of the trials a single, comprehensive explanation alone could satisfy both communist intellectuals and their opponents. It was difficult to believe that each of the perfectly sane-looking men whose confessions synchronised so well had succumbed to pressures and persuasions peculiar to himself. Consequently, it should not occasion surprise or suspicion that many found in the simplest answer the best. "They confessed because they were caught red-handed and there was no way out." This logic suggested itself to many observers who were by no means communists.[3]

In England sections of the press which had no reason to be pro-Stalin typified this attitude. The *Observer* Moscow correspondent wrote : "It is futile to think that the trial was staged and the charges trumped up. The Government's case against the defendants is genuine."[4] The *Spectator* correspondent supported this. "The guilt of the accused is completely brought home."[5] The effect in England was less pronounced than that of the Nazi-Soviet Pact of 1939. The left was not so shaken that it could not attempt justification. "What was frightening about these trials was not the fact that they had happened—for obviously such things are necessary in a totalitarian society—but the eagerness of Western intellectuals to justify them",[6] wrote George Orwell.

In *Darkness At Noon* Koestler maintained that for a man who had dedicated his life to the Party from his teens it was both natural and logical to obey the demands of the Party machine, even to the extent of confessing to crimes that had not been committed. But Koestler did not pretend to offer a complete explanation of the Trials. He says himself : "The confessions of the Moscow trials only appear mysterious to those who look for one uniform explanation of the behaviour of men prompted by heterogenous reasons."[7] He was concerned with the kind of man who had worked for revolution before 1917, who had known the enthusiasm and triumph of that year, and who had never allowed his conscience to come between him and the Party in the twenty years since. Koestler's theory of confession made little impact on the British public. Only a thousand copies of the book were printed and sold. In contrast, when the novel was published in France after the War at a time that coincided with the first wave of anti-Stalinist reaction (the reaction that Simone de Beauvoir describes in *The Mandarins*) four hundred thousand copies were sold.

The central character of *Darkness At Noon* is Commissar of the People Rubashov, accused of political deviation and treason.

The book is constructed so as to provide a solid background pattern to Rubashov's dialogue with himself, during which he gathers together the various strands of his past and concludes that the logic of his life's actions is that he must confess and die. Rubashov is not a leader of men, "one who receives prophecies", like Spartacus. He is not a phenomenon that has been created by events almost accidentally. He is not a revolutionary hero in the sense that Spartacus is. Spartacus's ability as leader was tested by moments of choice. The essence of Rubashov's life of devotion to the Party has been that he had no decisions to take, no choices to make. There were never any alternatives. Allegiance to the Party precluded such opportunities for individualism. "His past was the movement, the Party; present and future, too, belonged to the Party, were inseparably bound up with its fate; but his past was identical with it."[8] To question the Party amounted to questioning the value of his entire life. As Rubashov quickly discovers, he has come to the point when, after a life of not having to choose, he must make a choice that is crucial. He must decide whether to accept his past, accept the Party and the necessity of his confession and death, or whether to deny the value of his existence and refuse to confess. If he chose the latter he would have wasted his entire life.

These alternatives provide the novel's core, and inevitably the development and structure of the novel is very different from that of The Gladiators. The Gladiators is not without debate, but the conditions and the voices of the debate are continually shifting. Rubashov's interlocutor does vary, but the facts are constant. It is the immutability of the past that dominates. Rubashov, trained to ignore the possibility of alternatives, cannot really handle this new phenomenon and cannot shake off the grip of a creed that demands logical action. Rubashov's whole argument, the alternatives with which he faces himself, are themselves a direct result of the habit of thought that Marxism has planted so firmly in his mind. If he were able to break away from this habit, to see life on an entirely different plane, spiritual perhaps, or more homely, he might be able to move out of the small circle that the habit of logic, and the suiting of the terms to the exigencies rather than the other way round, confines him to. In fact, symbols and pictures which have nothing to do with logic begin to intrude on Rubashov's mind, but his intellect has no scope in the handling of them.

He remembers first the incident of Richard, a nineteen-year-old working in the German underground movement. Richard had criticised the material sent by the Comintern; it was therefore necessary to have him eliminated. It was Rubashov's job to tip off the SS so that they could do the job for him. He remembers the art gallery where he met Richard and can still see the Pietà that caught his glance as he intimated the consequences of Richard's deviation. The Pietà remains on the edge of his mind throughout the debate, but it does not divert its progress.

Before his arrest Rubashov had begun to find it difficult to react according to the Party's logic rather than his own conscience. He was being forced to acknowledge that he did have a conscience and that it functioned powerfully enough to disturb his allegiance. But it is not until the—ironical—security of prison walls that Rubashov can openly admit these doubts to himself. But even his doubts are sifted, categorised, channelled, by the habit of logical thought. They are built up into one side of the argument, the side that condemns his Party activities and therefore his life.

Rubashov has been trained to have faith in history, to believe that the movement of history, the action of the mass, dominates the importance of the individual. This training gives him the comforting thought that history will justify him if his doubts have been correct, if, in fact, his view of history has been incorrect. Yet at the same time he realises that those same memories that tend to confirm his doubts also challenge the rationality of this belief. Where is the individual massive enough to be taken account of by history?

History will rehabilitate you, thought Rubashov, without particular conviction. What does history know of nail-biting?
E

He smoked and thought of the dead, and of the humiliation that preceded their death. Nevertheless, he could not bring himself to hate No. 1 as he ought to. . . . The horror which No. 1 emanated, above all consisted in the possibility that he was in the right, and that all those whom he killed had to admit, even with the bullet in the back of their necks, that he conceivably might be in the right.[9]

The conflicting elements in Rubashov's dialogue are all there. He is dominated by a system of logical thought yet realises that he should try to tear himself away from it. History cannot take cognisance of the patch of blue sky he sees outside his cell, or of his secretary's white blouses, or of the thin brown arms of the man in the next cell. It is too large for these details and perhaps Rubashov himself is only a detail on the same scale. These are the very details that impinge on his conscience, that *seem* to influence his train of thought, but in fact they cannot penetrate the barriers that the Party has constructed. If Rubashov ceases to believe in No. 1 he reduces his life to a minute detail which, likewise, is unable to penetrate the Party's solidity—its achievements, its crimes, its power. Yet if No. 1 has been right, if the whole course of Stalinism is justifiable, Rubashov has sinned against both the Party and his conscience by allowing these doubts to exist. And if he has not sinned against his conscience he has failed his conscience, by not acting according to its prompting.

Rubashov is preoccupied with the individual's position in relation to history. His preoccupation is in fact much more dominant and much more precise than the attempt of Spartacus to come to grips with the problem. Spartacus, being leader, has to undergo experiences that Rubashov avoids. For him it is not a question of doing what he is told although it may go against his conscience. It is a question of making the decision to act contrary to his conscience. When Spartacus's forces split he has to demand "unconditional obedience and submission to his authority". He is laying himself open to the corruption of power.

Rubashov is corrupted by his recognition of power, not by his wielding of power. Spartacus says "I must keep to the road now. There were too many among us who would not obey orders . . . we must destroy them else they destroy us."[10] He is in precisely the same position as Stalin, as No. 1, who is convinced that Trotsky must be destroyed, although the risk from an old man with few followers, unable to move from Mexico and distrusted by Communist and capitalist alike was minimal. But Spartacus explicitly presents the paradox of revolution. He must demand absolute authority so that he can keep the revolution moving towards its goal, for he is the only man who has a clear vision of the goal. But this authority corrupts the revolution, for it inevitably leads to violence and murder in the revolution's name. The paradox of revolution is presented through the paradox of leadership. Koestler suggests the question: can such a being exist as a revolutionary leader? Revolutionary ideals seem to contradict the concept of leadership. Yet historic movements have always found, or been created by a leader. *The Gladiators* suggests that the revolutionary leader is an impossibility.

Yet the revolutionary follower is an essential feature of revolutionary action and heroism. Rubashov accepts the vision of the end that No. 1 presents. He has few opportunities for heroic action. His duties were often drab and distasteful. There was often danger, but seldom drama. There was no scope for spontaneous action because the carrying out of orders wiped out spontaneity. 1917 had been, for individuals, the grand climax of spontaneity. The long slow drag that came afterwards had to destroy much of what characterised and inspired the events of 1917; in other words, according to the terrible logic of Rubashov's interrogator, Gletkin, it had destroyed Rubashov.

Gletkin is a representative product of the Stalinist era. He is the new man who has no conception of the creative power of spontaneous energy and sees it only as a destructive force which must itself be destroyed. Trotsky's theory of permanent revolution went directly counter to this kind of thinking. It was anathema to the new age constructed out of a rigid and absolute

hierarchy. Gletkin is a vital link in the hierarchy. It is his business to bring about the self-destruction of the Rubashovs, "old
Bolsheviks" left over from a previous phase, who have not only
outgrown their usefulness but who, in their looking back to the
inspiration of 1917, are remembering energy and flux. Gletkin is
static and unchangeable, and belongs to a static and unchangeable system, that can only itself be influenced by some form of
revolution.

The figures from Rubashov's past, his two interrogators, Gletkin and Ivanov, who is himself eliminated for he is of the same
generation as Rubashov, the diary which Rubashov writes in
prison, become the second voice of his dialogue. In his diary
he tries to make sense of his thoughts. "A revolution conducted according to the rules of cricket is an absurdity,"[11] he
writes. Violence is a necessity of revolution. "The end justifies
the means" is the only rule by which revolution can live. But as
yet the ends have not been accomplished, and there is no guarantee that they ever will be, or that they will in fact turn out to be
what was anticipated and longed for. "For the moment we are
thinking and acting on credit. As we have thrown overboard all
conventions and rules of cricket morality, our sole guiding principle is that of consequent logic. We are under the terrible compulsion to follow our thought down to its final consequence and
to act in accordance to it. We are sailing without ballast; therefore every touch on the helm is a matter of life or death."[12]
Rubashov goes over and over the same ground, varying the details, the circumstances, switching his own tendencies. The case
of the logic of commitment versus the individuality of conscience is built up.

When Rubashov confronts Gletkin the factor of physical suffering intrudes, but this does not interrupt or confuse the progress of Rubashov's dialogue. The sight of Bogrov, hero of Kron-
stadt, led to his execution has a more radical influence. It provides a missing link in Rubashov's thoughts. It confronts him
with death. He had consigned his secretary Arlova to oblivion
because it would have been suicide for him to interfere and

give evidence in her favour. But he had felt remote from her death, although he had been her lover. But the confrontation with death seems to be offering an easy way out—the acceptance of fear. Fear cannot be dealt with logically. Rubashov refuses to allow it to intrude. If anything, the fact that both Ivanov and Bogrov are dead, personal friends and comrades, helps to convince him of the necessity of his death.

The revolution itself has created Gletkin. He has genuinely reached the point where choice is unnecessary, while Rubashov had only acted as if he had. His set of maxims are entirely adequate to guide his life for him, as are Nikitin's in a later novel of Koestler's, *The Age of Longing*. He is a symbol of the force that brings Rubashov to write this in his diary : "As the only moral criterion which we recognise is that of social utility, the public disavowal of one's conviction in order to remain in the Party's ranks is obviously more honourable than the quixotism of carrying on a hopeless struggle."[13] But the only way in which Rubashov can remain in the Party's ranks is to be executed.

Gletkin articulates with a precision that Rubashov would rather avoid exactly what Rubashov's duty to the Party demands :

Your task is simple. You have set it yourself : to gild the Right, to blacken the Wrong. The policy of the opposition is wrong. Your task therefore is to make the opposition contemptible; to make the masses understand that opposition is a crime and that the leaders of the opposition are criminals. That is the simple language which the masses understand. . . . Your task, Citizen Rubashov, is to avoid awakening sympathy and pity. Sympathy and pity for the opposition are a danger to the country.[14]

Rubashov confesses and he makes a speech at his public trial in which he approves the Party discipline. His speech is a modest and undramatic acceptance of guilt. But public confession solves none of his problems and does not reconcile him to his own logic. In the short space of life remaining to him he is still pondering the anomaly of his past:

> The Party denied the free will of the individual—and at the same time it exacted his willing self-sacrifice. It denied his capacity to choose between two alternatives—and at the same time it demanded that he should constantly choose the right one. It denied his power to distinguish good and evil— and at the same time spoke pathetically of guilt and treachery.[15]

Rubashov lunges at definition. He describes the logical extremes of the Party as "the running-amok of pure reason". He returns to the conclusion that "we are sailing without ethical ballast". But in reality he is no further than he was when the cell door first clanged shut. He has succeeded in confirming the paradox of his own life, of revolution, of allegiance to a single creed and discipline, and the result is that at the moment of death he no longer knows for what he is dying.

Rubashov acts always according to a code that is too rigid to allow scope for heroism, a code in which honour is to serve, to do what is demanded. Although he retains a wavering faith in history he is not a hero in the historic sense, and cannot be until there has been time for judgment to be passed on the Gletkins as well as on the old Bolsheviks—until history itself has confirmed or rejected Rubashov as hero. If there is an element of tragedy in *Darkness At Noon* it is not personal tragedy, but is contained in the self-destruction of revolution, in the men of genuine good faith who made the mistaken attempt to use their power over people as a means of controlling circumstances. Koestler, of course, cannot use *Darkness At Noon* as a vehicle for offering an explanation of the failure of the 1917 inspiration, but he continually reminds us of the presence of this much larger and more complex question.

Rubashov dies still in the midst of his debate almost pathetically. The death of Spartacus is equally without fulfilment. He is killed ignominiously and without drama as he tries to make a final heroic gesture—his first self-conscious attempt to act out the hero in action. The revolutionary hero, Koestler's focal point in the debate about the failure of revolution, dies with no sense of achievement, no sense of having made an individual contribution. It is almost as if death deprives Spartacus of his heroic qualities. He and Rubashov are both cut down to unheroic size. Ultimately, they are neither of them more remarkable as men than Orwell's Winston Smith, a hero who never was. Spartacus could not afford to care about individual lives; nor could Rubashov. Therefore their own lives are placed by the logic of the revolution in a subsidiary position. If Richard was no loss, nor was Rubashov. He only mattered more when he was being of greater use to the Party.

In Koestler's novels revolutionary activity comes near to debasing human life. History is able to argue the individual in anonymity. In the novels of parallel European writers, of André Malraux and Ignazio Silone for instance, the opposite process occurs. Malraux's characters seek personal salvation through political action. Their allegiance and activity is intimately involved with their background, their experiences, with their moral development. While Koestler will offer a single incident as an explanation of a man's political commitment, Malraux's heroes are fully aware of the threads connecting moral and intellectual dissatisfaction and violent action. They are continually seeking the action that is relevant to their lives rather than to their creed. When Chen, in *La Condition Humaine* (first published in London as *Storm in Shanghai* in 1934), turns to terrorism, it is not only because the logic of the situation seems to demand the death of Chiang Kai Shek. It is primarily because Chen becomes certain that this is how he must fulfil himself. It is a confirmation of individuality. Katov is doing the same when he gives away the cyanide capsule with which he was going to anticipate death in the furnaces. He is performing an act of moral as much as physical heroism and he is confirming his right to act according to individual dictates. Spartacus is confused by the distinction between personal affirmation and collective achievement. He is confused by the fact that he is leader and that therefore personal affirmation must represent collective achievement. When he has to face the climactic crisis he fails because his single-minded determination and his humanity pull in different directions. He makes the decision to arrest and crucify the instigators of defection, but when the horde rebels and demands that the victims be freed Spartacus submits to the collective will and no longer embodies it. His decision to destroy defection represented his acceptance of his position. When he turns back on himself it is the final failure.

The whole question of the relationship between the revolutionary hero and the revolution itself is hardly tackled by Malraux. The relevant relationship is that between the individual and his own morality. Even strictly political arguments are seen in these terms. When Chen and Kyo go to Hankow to consult those in direct contact with the Comintern, they are desperate to clarify the situation, to find out whether the Comintern is going to oppose Chiang Kai Shek, the Communists' one-time ally, or whether they will allow him to take over control of Shanghai and almost inevitably destroy the Communists there. But they want to know not so much because they want to ascertain what their political duty is, but because they each must work out a mode of individual action. Chen commits himself to terrorism, Kyo to not running away.

Malraux's heroes are intellectuals; their thinking, unlike Rubashov's, encompasses areas beyond the immediate political horizon. Partly because of this the act of killing comes to have an almost spiritual significance. In the opening sequence of *La Condition Humaine* Chen steels himself to murder for the sake of the cause. A minor detail makes him feel "desperate in his inability to decide". He is committed to action, but to kill a sleeping man, which is what his commitment demands, is not the same as meeting an enemy face to face. "If only he could fight, fight an enemy who was on his guard, who gave blow for blow—what a relief that would be!"[16] Chen is assailed by doubts and fears from all sides, but this assassination is "his offering to the Revolution". Later he acts for himself, and kills himself. He is filled with a moral exultation as he prepares to throw the bomb at Chiang Kai Shek's car. He is going to throw himself with the bomb, and his death will mean redemption :

> This night of fog was his last night, and he was satisfied. He was going to be blown up with the car—head over heels in a flash which would illumine the hideous thoroughfare and splatter its walls with blood. The most ancient of Chinese legends came into his mind : men were but vermin on the earth. Terrorism must be made a mystic faith. Solitude before the event : let the terrorist first take his resolve alone, and act alone.[17]

Spartacus acts alone and is reduced to an ordinary level. Chen acts alone and dies a hero in his own eyes. It no longer matters, as it did when he first killed, how the revolution judges him. Chen as a revolutionary finds a meaning in his commitment through death. Kyo also kills himself and thus preserves his individuality. Katov makes a last moral gesture and is thus true to his individuality.

Koestler does not allow his heroes such glory—his individuals cannot see their own actions in such a light—but he does share Malraux's emphasis on the aloneness of the revolutionary hero. Spartacus is aware of the distance between himself and the men he leads. It is his duty to preserve this distance. Rubashov is isolated from the generation that he was a part of and cannot make real contact with the new generation. Malraux's heroes are cut off from collective action by a sense of personal destiny. But their isolation is more than this; they are isolated even in their most intimate relationships. Kyo, as he approaches the climax of his commitment, cannot break down the barriers between himself and his father, Gisors, and May, his wife.

Jean-Paul Sartre, too, writes of individuals whose preoccupation with making their actions meaningful only serves to cut them off from others. Matthieu in *The Age of Reason* (1947) has a restlessness and undirected will to action which leads him to resent intimate claims on his personality, the claim of the pregnant Marcelle, for instance, while he seeks an end to his isolation. Intimate relationships seem to hold him in a trap. He longs to be able to clarify his ideas and translate them into action.

But Koestler, in *The Gladiators* and the later novels, is concerned primarily with the progress of revolution itself, and his handling of individuals is geared to this. While Malraux uses revolution and political commitment as the situation of his individuals' dilemmas, and presents through these dilemmas an essentially tragic view of humanity, Koestler's characters are fulfilling an historic function. This eliminates the tragedy of the individual, although there is a suggestion of the tragedy of the mass. The political role dominates, and the revolutionary hero's childhood, his love affairs, his private misfortunes are seen only in their relationship to this role. In Malraux's novels commitment is a reflection of these areas of the hero's life, an aspect of his thought and behaviour. The political role dominates only in so far as Malraux sees an involvement with politics as being characteristic of the age. The Communist betrayal in Shanghai or the reasons for the Kuomintang's success were not so important as the fate of his heroes. The quality of their deaths is crucial. But while Malraux's heroes give away their cyanide, or man the barricades and face the firing squad with a full sense of individuality and pride, while Sartre's heroes fight on against fantastic odds with resigned desperation but a feeling that action equals achievement, the deaths of Koestler's heroes come as a logical full-stop to their lives. Koestler witnesses their deaths and records their final thoughts with an objective eye, and allows them no more individuality or justification than history itself gives.

A novel in which revolutionary character is presented on a very different plane is Silone's *Bread and Wine*, first published in this country in 1937 and again, in a revised and rewritten form, in 1964. The mood of *Bread and Wine* is one of inaction. The underground resistance to Fascist Italy could crawl only by inches towards liberation. But the situation in which Pietro Spina, an exile who has returned illegally to Italy, finds himself is not only that of resistance to Fascism. It is his forced inactivity, his necessary anonymity and disguise, that generate his examination of his own position and personality. Spina as a revolutionary hero is very different from both Koestler's and Malraux's heroes. He is a contemplative rather than an active hero. He is so alone that he has to start from scratch in his attempts at communication with others. His disguise as a priest forces on him a habit of speech and action that are not his own—and yet as the novel progresses we can see that Spina is much nearer to a Christian morality than the corrupt and careless Church that functions around him.

Few escape the blanket of suffering that lies over the Abruzzi. Only those who directly collaborate with the régime can expect to do well. Most of the villages are sunk in a hideous apathy, or an equally hideous and often useless drudgery. Their inhabitants instinctively, but remotely, dislike the régime, but just as instinctively join in the cheers when the war against Abyssinia is declared. Spina, ill, hunted, disillusioned, feels a compulsion not only to stay in Italy but to remain in order to devote himself to the resistance movement. He feels a compulsion to communicate with the people around him although the task of injecting them with some kind of political understanding and vigour is virtually hopeless. More than this, he feels moved beyond anything that Rubashov or Spartacus or any of Malraux's heroes can express by the suffering that is so close to him. Ironically, as a priest he comes much nearer to suffering than he ever did as a revolutionary. People come to him. His political role detached him from its reasons. His new, more savage yet more compassionate, understanding revitalises his tired commitment.

When Spina returns to Italy he finds that most of the young men he had been brought up with, except for those who actively support the régime, are dead or dying. The causes have been starvation, the police, moral and physical disintegration. The task of bringing together a movement when personal contact points the way for the police has little chance of success. There is little Spina can achieve, yet he feels that he is engaged in an activity that is essential to human dignity, to self-respect, to his entire existence as a human being. Spina cannot resist making the fumbling human contacts that are necessary—but the necessity is not only that of the revolution. It is also the necessity of his own personality and the demands he makes on himself for reasons that are personal rather than political. His relationships with Cristina and Bianchina are not political; they are personal, and grow to have political meaning through his own personality. They learn from his personality rather than from his politics, because he can only express his politics through his personality.

Pre-eminently *Bread and Wine* is a novel about attempts to communicate, and it is this that distinguishes it from the novels of Koestler and Malraux. Spina achieves nothing politically, but he has made his mark on the community and inspired individuals to a new awareness and a faith in him. As long as he is true to his commitment faith in him is the next best thing to faith in political activity. And Spina of course must have faith in himself, and that is perhaps the most important thing he achieves. The only man whose political commitment is effected by Spina is killed before he has a chance for action. But this is better than to have remained in selfish apathy.

Spina is one of the few revolutionary heroes for whom being true to himself coincides with being true to the revolution, but it is an identification that takes time and thought and suffering to achieve. Spina, isolated, cut off from his family, most of his friends dead, struggling to reorganise a disintegrating movement, is forced into a penetrating self-examination and a new kind of courage. He himself writes in his notebook :

He is saved who overcomes his individual egoism, family egoism, caste egoism, does not shut himself in a cloister or build an ivory tower, or make a cleavage between his way of acting and his way of thinking. He is saved who frees his spirit from the idea of resignation to the existing disorder. Spiritual life has always meant a capacity for dedication and self-sacrifice. In a society like ours a spiritual life can only be a revolutionary life.

. . . one must not be obsessed with the idea of security, even of the security of one's own virtue. Spiritual life and secure life do not go together. To save oneself one must struggle and take risks.[18]

Spina, of course, takes risks and, it is suggested, dies. But the drama and danger of *Bread and Wine* are subdued. The hunt for Spina is not made much of. And yet we are made as acutely aware of the nature of totalitarianism as we are in *Darkness At Noon*. But it is an awareness that seems to seep from the conditions of life at its lowest level rather than from the authorities above. Spina carries on his own debate, yet his situation is not intellectually articulated. It is expressed through the lives of the people, through his relationships and through his personality. Spina would be the same man, though perhaps unrecognised, wherever he was placed. We cannot detach Rubashov from the Russian Revolution nor Kyo and Chen from the particular agonies of China.

The examination of political theory is not an object of Silone's writing. Political theories are of course discussed, as they would be natural to the conversation of a revolutionary, but the tone, the mood and the intellectual content are at a great distance from anything Koestler wrote. The third novel in what Koestler saw as "a trilogy concerned with the ethics of revolution, the problem of ends and means"[19] was published in 1943 : *Arrival and Departure*. In it we have a third example in Koestler's gallery of revolutionary heroes. Koestler says that in this novel the problem of ends and means "is shifted to the psychological level".[20] It is perhaps this shift that diminishes the size of the hero. Peter Slavek is not of the stature of Rubashov or Spartacus.

In Peter, Koestler is presenting a typical product of the "Euro-

pean laboratory". He is typical, although he is younger, in the
same way as Koestler presents himself as a typical product in
Scum of the Earth. He arrives in Neutralia, a rather pathetic,
dogged, truculent figure, a minor hero of the resistance movement in a small central European country. Peter is the only one
of Koestler's heroes whom we can relate to Spina; he feels compelled to act to the contrary of all logical argument. He is an
exile, he has earned his retirement from politics, he is encouraged on all sides to leave the political scene. His attempts to
work for the British, the only country that is still fighting
Fascism, are met with aloofness and barriers of bureaucracy.
They are considered to be a sign of psychological peculiarity.

Peter's brief, futureless affair with Odette is the prelude to a
psychological reaction to what he has been through—torture,
guilt and exile—for which he cannot feel intellectually responsible. Sonia, the large, oppressive psychoanalyst, confident and
cynical, who takes charge of Peter when his leg becomes paralysed, provides him with a rational excuse to abandon his
political commitment. Peter feels that he has betrayed his commitment in his feelings about his working-class comrades—
Peter himself comes from the intellectual bourgeoisie. Sonia explains his heroism, his refusal to speak under torture, in terms
of guilt feelings, but guilt feelings that have their root in a childhood incident. "The clue to your past adventures is that feeling
of guilt which compelled you to pay all the time imaginary
debts,"[21] she says. At first Peter accepts this because he is seeking
explanations.

Sonia eliminates the idea of the hero altogether. She degrades
modern heroism : ". . . in this age all crusaders are stigmatised.
They try to hide it by being doctrinaire, or matter of fact and
tough, but when they are alone and naked they all sweat little
drops of blood through their skins."[22] It is not until Peter's story
of the mixed transports that the hero is redeemed, and heroic
action is seen to make any kind of sense in the face of the explanations Sonia is presenting. The Jews singing as they step into
the gas wagon transforms an incident of the utmost horror and

bestiality into an expression of the triumph of human will. It may be a meaningless triumph, but it is none the less magnificent. Peter's silence under torture is also meaningless—the information that he refuses to give is already known—but it is a triumph of the same kind. Yet this means little to Sonia, for whom the quality of the motive determines the quality of the act. The circumstance that determined Peter's behaviour was such that his revolutionary action could be dismissed as gesturing.

Peter's leg returns to life and at first he accepts his cure. "He was cured; never again would he make a fool of himself. He was cured of his illusions, both about objective aims and subjective motives. The two lines had converged and met. No more debts to pay, no more commands to obey. Let the dead bury their dead. For him, Peter Slavek, the crusade had come to an end."[23] But ultimately Peter realises that he has no choice but to carry on the fight as best he can. His old inspiration comes to the rescue and does not allow him to retire. When he leaves the boat that is to take him to America to join Odette his action has, like previous actions, nothing to do with illusion or motives, but with compulsion and spontaneity. It is nothing so specific as conscience or theoretical commitment that leads Peter to rejoin the battle. It is an impulsive act.

We have a lingering feeling, which Peter shares, that "hero" is an inconvenient label that others have pinned on his irrational and unpremeditated behaviour, a label which at first he felt constrained to live up to, but when the moment for action arrived was forgotten. What is made clear is that, in Peter's case at least, the initial commitment is not rationally worked out. It is a compulsive reaction to circumstances—the same kind of reaction that Koestler himself experiences, and which he describes in *Arrow in the Blue*.

Peter is a more ordinary man, and perhaps in a more ordinary predicament, than either Rubashov or Spartacus. He is not in the extreme position of Rubashov nor does he have the responsibility of Spartacus. He is in fact in a position where he can and must decide for himself and act for himself. There is no person or creed to guide him in these particular circumstances. At this stage in the war against Hitler it was possible for an individual like Peter to feel that the war against Fascism dominated every kind of political allegiance. When Peter is parachuted from a British plane the revolution is of secondary importance. And it was this that Sonia left out of her assessment. Hatred of all that Hitler represented could be a much more powerful force than guilt though much more difficult to categorise in psychological terms.

Koestler had intended to present a psychological explanation of revolutionary action. In fact he shows that psychological explanations are not all that relevant when it comes to the action of the moment. Peter submits to the necessity of action. The problem of ends and means recedes. The problem of the individual in extreme circumstances forced to make a choice dominates. In this sense *Arrival and Departure* does not really belong to a trilogy about the ethics of revolution. It *is* about the relationship of conscience and action, an essential part of this discussion, but the relationship is not itself an intimate part of the theory and progress of revolution, as is the case in both *The Gladiators* and *Darkness At Noon*. Peter is the closest Koestler gets to Malraux's characters, although he is more limited and much more confined. He is involved with the morality of commitment rather than the ethics of revolution.

7

THE THIRD DIMENSION

Koestler's heroes grew out of the political predicament of his times. They grew out of his own confrontations with facts and ideologies, and they are placed in dilemmas of which Koestler himself had direct and intimate experience. Their situations, even in the case of Spartacus, had a contemporary immediacy that it was hard to resist. Critics and reviewers described Koestler's writing as "journalistic", but they conceded that the journalistic approach could respond more quickly to political facts than a slower-paced fictionalising—and that the growing intrusiveness of political facts made them a proper, if not a necessary, subject for the artistic imagination. After the War, when there was a mood of retreat from politics, looks were cast back doubtfully to the thirties, and the doubt extended to the place of the political novelist. The "political novel" as such came under attack. Politics, it seemed, inevitably damaged the more subtle qualities of characterisation and interpretation that one looked for in a novelist. The kind of reality represented by political and economic facts interfered with the imagination's striving to arrive at a more "real" reality.

Koestler, as we have seen, was conscious of the difficulties that lay before the writer who based his fiction on politics. He was perhaps over-conscious of these difficulties. His fiction is very deliberate, painstakingly put together. He was torn between his understanding of the conventional ingredients of fiction and the urgency of what he had to say. The result is that he is very meticulous in his handling of character and construction even when neither is particularly successful. But the compelling force behind Koestler's novels is that they were conceived as a demonstration, contemporary and historical, of a group of theories and interpretations concerning the dominant facts of the contemporary political climate.

The Gladiators is Koestler's only historical novel and he did careful research to get the social details as accurate as possible. The particular facts had in most cases to be conjecture, and so to a great extent the novel's power to convince lay in the reality of its background. In general one does not question this background—the small details of daily living mingled with those of the institutions and conventions of the time. It is the way in which Koestler slots his individuals into this background that is not wholly successful. He almost seems to have some scheme whereby individuals are given particular prejudices, longings, likes and dislikes. It is almost as if Koestler has accumulated a plausible collection of characteristics of this kind and then distributed them among his characters. One is not always aware of this, but it is occasionally striking.

Spartacus himself, partly because of his isolation, partly because of his vagueness, is outside any such scheme. Koestler deliberately presents him as an enigma, and we see him more often through the eyes of others than through his own mind. No explanation is attempted either of his motives or his actions, and this, paradoxically, allows Koestler to suggest depth rather than analysis. Koestler avoids the common inclination of historical novelists to supply too much unconfirmable detail. Practically nothing is known about Spartacus, and Koestler reins in his imagination in his presentation of his central characters. Other characters, invented, can be handled in any way he likes. Spartacus has his place in history, his place in a movement, and it is in this that his importance lies.

Koestler's approach to Spartacus could be isolated as a common fault of political novelists—the subjugation of the individual to history. But here it works admirably. The vagueness, the bare simplicity, the lack of intrusion into Spartacus's mind mean that Koestler does not intellectualise. His metaphorical phrasing of Spartacus's predicament is not always convincing, but the shadowy force of Spartacus himself is. This is not to say that there is no intellectualised argument in the novel, but that it is contained in the dialogue of characters other than Spartacus— the Essene, Fulvius the commentator, and Zozimos the philosopher. These dialogues emphasise Spartacus's isolation. He finds it difficult to make contact with the arguments and the theories that surround his actions.

Koestler pictures Spartacus at a distance, as if he himself were one of his followers speculating about his leader, overhearing an occasional conversation. This can be a powerful and teasing device, and the very fact that Koestler does not attempt to explain every facet of Spartacus's character gives depth to his simplicity. Spartacus barely develops as a character, but development hardly matters as we look at him from so many different angles. Koestler employs a different technique in his presentation of the other characters. They too are static, and this is much more troubling in creations of the imagination than in a clouded historical figure. They tend to be pictured, both physically and intellectually, through the emphasis of a single characteristic— Crixus through his brawny bulk and his longing for Alexandria, the Essene through his bullet head and his sardonic manner. The technique is complemented by the representation of the various stances in the debate about revolution by a single character who maintains this stance. With more colour and more imaginative depth they would be almost allegorical figures. Only Spartacus is outside this kind of classification.

In *The Gladiators* and *Darkness At Noon* Koestler is concerned with the progress of revolution itself, and this means that the emphasis on individuals is different, though not necessarily less, than what we expect in the non-political novel. While a writer such as Howard Fast writes a novel about Spartacus which is an imaginative portrayal rather than an historical interpretation, and therefore tries to circumvent history by bringing his characters as close to our own imaginations as possible, Koestler is concerned with history itself. In Koestler's novels personal relationships are seen in the light of the influence of political action and pressures : if there is something stilted and unsatisfactory in the affair between Peter and Odette in *Arrival and Departure* it can legitimately be seen to arise from the genuine pressures of commitment of the characters themselves rather than the result of the effect of politics on Koestler's writing. In *The Gladiators* the characters are reflections of the growth and decay of revolution. We see them in relation to their commitment and the dilemma that commitment brings. We see them forced to act, forced to choose, in situations that were characteristic of Europe in the thirties. First came the necessity of choice—and apathy was as much a question of choice as action—for everyone from the German who had to choose between Hitler and the concentration camp to the socialist who had to choose between Stalin and political impotence. And with certain choices came the necessity of action. It is the gradual realisation of this that Koestler portrays in Spartacus.

Koestler's methods of characterisation are not the inevitable result of political fiction. Malraux's characters are much more fluid, for Malraux is not concerned with revolution so much as with revolutionaries. Argument is revealed through personality rather than represented by personality. It is a method of illustrating historical forces rather than interpreting them. After reading *La Condition Humaine* we have only the vaguest grasp of the Shanghai revolt and the political situation in China. We have learnt something only about a few imaginatively created individuals who were involved in certain events. Most critics would say that Malraux's approach provides the more legitimate subject for fiction.

The question of what *is* the legitimate content of fiction is inevitably a red herring. It is possible for the imagination to attempt to handle any aspect of modern life. As we have seen, when the imagination is faced with the more violent and horrific aspects of reality it is strongly challenged. The greater the challenge the more rewarding the effort, and, in some cases at least, the more impressive the result. Koestler is often accused of a failure of imagination. In fact, Koestler faced his imagina-

tion with difficulties that were greater than those Malraux tried
to handle. Koestler dealt primarily with facts, with reality, and
it is exactly this that the imagination has to struggle with most
fiercely if it is not to retreat altogether. Why write fiction about
fact? Because fiction is a method of interpretation, of placing in
perspective, of relating facts intimately to individual lives. It is
also a method of making facts acceptable and comprehensible to
the reading public.

Darkness At Noon is the most intellectual phase of Koestler's
argument: it is also the most compelling. His static technique
is more exaggerated than in other novels, but one questions the
method of characterisation the least. The physical confinement
of the novel, the action almost entirely held by prison walls and
the memories of a single character, inevitably intensifies details
of personality. We come to know important aspects of Rubashov's personality through a few idiosyncratic gestures—his
fiddling with his pince-nez, for example. These gestures become
obsessive, they threaten to engulf his whole personality, but this
is psychologically convincing. It is the minute focus of the
prison cell that is responsible. Rubashov is physically imprisoned,
but most of the other characters are also trapped in some way.
They become specimens not only because Koestler uses them as
examples and illustrations, but because circumstances force
them under the microscope. In Little Loewy and Richard we see
men, who like Rubashov himself, half-voluntarily walk into a
trap that means death. Both characters are impressively memorable, and we remember them for the same reason as Rubashov—
for their small betraying gestures, for the surrounding details.
The vehicle of memory, which picks out certain details and impressions but is rarely comprehensive, makes these characters
convincing. although they remain static and without development.

Koestler accused novelists of the thirties of ignoring the third,
irrational dimension of character (in "The Novelist's Temptations", *The Yogi and the Commissar*, 1945), but he was thinking
chiefly of the connection between psychological development

and commitment, the connection he himself tried to explore in *Arrival and Departure*. He does not touch on the relation between the irrational and personality. In his own novels explanations of personality become explanations of action. In a free-ranging novel such as *The Gladiators*, or later in *Thieves in the Night*, the dominance of action over personality works more effectively than in the constriction of *Darkness At Noon*. The advantages that memory and a trapped atmosphere give Koestler's characterisation are not enough to make the presentation of Rubashov himself completely successful. There are gaps in response which are all the more evident as we are led to believe that they will in fact be filled in. Some of these are filled in by Rubashov's dialogue, but this is geared, again, to providing a context for action, past and present, and an explanation rather than a portrait of personality. Rubashov's individualism is presented as a foil to the Neanderthal Gletkin yet many aspects of the contrast remain unexplored. We come to know Rubashov's mind and his nervous gestures well, but find it hard to believe that even the most dedicated revolutionary of the old generation would have reduced subjective response to the level of seeking only symbols and illustrations of formulae.

These symbols are often powerful—the outstretched hands of the prisoner opposite, Arlova's white blouse—but their representative importance confines their significance. Their precise meaning to Rubashov is only too clear, and their suggestiveness is therefore curtailed. Rubashov is pre-eminently a character *à thèse*, and it would be a mistake to dismiss him or the novel on grounds of incompleteness of presentation. To some extent the very intensity that emphasises the flaw in his characterisation also carries us over it. There is a strength of movement and suspense in the novel that matches the hard clarity of the dialogue, both actual and internal. The variety of character breaks the constriction without breaking the intensity. Small incidents, such as the visit to the barber, or merely the walk along the prison corridors to the interrogation room, assume a momentum of action almost comparable in function to the climactic execution of Bogrov. The novel is full of such incidents, and we react to them in the same way as the prisoner in solitary confinement reacts to the slightest variation in routine. We have seen the reaction in Koestler himself in his *Dialogue with Death*. These incidents encroach on and expand Rubashov's debate with himself, the pulse of the book, so that, although his mental position remains essentially static throughout, the combination of incident and relentless dialogue gives pace to the novel.

Darkness At Noon represents an approach not only to a particular period in Russia but to a particular phase of revolution. Another novel that handles the same period but without placing it historically is Victor Serge's *The Case of Comrade Tulayev* (1951). Serge approaches the Moscow Purges from a position politically similar to Koestler's but in a rather different mood. Koestler's fiction is close to the tradition of the French *roman à thèse*; Serge writes in the expansive perspective of the Russian tradition. The situation has an almost comic irony. Comrade Tulayev is shot, and this becomes the starting point of rigorous purges, in much the same way as the assassination of Kirov initiated the Moscow Purges. But Tulayev is shot almost by accident by a depressed and angry young man, Kostia, who did not premeditate any such action. There was no widescale plot, but such a plot is created by the authorities and the layers of implication go deep. Kostia is never discovered, and is the only character with any prospect of happiness when the novel ends.

Tulayev's death provides the excuse for getting rid of unreliable elements in the Party. The process escalates: Party leaders, Old Bolsheviks in exile, Trotskyist elements in the Spanish Civil War are drawn into the net of victimisation. In fact, Serge is fictionalising fact exactly. He is merely changing the names and giving the initial situation an ironic twist. Makeyev, a Party official, sums up the essence of Stalinism, or rather the attitude of those forced to choose between Stalinism and death: "Men like myself have to have hearts of stone. We build on corpses, but we build."[1] These are Serge's Gletkins, but with a self-comprehension, and therefore vulnerability, that Koestler's character is without.

There is a wide range of character in *Comrade Tulayev*, and this helps Serge to convey a sense of the vastness of the Russian territory and the warmth of the Russian people. He uses his characters to picture the growth of the Russian Revolution in its different aspects—in different localities, spheres of action, ways of thinking. His rich personalities cannot be categorised—they are not being used as illustrations—but are suggestive of a complex and deeply rooted life. Their doubts do not have the hard clarity of Rubashov's, but are mingled with the uncertainty of personal relationships and an emotional patriotism, loyalty and sense of justice. Where there is irrationality it cannot be analysed, as Koestler's characters invite analysis, but is a part of their lives and traditions.

Serge is handling fact, but his style is very different from Koestler's. The quality of his writing can be turbulent and impressionistic. It is sometimes hard and biting. Here, as Serge describes the bombing of Barcelona, it combines all these qualities:

> . . . one morning the morgue was filled with children in their Sunday clothes; the next, with militia men in blue tunics, all beardless, all looking strangely like grown men; the day after that, with young mothers nursing dead babies; the next, with old women whose hands were hardened by half a century of toil—as if the Reaper enjoyed choosing his victims in successive series. . . . The placards kept proclaiming, THEY SHALL NOT GET THROUGH—NO PASARAN!—but we, shall we get through the week? Shall we get through the winter? Get through, get on . . .[2]

The progression of phrases is similar to a technique Koestler sometimes uses, but Serge's prose is both more flexible and more permissive. The language is more suggestive, it contains more meaning. Serge does not express horror by the straightforward accumulation of detail. His words react upon one another. He speaks of militia men "looking strangely like grown men" and we realise with a shock that they are boys. When he writes "young mothers nursing dead babies" it is almost as if he is ironically suggesting that the mothers are not also dead. It is this irony in the presentation of normally conflicting facts that impresses. The final discrepancy between the determination of the placards and the hopelessness of fact, and the movement from the certainty of observable detail to the uncertainty of human endurance give this passage a power—emotional rather than intellectual—which Koestler rarely achieves.

Koestler's descriptive prose is always direct and precise, but at times his very precision narrows its scope. He presents his characters with a selected list of details, which are all offered at once:

> A certain Paul was amongst them, the section's organisation Secretary. He was an ex-wrestler, bald-headed, pock-marked, with big sticking-out ears. He wore a sailor's black sweater under his coat, and a black bowler on his head. He had the gift of wagging his ears, thereby lifting his bowler and letting it drop again.[3]

This is all that we are told about Paul. He is not an important character, but he is mentioned again with the same details present. The language is very explicit and very limited in function; it is efficient rather than powerful or suggestive, and its rhythm also is functional. Even in the description of Bogrov being led past Rubashov's cell, where there is impetus and vigour, the force is achieved by reiteration, by the accumulation of strong, hard-sounding vocabulary, rather than by the association of words. And Koestler's prose essentially does not vary. What variations there are are variations of speed and quantity of detail, not of quality or density of meaning. Koestler frequently picks up a detail—the Pietà, for instance—and hammers it into a recurrent symbol, but in most cases the power of suggestion is limited, and repetition does not involve widening implications.

Albert Camus, in *The Rebel*, makes a distinction between rebellion and revolution. Revolution is an enactment in the name of an ideology; it almost inevitably involves a belief that the end justifies the means. Rebellion is an assertion that transcends the individual and necessitates a belief that the means justify the end. Spartacus moves from rebel to revolutionary. Peter Slavek is essentially a rebel who can only fulfil himself in acts of rebellion, since the potentialities of revolution have faded.

In his discussion of the character of the rebel Camus writes: "the affirmation implicit in each act of revolt is extended to something which transcends the individual in so far as it removes him from supposed solitude and supplies him with reason to act."[4] Peter is a fine example of this. Having been shown that his commitment has an irrational and irrelevant origin, having decided that the sensible way to behave would be to remove himself from the area of battle, at the last minute he throws himself back into the fight. It is an attempt to eliminate his isolation and his lack of contact and to give his life something more solid than mere security. He obeys an impulse and the analysis of motive decreases in importance.

We have to remember that, like Camus, Koestler was trying to characterise the rebel and the revolutionary (without making an explicit distinction) in general terms as well as in particular detail. As he eased the gladiatorial revolt into the shape of the Russian Revolution so he eased essentially representative figures into the shape of individuals—or vice versa. The process was not always accomplished without damage. But Koestler's purpose was quite legitimate; he wanted to make absolutely sure that his readers would not interpret an individual personality as indicating an isolated incident. Without using large numbers of characters he had to try to present quantity. The fact that Peter is typical, that is that there were many others from his kind of background who had similar experiences, is as important as the details of what he goes through.

This fact inevitably complicates Koestler's methods of characterisation. Another complicating factor is that it is important in the context of time and place for Koestler to present and explain an individual's political role as well as his private personality and actions. In fact in *Arrival and Departure* Koestler is explicitly trying to make the connection between all these levels of characterisation. But the connections he makes become a little too formalised, a little too schematic, to be entirely convincing.

Peter's identity in his own country was quite clear. It rested on what he had done for the revolution. He was known for his courage. As far as the revolution and the fight against Hitler were concerned his private confusions were an irrelevant part of his personality. In Neutralia Peter very nearly becomes absorbed into the grey dejection of men and women who are no longer capable of hope. They only long to get as far away from the conflict as possible, yet America does not represent a new life, but rather a further and equally depressing phase of exile and a rejection of the European conflict and all that it means. In so far as Peter's present situation cannot be separated from his past, which has left him emotionally as well as physically damaged, his political role is a dominant part of his personality. By the end of the novel we have been shown the way in which his personality, and the subconscious and psychological activities behind his personality, have governed his political role. The facts of political life have shaped Peter's life more roughly than the particular psychological pressure that Sonia Bolgar detects; the point is that for Peter the crucial pressures arise from the facts, events and actions of the present. It is these that he responds to.

The pressures of the present have been such that Peter finds himself in a world whose different aspects bear no relation to one another. Each moment of awareness is a moment of deception. He is deceived into thinking that he has made his way into a rational world where the issues are straightforward. (He finds that the bureaucratic machine will take months to allow him to enlist; he is advised not to bother by the country he wants to fight for.) Later, he is deceived into thinking that self-knowledge has solved his problems. On both occasions the moment of awareness, which ought to be exciting and regenerative, over-reaches itself and plunges Peter straight back into the old areas of conflict. The question implicit throughout the book is : where is Peter to look for a basis for thought and action? He has no all-embracing metaphysic of the kind that sustains Malraux's heroes, not even the savagely channelled hatred of Orwell's characters. He does not know to whom or what he can allow a response. At a distance from the conflict that claims his conscience he is adrift.

Peter's fight with apathy is something quite different from his fight with the secret police. Then, he was sure of his ground. Now, there are sinister complexities that intrude on the straight-forward. Peter has been taught to see conflict in terms of black versus white. Like Rubashov he has been educated to avoid making a choice. In Neutralia he is swamped first with apathy, then with the necessity of making decisions. We meet Odette first as a part of this apathy. She is as colourless as the other refugees; she is in transit, stateless, almost without identity. But her relationship with Peter gives her some energy and purpose, and gives him a focus for his neutral life. Beside Sonia, Odette is overshadowed; she becomes inanimate and negative. But with Peter, because of their knowledge of shared danger, because of their complete inadequacy towards each other, and because of the almost disproportionate and desperate enjoyment of their ten days together she achieves a kind of affirmation. Their rela-tionship fluctuates in a way that seems to be beyond Koestler's control. There is a chilly warmth which grows when they are, for instance, deciding where and what to eat, but subsides when they are talking of themselves. Peter clings to Odette and the atmosphere of her presence much in the same way as he clung to silence under torture. He finds in their relationship a justifica-tion of the present. It enables him to isolate himself, momen-tarily, from both past and future.

But Peter needs to live according to his original impulse and the affair with Odette can only be pathetic, doomed by the fact that Peter and Odette have been deprived of the right, even the ability, to expect anything from the future. But it is doomed by another factor also, and this is Koestler's distinct failure in his characterisation of Odette. He has been criticised more than once for his inability to handle women. Strangely, it is one of his less important woman characters, Arlova in *Darkness At Noon*, who remains most impressively in the memory. She has a solidity and a warmth that makes up for the fact that one is told practically nothing about her personality. But Odette is a figure washed in grey, expressionless, actionless. We always seem to see her motionless. We can believe in Peter's rather jerky passion, but it is hard to accept that Odette has even the physical ability to make love, let alone any kind of passion. Part of Odette's greyness is a legitimate aspect of her character. But it is a much more difficult job to render convincing a personality that has been bludgeoned into a stunted form by events than to present the normal and the conventional. It is a difficulty that cannot be overcome by mere negativity in the method of characterisation. The negativity must be actively moulded by the author.

Sonia Bolgar is unsatisfactory through overemphasis rather than underemphasis. She remains nothing more than a large, clever woman in a white suit. Even her largeness has no density —it is as if the cold precision of her attitudes had coated her in shiny plastic. If she had been developed into caricature she might have been successful. But as it is the reflection of her attitudes in her appearance restricts her, and rather than this making the psychological explanation more convincing it makes us suspicious of it. It seems as if Sonia has taken a series of psychoanalytical watchwords and applied them to Peter just as Peter has applied revolutionary watchwords to the political situation. They have both had resort to utilitarian short-cuts and generalisations. Peter survives more successfully as a character because he has weaknesses, bursts of romanticism, moments of helplessness, and suffering is always with him, at the same time both haunting and repulsive. Even so, he is a stiff-legged character. Koestler seems to have been so anxious to explain him, in a way he was not with Spartacus, for instance, or even with Rubashov, that he left no room for fluidity. He has erred in a way that he himself was to criticise later :

> Some novelists give meticulous descriptions of the visual appearances of their characters; others give little or none. Here again the general trend is away from the over-explicit statement towards the suggestive hint which entices the reader to build up his own image of the character. I am always annoyed when the author informs me that Sally Anne has auburn hair and green eyes. I don't particularly like the combination, and would have gone along more willingly with the author's intention that I should fall in love with Sally Anne if he had left the colour-scheme to me. There is a misplaced concreteness which gets in the way of the imagination.[5]

In the case of Peter it is psychological "appearances" that Koestler over-describes. In striving to emphasise the irrational dimension which he accuses "pink" novelists of the thirties of neglecting he becomes guilty of "misplaced concreteness". He is in danger of explaining Peter's personality away altogether, of saying that personality is irrelevant because it depends on obscure childhood incidents. But if we have in Peter an anatomical drawing of a personality, we can still see the possibilities : and there is still a great deal of power in the novel. It is tough and clear, and toughness and clarity answered a need that Orwell also recognised.

Koestler's hard, precise conflicts contrast sharply with Orwell's drab scenes of the dissatisfied individual sinking in a mire of sticky facts which he can neither grasp properly nor let go of entirely. There is no vivid area of action to bring the problems of Orwell's heroes into focus. *Burmese Days* is the only novel in which this comes near to happening. There is no ready-made system of logical belief to help out Orwell's heroes. The circumstances of Koestler's novels are more drastic than those of Orwell's earlier books, yet they are also more black and white. In spite of Peter's difficulties it is easier for most of Koestler's characters to know how to act. In his own life Orwell experienced the relief of being plunged into a situation, in Spain, where the course of action was clear. Conversely, Koestler later expressed his relief at being in a country, Britain, where such exhausting opposites did not pertain. But Koestler's attempt to write about people confined in a heavy, static atmosphere (*The Age of Longing*) was a failure, while Orwell's use of those elements of political life that were outside his own experience was more successful, perhaps because more purposeful. Orwell's consciousness of his lack of experience made him more sensitive to its literary possibilities.

Koestler tells us how the fact that he had lived through the experiences that were his subjects damaged his novels. "Emotion and intuition, dialogue and analysis of character, were all spent in lived relationships. By the time they had become dead relationships I felt no urge to record them; the experience had been too completely consummated and burnt out."[6] Yet this does not quite explain the particular quality of his novels. The fact that Koestler continually intellectualises, handles people as if they were arguments, and by this intellectualisation flattens his fiction's dimensions, is not necessarily the result of the searing effects of real experience. We can explain this flat quality by suggesting that it is Koestler's mind that responds to both people and events, that the fierce feeling that seems to be emotional comes from his understanding of injustice, of pain, of loss, for instance, not from a subjective apprehension of these things. It is curious to criticise a writer for having a finer understanding and intellect than most, but it does seem to be Koestler's very intelligence that gets in the way of his fiction.

This is one factor. Another is the difficulty already discussed of translating the effects of extremity, its power of, precisely, flattening the personality, into fiction without losing a dimension. A problem here is that because we can clearly see Koestler's intellect at work we are only too aware of his attempts to round out his characters. If he, and we, accept the limitations of his characters, it must be accepted also that they should not be forced to carry too much weight. In fact they frequently are, and this destroys some of their fictional strength. Peter suffers from this. In *The Age of Longing* the heroine Hydie suffers to a far greater extent. The context of *The Gladiators* and *Darkness At Noon* helps Spartacus and Rubashov to survive. *The Gladiators* has a vigour generated by its scope of action. *Arrival and Departure* is cramped not merely because of its confinement of place, but because too much emphasis is placed on a single character who is not adequate in performing the function required of him. We notice this inadequacy because Koestler has made his function so clear.

It is not the fact that Koestler writes political novels, that he tries to fictionalise fact without losing anything of the fact's original force, that is responsible for the flaws that have been discussed. As we have seen, two important political novelists, Silone and Malraux, do not encounter the same kind of difficulties. The difficulties arise primarily from Koestler's approach, his own response to events and people. To attribute Koestler's partial success in solving them directly to the encroachment of politics is short-circuiting both Koestler's understanding and the content of his fiction. The literary critic approaches Koestler's novels, especially at this distance, from a standpoint that is almost inevitably conventional. He knows what he is looking for. Koestler was really writing fiction for readers who did not know what they were looking for : many readers in the thirties and during the War were in this position.

This points to the question whether fiction that is written in response to and for a particular period can endure. The answer can only be that as long as we retain any awareness of history there is no intrinsic reason why it should not. It was Orwell who said that Koestler was writing the kind of literature that is an attempt "to write contemporary history, but *unofficial* history, the kind that is ignored in the text-books and lied about in the newspapers".[7] Orwell was clearly thinking of Spain when he wrote this. Koestler's own experiences had made him only too conscious of the value of unofficial history, and unofficial history is perhaps exactly what documentary is.

But unofficial history has its tradition in fiction also, which counteracts the tendency to think of the political novel as an invention of the thirties. Scott is an example. Koestler digested and interpreted events that his readers were not able to come close to. In one novel at least, *Redgauntlet*, Scott was doing exactly this. He presented the thoughts and actions of a group of political conspirators who, in spite of the fact that history had left their movement behind, continued to work for their aims. He placed them in contemporary society, showed their effects on citizens who assumed that such movements were not a part of contemporary life. Scott was in many respects a political novelist with an interpretative function similar to Koestler's. And he solved, or avoided creating, many of Koestler's problems. Much of his history lies in his characterisation. Koestler did not have the ability to present society in and through people.

Some of his problems Koestler was able to solve in his fourth novel, *Thieves in the Night*. In it he dealt with issues that were still alive and uncertain, issues in which his emotional involvement emerged as clearly as his intellectual grasp. His own passage through Communism did not dominate them. The result was that he wrote a novel that was a little more rounded and a little less confined by intellectual assessment than his others.

F

8

A FAITH TO FIGHT FOR?

The Spanish Civil War had strengthened Orwell's commitment as it had pointed to the necessity of Koestler releasing himself from Communism. But for a brief period, as war on a large scale became more certain, Orwell's condemnation of war outweighed his hatred of Fascism. He associated himself with the ILP which at that time, and throughout the War, followed a pacifist line. When war became a reality it found many others on the left in a similar predicament. It was not simply a question of distaste for what it was imagined would be an imperialist war, both politically and physically a re-enactment of the First, but of a mood of defeat and withdrawal that followed Spain. Munich, the Nazi–Soviet Pact, and the fact that Chamberlain was still in the saddle when war broke out did nothing to encourage optimism. However, although Orwell remained pessimistic, his pacifism did not last long—probably only a matter of months—and he was rapidly again convinced that the military destruction of Fascism was essential.

The post-Spain withdrawal symptoms affected Orwell's writing. In a letter to Cyril Connolly he wrote: "This bloody mess-up in Europe has got me so that I really can't write anything. . . . It seems to me we might as well all pack our bags for the concentration camp."[1] Nine months earlier he had written: "I have seen wonderful things and at last really believe in Socialism, which I never did before."[2] Then Orwell had before his eyes proof, however brief, that a socialist society was viable—he could believe that it was possible. But the threat of war and Fascism mingled in his imagination. An overwhelming sense of futility, of not being able to take effective action, of being always on the defensive, is revealed in letter after letter. "Every-thing one writes now is overshadowed by this ghastly feeling that we are rushing towards a precipice, and, though we shan't actually prevent ourselves or anyone else from going over, must put up some sort of a fight."[3] Whatever the depth of his pessi-mism Orwell never ceased to believe that one "must put up some sort of a fight".

The novel that Orwell was writing at this time survives this mood with remarkable vitality. The book itself, *Coming Up for Air* (1939), is concerned with the imminence of war and the per-versions of modern civilisation, but it is a much more cheerfully toned novel than previous ones. The main character has a frank-ness and energy that takes him right out of the depression-bound confines of Gordon or Flory. George Bowling, shabby middle-class with a dull, bad-tempered wife, in his escape to the village of his childhood finds it built up and commercialised beyond recognition, but the power of his memories enables him to sur-vive. Orwell himself was dubious about the use of the first-person narrative but in fact it is largely responsible for the wry humour and good nature which is present in such quantities in no other of his novels. George Bowling's character has a resili-ence that Gordon Comstock's has not, and so we feel that he will survive his stultifying home, his dried-up wife and the bombs being dropped on London, while Gordon would just turn his head to the wall or make some ineffectual gesture of revolt. Bowling's revolt is perhaps little more than a gesture also, but it is at least a meaningful one. His dream of recapturing his child-hood in the country is shattered but he retains the sensitivity and warmth this childhood gave him.

George Bowling returns to a "vulgar low-down row in a smell of old mackintoshes" and feels his dreams of the past and his worries about the future fade into the background as he faces the sordid present, but there is salvation in his own personality. *Coming Up for Air* is in many ways the most convincing of Orwell's novels. The detail is breathtakingly exact, the frank-ness almost shocking in its portrayal of middle-class tedium.

The first few pages in which Bowling casts a critical eye at himself while taking his morning bath are more ruthless than the cruder condemnations in the earlier novels.

In *Coming Up for Air* Orwell is able to strike a happier balance between the reality of fact and the resilience of human nature. Bowling's brief revolt is meaningful because it is genuine, more genuine than Gordon Comstock's even though it is no more clearly directed. His defeat is not pathetic because it is not apathetic. He remains aware of adversity, his experience of escape has rubbed his nose in the impossibility of escape, yet his personality survives energetically. We feel that he might well make the attempt again. Neither Flory nor Dorothy nor Gordon have this energy of character that has made *Coming Up for Air* a hopeful book in spite of itself.

The attack on modern society and the middle-class position is in fact much more precise and more controlled in *Coming Up for Air* than in earlier books. The account of the Left Book Club meeting in the novel has a sharper edge to its criticism than the outbursts in *Wigan Pier*. Mrs. Bowling's neurotic penny-pinching is shown to be ludicrous as well as intolerable. Through the first-person narrative George Bowling's hatreds and criticisms are solid, a direct confrontation with reality. The instant, violent disgust at the fish-filled frankfurter stabs home much more surely than Gordon's morbid fry-up in his digs. The nostalgia for an unspoiled world that hovers at the edge of earlier books takes on a warm reality. And the appeal is very direct. George Bowling chats and grumbles to his readers as if he were not functioning through the printed word. With humour and without losing his sense of the injustices of the old world he recalls it in much the same way as Orwell does in his essay "Boys' Weeklies" which was written at about the same time:

Uncle Ezekiel is cursing Joe Chamberlain. The recruiting sergeant in his scarlet jacket . . . is strutting up and down twisting his mustache. The drunks are puking in the yard behind the George. Vicky's at Windsor, God's in heaven,

Christ's on the cross, Jonah's in the whale, Shadrack, Mesach, and Abednego are in the fiery furnace, and Sihon king of the Amorites and Og the king of Bashan are sitting on their thrones looking at one another—not doing anything exactly, just existing, keeping their appointed places, like a couple of fire-dogs, or the Lion and the Unicorn.[4]

The characterisation suffers from some of the faults present in the earlier novels, the construction is a little clumsy—both too straightforward and too contrived—but *Coming Up for Air* reveals the same fine touch that illuminates *Homage to Catalonia*. Paradoxically these two books mark the height of Orwell's cheerfulness. It is curious that this should be so at a time when Orwell was so profoundly affected by the political situation. But he was also at this time condemning a pessimistic outlook, and frequently discussed the relationship between pessimism and right wing beliefs. His essay "Second Thoughts on James Burnham" is particularly concerned with this. Many of his "As I Please" articles in *Tribune* touched on it. He found the novels of the 1920s both reactionary and pessimistic because they contained no belief in the possibility of change for the better. He could not tolerate the shrugging acceptance that led to apathy, although, as his novels make clear, he could understand it. Although from the middle of 1937 to his death Orwell consistently expressed his conviction that nothing could stop the growth of totalitarianism and the decay of democracy he never entirely lost his very deep faith in human nature. He felt both a compulsion and a duty—usually synonymous in Orwell's case—to alert humanity to the dangers he saw, and to carry on the struggle for improvement. When war broke out the issues became concrete and vigorous. A large section of the left wing in Britain experienced a reluctant but invigorating optimism. The sense of urgency which had grown stale with the steady decline in the political situation became alive again. Once the period of "phoney war" was over and Chamberlain was out gloomy pacifism gave way to a reaffirmation of the necessity of action. Perhaps the war would not be won, but at last Britain was fighting Hitler, and there was an opportunity of translating words into deeds. As Britain became hard pressed and better organised the left became sure that the war against Fascism would necessitate radical changes in the structure of society.

When war was declared Orwell was writing one of his most acute and judicious pieces, the essay on Henry Miller "Inside the Whale" in which he discusses the position of the artist in relation to public events, and makes clear the dual role he himself was always trying to play as writer and propagandist. He continually urged that a writer must pay attention to the world of politics and government—"a novelist who simply disregards the major public events of the moment is either a footler or a plain idiot"—and yet insisted equally that the small details of everyday life were of vital importance. Koestler was later to describe with a far more intellectual moral sense the role of responsibility of the intelligentsia in Europe. Here Orwell's morality is of a much more down-to-earth nature.

In this essay Orwell's moulding of a combination of literary and social criticism can be seen at its best. They do not lie parallel but grow out of one another. He cannot discuss Miller without examining the meaning of his a-political outlook just as he cannot write of Auden or Spender without trying to make sense of the extensive intellectual gravitation towards Marxism. This was a part of Orwell's moral sense. Primarily he enjoyed Miller's "friendly American voice, with no humbug in it, no moral purpose, merely an implicit assumption that we are all alike"[5] and the fact that Miller's concern for everyday things is transformed into a profound feeling for life by his energetic and attractive prose, which Orwell describes as "flowing, swelling . . . a prose with rhythms in it, something quite different from the flat cautious statements and snack-bar dialects that are now in fashion."[6] Orwell commends Miller because of his way of "owning up to everyday facts and everyday emotions"; yet Miller sees nothing beyond his own experiences, his immediate world is tiny, and he accepts everything around him as unchangeable. Orwell says "We live in a *shrinking* world. The 'democratic vistas' have ended in barbed wire. There is less feeling of creation and growth, less and less emphasis on the cradle, endlessly rocking, more and more emphasis on the teapot, endlessly stewing. To accept civilisation *as it is* practically means accepting decay."[7] Miller has no eye for democratic vistas, he is only interested in his own minute sector; his compassion is general and uncritical rather than particular and constructive. But he can write "astonishing" prose, he has "chosen to drop the Geneva language of the ordinary novel and drag the *real-politik* of the inner mind into the open",[8] and this makes him, for Orwell, a valuable writer.

This affirmation is an important part of Orwell's belief. He admired Miller's concern with humanity infinitely more than Auden's rather marginal concern for Marx. Orwell's own eye never left "everyday facts and everyday emotions" even when he was nearest to writing for a narrowly propagandist purpose. He used "Inside the Whale" as a vehicle for condemning dogmatic propagandists. If he found pessimism and acceptance a symptom of right-wing beliefs he found facile Marxism a symptom of inhumanity, and inhumanity was one of Socialism's worst enemies. He was deeply concerned at what literature had lost to politics. "During the past ten years literature has involved itself more and more deeply in politics," he writes, and condemns the results:

. . . there is now less room in literature for the ordinary man than at any other time during the past two centuries. One can see the change in the prevailing literary attitudes by comparing the books written about the Spanish civil war with those written about the war of 1914-18. The immediately striking thing about the Spanish war books, at any rate those written in English, is their shocking dullness and badness. But what is more significant is that almost all of them, right-wing or left-wing, are written from a political angle, by cocksure partisans telling you what to think, whereas the books about the Great War were written by common soldiers or junior officers who did not even pretend to understand what the whole thing was about.[9]

Of course some of the reasons for the differences in the literature of these two wars lies in the differences between the wars themselves, but Orwell has a legitimate point here, and it is a point that his own book on Spain underlines. He insists that this loss must be remedied. It is a theme he returns to again and again. He himself went some way towards doing so, although he was always fumbling in his attempts to handle personality. Like Koestler, his very consciousness of the problem may have interfered to some extent with his effort to overcome it.

May 1940 brought a change in political mood. It saw the fall of France, Churchill replacing Chamberlain, and Dunkirk. It was the time when Koestler was making his erratic escape to Britain. The struggle for survival put all other issues in the shade, but it was at this time that the left reawoke to the political challenge. As the situation became grimmer—and between September 1939 and the fall of Tobruk in October 1942, Britain did not secure a single major offensive victory against Germany, and suffered severe defeats in North Africa, Crete and Singapore—the left united in its demand for social equality and an elucidation of war aims. Orwell never lost his bitterness against those he termed "the orthodoxy-sniffers". Both *Animal Farm* and *Nineteen Eighty-Four* were directed against them. But the War brought him some hope that the rigidity of orthodox Marxism would melt away in the common effort towards social change, and the disappointment brought about by lack of change and increased constriction permanently affected the remainder of his writing life. Meanwhile he entered if not wholeheartedly with all his energies into the freshly tackled campaign for social revolution. The general feeling on the left was that in order to defeat the evils of Nazism Britain must put her own house in order. Britain must commit herself to fighting for a better world and prove it by comprehensive social reconstruction at home.

This was necessary both to get the most out of Britain herself and to convince the peoples of Europe that the War was still worth fighting—that, in fact, with their help, the War could be won.

Miller had written as a victim of society rather than as a propagandist for a particular way of life, and Orwell's natural sympathies were with the former. He was deeply suspicious of the propagandist. Yet he himself managed to combine the outlook of both victim and propagandist in *Down and Out* and *Homage to Catalonia*, and in 1940 he committed himself to a propagandist role even more unreservedly. Fredric Warburg and T. R. Fyvel were the originators of *Searchlight Books*, a series devoted to doing "all in their power to criticise and kill what is rotten in Western civilisation and supply *constructive* ideas for the difficult period ahead of us".[10] They asked Orwell to enter the project as joint editor with Fyvel. The first book, *The Lion and the Unicorn*, was written by Orwell himself. In it he discusses the English national character and the nature of the English revolution, which he believed was imminent. The predominant note is optimistic. (T. R. Fyvel says that Orwell was *not* optimistic at this time, but it was felt to be strategically necessary for the first book in the series to strike a hopeful note.) He sketches with a slightly wry appreciation the quality of life in England, the decay of the ruling classes, the privateness of English life, its essential democracy (and its lack of understanding of what it would mean to have this democracy destroyed)— all the qualities that Koestler appreciated so much as he viewed the English from the relative safety and comfort of Pentonville prison—and its extraordinary cohesive behaviour in moments of crisis. "In moments of supreme crisis the whole nation can suddenly draw together and act upon a species of instinct, really a code of conduct which is understood by almost everyone, though never formulated."[11] Again he attacks left-wing intellectuals, although politically most of them were at this time sharing his own position, and points out their lack of sympathy and their unsuitability. He talks of their "generally negative, querulous attitude", "the emotional shallowness of people who live in a world of ideas and have little contact with physical reality".[12]

The Lion and the Unicorn is a plea to the left to abandon this attitude as well as a document intended to rouse the conscience and consciousness of the non-political. The main contention is that "We cannot win the war without introducing Socialism, nor establish Socialism without winning the war. At such a time it is possible as it was not in the peaceful years, to be both revolutionary and realistic."[13] It was a widely held belief—Laski's *Reflections on the Revolution of Our Time* embodies it—that the alternatives before Britain were social revolution or defeat by Hitler. Orwell believed that war presented an opportunity of shaking sense and action into the left. "We have got to make our words take physical shape, or perish. We know very well that with its present social structure England cannot survive, and we have got to make other people see the fact and act upon it."[14]

The simultaneous shock and relief of the outbreak of war stimulated a heightened sense of drama. Orwell at once took hold of a situation that he saw as being one of straightforward alternatives and communicated it in dramatic terms. He plunged confidently into explicit assumptions and predictions—it was a clear and tough response. But, as always, his demands for action never became remote from the actual details of the situation as he saw them, nor from his understanding of the English character and his experience of English life. His immense and profound affection for England is continually present. He writes of "the crowds in the big towns, with their mild knobby faces, their bad teeth and gentle manners . . ."[15] and much that is out of date he is clearly reluctant to do away with. Many anachronisms will remain, he anticipates, when the revolution is complete, and this fact is itself a tribute to the humanity as well as the muddle-headedness of the English character.

Orwell's demand for "a simple, concrete programme of action" was in tune with the general feeling of the left, and the interpretation of what was necessary was clearly legitimate. The feeling of hope was itself legitimate. He says "War is the greatest of all agents of change" and "Above all war brings it home to the individual that he is *not* altogether an individual".[16] He urged the left to exploit this sense of common danger, to take advantage of the opportunities that the state of war was creating. His experience of the Spanish Civil War had been vitalising as well as bitter, and he was sure that something good—the destruction of class privilege, the acceptance of nationalisation —could result from the War. He realised, though, that revolution would not simply occur with ease and spontaneity :

> It is a struggle between the groping and the unteachable, between the young and the old, between the living and the dead. But it is very necessary that the discontent which undoubtedly exists should take a purposeful and not merely obstructive form. It is time for the *people* to define their war-aims. What is wanted is a simple, concrete programme of action, which can be given all possible publicity, and round which public opinion can group itself.[17]

Orwell tried to fashion this concrete simplicity himself in the form of a six-point programme demanding nationalisation, limitation of income, educational reform, and devoting three points to Britain's international responsibilities. It was the first and only time Orwell presented such a programme of action. The proposals are straightforward and clearly articulated. The measure of their acceptance can be somewhat ironically assessed by the fact that by the summer of 1941 the Government had taken over total control of industry and manpower. Churchill adopted on his own terms many of the left's most pressing proposals. As he did so it became quite clear that Britain was not moving towards Socialism.

Orwell continued his temporary association with the more orthodox left by contributing articles to *Left News*, the organ of the Left Book Club, which were later included in *The Be-*

trayal of the Left, edited by Victor Gollancz. This was a pained outcry of those whose illusions about Soviet Communism had been shattered. Orwell, of course, had never shared these, but Gollancz and Strachey, the other contributers, had been confirmed fellow-travellers. His *The Coming Struggle for Power* and *The Theory and Practice of Socialism* had provided the language of political expression for the thirties. His movement away from the CP, which was gradual but definite, was all the more significant. Most significant of all was its culmination in the publication of *The Betrayal of the Left* and *A Faith to Fight For* in 1941. The language of the latter, an affirmation of Britain's combative role and a belief in democracy, is simple and passionate, far different from the reasoned Marxist phraseology of his earlier books. Strachey, a guiding light of left-wing intellectuals, helped to clear their political confusion with this condemnation of the Communist position.

For those Marxists who had survived Spain and the Purges the Nazi–Soviet Pact of 1939 was the final test. Communism, which had led the way in the anti-Fascist battle, made its peace with Hitler. Russia, which had condemned so vociferously imperialist aggression, moved into Finland. Meanwhile Britain, after the fall of France, was fighting a lonely war. *The Betrayal of the Left* was published before Russia entered the War. It conducts a detailed examination of the behaviour of the CP from the outbreak of war to the beginning of 1941. Behind it were the feelings of betrayal which had built up over the last years of the thirties. For the first time Orwell spoke with the same voice as the high priests of the left. It was a subject about which he felt particularly deeply, to which much of his later work was devoted. The examination was conducted by methods at which he was an adept. It was surrounded by a framework of straightforward description of Communist inconsistency and hypocrisy, from the change of line early on in the War to the birth of the People's Convention, a Communist-backed organisation which opposed the War. Into this framework was set a variety of analytical essays of a more calm and careful approach than much of left-wing journalism was used to. Victor Gollancz illustrated the combination of deliberate misrepresentation and bluff by exaggeration that the Communist press indulged in. He compares the bloated invective of Harry Pollitt's 1939 May Day manifesto, in which he condemned Hitler in phrases teeming with colourful clichés, with the cold-blooded attempt of the *Daily Worker* to hold Britain responsible for the Nazi invasion of Norway. This is the first essay, and the tone of controlled but bitter reproach spreads throughout the book. It was the first time that condemnation of the CP changes of line had been so ruthlessly articulated. On the whole the left had remained quiet, but the War was again a stimulant. Political allegiance began to be seen in a different perspective and the left (apart from the ILP) was more or less united in its attack on revolutionary defeatism.

Orwell's essay in the book extend the discussion he began in *The Lion and the Unicorn*. He examines in greater detail the nature of democracy in Britain, and suggests that it is completely vulnerable to the threat of deterioration in the face of a large area of discontent, and that "it can only save itself from destruction by ceasing to be democratic. The things it is supposed to be fighting for are always scrapped as soon as the fighting starts."[18] Democracy relies on force for self-preservation, and loses its essential character when it uses force. In a crisis democracy is almost inevitably confused and fumbling. Orwell reiterates his belief that "the choice is between socialism and defeat", and he sketches, for the first time so explicitly, his picture of socialism :

When the real English socialist movement appears—it must appear if we are not to be defeated, and the basis for it is already there in the conversations in a million pubs and air-raid shelters—it will cut across existing party divisions. It will be both reactionary and democratic. It will aim at the most fundamental changes and be perfectly willing to use violence if necessary. But it will also recognise that not all cultures are the same, that national sentiments and traditions have to be respected if revolutions are not to fail, that England is not Russia—or China, or India. It will recognise that British democracy is *not* altogether a sham, *not* simply "superstructure", that on the contrary it is something extremely valuable which must be preserved and extended, and, above all, must not be insulted.[19]

Into this description are drawn all the elements of Orwell's socialism : his belief in democracy and his longing for physical revolution, his respect for tradition, particularly English tradition, his abhorrence of Marxist dogma, his reliance on ordinary people, his admiration of the short-lived revolution in Spain. All these profoundly coloured Orwell's attitudes, and their influence was constantly felt in the articles he wrote during the War.

As in *The Lion and the Unicorn* there are flaws not so much in the argument itself as in the manner in which Orwell dismisses his opponents, in particular the "doctrinaire Marxist". He does this by attacking the language they use, indicating its shallowness and lack of value. But in his haste to sweep away opposing arguments there are times when he does not pause to illuminate sufficiently the precise reasons for dismissal. For instance, he brushes away the word "realism" as being irrelevant and therefore meaningless. Certainly he was right in saying that it was a word used too frequently and too thoughtlessly, and that it had become debased by jargon. But Orwell does not emphasise that it is the manner in which the word is used, not the word itself, that is at fault. In his essay "Politics and the English Language" he was to make this distinction very acutely. But here he is sometimes too precipitate. His technique of exposure relies on precision, and there are moments, in both *The Betrayal of the Left* and *The Lion and the Unicorn*, when his enthusiasm and impatience do not allow him to take enough time over revealing jargonistic frauds. There are inconsistencies also. He constantly reveals his nostalgia for the simple life and his hatred of machines, and the way in which this influences his socialism is clear, and yet he accuses the middle-class socialist of being "out of date", and blind to the "modern technical middle class". It is true that this accusation arises out of the left-wing intellectual's advocacy of proletarian revolution, and Orwell is making a valid point, but it is a point that his critics could, and did, make against Orwell himself. He was continually in danger of allowing his distrust of the complex industrial world that he investigated to interfere with the logic of his conclusions.

The Lion and the Unicorn marked the beginning of a concentrated period of comment and criticism of every kind, of observation and investigation, which Orwell kept up throughout the War. He had by this time many more opportunities to be published, and he took advantage of every outlet he could find. By 1940 Orwell's articles and reviews were appearing frequently in a number of periodicals. Early in the year the magazine *Horizon* had been launched by Cyril Connolly, and a number of Orwell's best-known pieces first appeared there. They reflect his continued wide range of interest, but they also show him, in spite of the present challenge of war, still returning to the pre-First War legend. The tone differs but the sentiment is the same as George Bowling's:

The year is 1910—or 1940, but it is all the same. You are at Greyfriars, a rosy-cheeked boy of fourteen in posh tailor-made clothes, sitting down to tea in your study on the Remove passage after an exciting game of football which was won by an odd goal in the last half-minute. There is a cosy fire in the study, and outside the wind is whistling. The ivy clusters thickly round the old grey stones. The King is on his throne and the pound is worth a pound. Over in Europe the comic foreigners are gesticulating, but the grim grey battleships of the British Fleet are steaming up the Channel and at the outposts of Empire the monocled Englishmen are holding the niggers at bay. Lord Mauleverer has just got another fiver and we are all settling down to a tremendous tea of sausages, sardines, crumpets, potted meat, jam and doughnuts. After tea

we shall sit round the study fire having a good laugh at Billy
Bunter and discussing the team for next week's match against
Rockwood. Everything is safe, solid and unquestionable.
Everthing will be the same for ever and ever.[20]

Orwell enjoyed this picture. He was also right in suggesting that
it represented an important facet of the English character. Even
during the War, while the picture itself was fictional, the instincts and inclinations continued to be real. It seems that
Orwell himself was directing his efforts towards establishing a
situation in which everything was "safe, solid and unquestionable". This companionable calm, the steadiness of an established
order, had a profound attraction for him, even though it was
built on inequalities. Yet he says repeatedly that such a companionable feeling has gone for ever. The picture that he gives is
not satiric, and though it is clear that he does, really, disapprove
of the British Empire and holding niggers at bay his tone is
regretful. In spite of everything, sitting around the fire having
tea, even in a public school, is a good, human occupation, and
when Orwell thinks of the threat of Fascism it is the destruction
of this kind of warmth that most appals him.

This nostalgia does not interfere with Orwell's socialism. It is
in fact an important element of what gives Orwell's brand of
socialism its particular warmth and humanity, a solid contact
with human situations, which the theorists so often lost track
of. Orwell condemned savage nationalism, but neither had he
any time for the sophisticated intellectual who disparaged his
own country as a matter of course. The War, though, brought
unfashionable patriotism back into favour, as Strachey's *A Faith
to Fight For* reveals. Orwell's love for England was profound, if
critical, and the socialism he was after was an English brand,
including all the anomalies and anachronisms that he found
typical. In many ways he was sad that it was not possible to
include all the features of the Greyfriars tea in a vision of
socialism. Koestler, too, warmed towards these anomalies of the
English character.

Although Orwell's eye was throughout the War acutely fixed on immediate problems he was able to write on Dickens, Kipling and Donald McGill's postcards with ease and humour. Almost always such subjects became the bases for a discussion of the relationship between art and politics, and between people and public events. Most political writers he condemned, not so much for their opinions as for the fact that they wrote badly. But there were some that he admired : Trotsky, Borkenau, Silone and Koestler were among them. He did not agree with all they wrote but they wrote well, and they seem to have been a genuine inspiration to him, perhaps the only contemporary inspiration that he had. A writer such as Silone had an intensity and depth that grew from his particular experience of European politics, an experience that Orwell lacked. Britain's isolation had made that jolly tea possible; it had also cut her writers off from springs of vitalising energy.

The first year of the War was financially difficult for Orwell and he could not afford not to write, although he found it difficult. But later he worked with the BBC, broadcasting to India. In his attempt to present English life and letters to the Indians Orwell again had occasion to return to the question of art and propaganda. He reinforces his rejection of political propaganda while making the writer's responsibility clear :

> I have always maintained that every artist is a propagandist. I don't mean a political propagandist. If he has any honesty or talent he cannot be that. Most political propaganda is a matter of telling lies, not only about the facts but about your own feelings. But every artist is a propagandist in the sense that he is trying, directly or indirectly, to impose a vision of life that seems to him desirable.[21]

Yet Orwell did except those writers mentioned above, and presumably he excepted himself, from these criticisms. He makes an implicit distinction between well-written and truthful presentations of facts and sloppy and dishonest bullying. And he commends the fact that so many writers in the 1930s were politically conscious even though in most cases their literary handling of this consciousness was inadequate:

The writers who have come up since 1930 have been living in a world in which not only one's life but one's whole scheme of values is constantly menaced. In such circumstances detachment is not possible . . . literature had to become political because anything else would have entailed moral dishonesty. One's attachments and hatreds were too near the surface of consciousness to be ignored. What books were *about* seemed so urgently important that the way they were written seemed almost insignificant.[22]

As Orwell was to make more explicit later it was precisely the way books were written, their language, that was to decide their success or failure, both as literature and as methods of political persuasion. It was through his analysis of the use of language that Orwell finally resolved his ambiguity over propaganda. He conducted this analysis in the course of writing for a number of papers and periodicals—the *Observer*, the *Manchester Evening News* and the *New Statesman*—but it was through the columns of *Tribune* that he found his most congenial outlet.

Tribune had been founded by Stafford Cripps in 1937, a product of the enthusiasm of the People's Front. It was the mouthpiece of the Labour left, and in its first years it was hardly likely that Orwell would have written for it. But by the end of 1940, when his first pieces appeared, Orwell was no longer isolated in his opinions, and he found a place on *Tribune*'s platform of leftwing criticism of the Coalition and electoral truce. Russia's entry into the War in the summer of 1941 did not remove Orwell from its pages, although he never joined in the adulation of Stalin that mounted through the War's second half. He was suspicious of the Americans also, who entered the War at the end of that year. They were characterised for him by the cruder representatives of American troops in Britain, and he was in-

stinctively repelled. Others were also. But what was more important for Orwell were the left's cries for more efficiency in
war industry, and the speculations and proposals concerning
the War's end.

Orwell provided an unceasing monologue of criticism and
protest. His book reviews were bound in a web of social comment. He tried to place literature in a context of living experience, and if it did not fit he made it his business to investigate
the reason. His passion for language guaranteed that however
social his moral stance his criticism was always sharply literary,
and he always admired the writer who could, like Richard
Wright, author of *Black Boy*, illuminate the interior of men's
minds without losing sight of social context. Language and
politics, language and morality, became more and more closely
fused, as the pressures Orwell responded to increased.

Scattered throughout the *Tribune* pieces, even in the early
years of the War, are frequent indications of the pessimism that
had become rooted in Orwell's outlook. A private indication of
his state of mind is given in his Notebooks. He was finding it
difficult to write and longed to be more active. He was kept out
of the Army by his Spanish wound and generally poor health,
and he felt this bitterly. He gained some satisfaction from his
involvement with the Home Guard. As a sergeant he was, it
seems, faultless in theory but hopeless in practice. But he was
one of the few men who recognised the potentialities of the
Home Guard. Tom Wintringham, an experienced and respected
veteran of the Spanish War, wanted to create a genuine
"people's army", skilled in the tactics of guerrilla warfare.
Orwell was quick to grasp the revolutionary potential of such
an organisation. Composed of men who were prepared to fight
the Nazis to the last ditch and dispensing with the traditional
and hampering stuffiness of British Army discipline, the Home
Guard could have been a vital force. But as quickly as the possibilities were recognised the hopes of its original organisers were
demolished. The Home Guard became riddled with an exaggerated blimpishness which infuriated Orwell. It seemed to be

taken seriously by the Government only in so far as it provided opportunities for men, like Orwell, with experience gained from Spain and a background of leftist thinking which encouraged them to try and make the Home Guard a useful force. Orwell and those like him were deeply distrusted.

This was the first real disappointment of the War that Orwell was involved in. But in fact the War brought into focus all those aspects of modern life that most tormented and disgusted him, and this reinforced a profound feeling of disintegration. The only antidote to such a mood would have been action of some kind, but there was no effective opportunity for this, and the fact that his services were not required deepened his gloom. In July 1940 he wrote to John Lehmann: "What is so terrible about this kind of situation is to be able to do nothing. The government won't use me in any capacity, not even a clerk, and I have failed to get into the army because of my lungs. It is a terrible thing to feel oneself useless and at the same time on every side to see halfwits and pro-fascists filling important jobs."[23] The mood was reflected in his writing. But his fervent hope that the War would destroy all the "rubbish" of daily living survived.

Orwell writes of the growth of totalitarianism and the loss of liberty as if they were permanent features of life. Yet he continued to condemn pessimism, while revealing an interest in the way in which it could be used in literature. In a discussion of Hardy's The Dynasts he says: "One might wonder how any truly tragic effect can be produced by Hardy's morbid and almost superstitious view of life" and "Hardy's pessimism was absurd as well as demoralising, but he could make poetry out of it because he believed in it; thus showing, like Poe, Baudelaire and various others, that even a half lunatic view of life will do as a basis for literature provided it is sincerely held."[24] His repudiation does not preclude a consideration of how this kind of pessimism could be worked with, and, although he himself condemned such a view of life as "half lunatic" there are many who would say that it was a view Orwell shared. He was certainly at this time aware of the possibilities of writing a "hopeless" novel. It is likely that he was already quite far advanced in his planning of *Animal Farm*, and although *Animal Farm* is very different in tone from *Nineteen Eighty-Four* it is no less absolute in its lack of escape. And Orwell was also becoming preoccupied with the generation of *Nineteen Eight-Four* itself.

1942, in spite of America's entry into the War, was a difficult and shattering year. The Japanese were victorious in the East, Rommel in the North African desert. Churchill and the Coalition Government survived the left's criticisms without making the major adjustments demanded—and with some of the "Munich men" still there. A Ministry of Production, which the left had long insisted on, was created, but it did not have the powers the left felt were necessary. The worst disappointment of 1942 for Orwell and left-wing opinion in general was the failure of Cripps to live up to the image he briefly presented. He returned from Russia in the beginning of the year after a long absence from the inevitably drab scene the War had brought. He was seen, misguidedly, not only as the cementer of the Russian alliance but as a new and vigorous face in politics. His criticism of the war effort over the radio brought enormous public response. For a brief moment the left seemed to have a leader. The image faded when Churchill welcomed Cripps into the War Cabinet, thus stifling his potential.

The fall of Tobruk in June was the grimmest moment in a grim year. But in the autumn the military tide began to turn. Victory at El Alamein marked the beginning of the long haul towards victory over Hitler. But the left's optimism had not survived 1942. It had long been clear that Churchill could win the war without any radical alteration of Britain socially or economically. Orwell surveyed the scene with bitterness.

In December 1943 he began to write a regular weekly column for *Tribune* entitled "As I Please". It provided a continuous outlet for his efforts at assessing the political situation and the social scene. At the same time he did not fail to keep a lively eye on the people living around him and on the natural world. The fact that he saw a heron flying over Baker Street is as worthy of comment as the murder of Trotsky.

In spite of the fact that the prospects for social change were so much less favourable, that so many opportunities had been missed, and in spite of the fact that his own gloom was beginning to lie thickly on his discussions of the political situation, Orwell was again attacking pessimism and associating it with right-wing beliefs at the end of 1943. He saw that pessimism could be a subtly dangerous force. He connected it with what he called the "neo-reactionary school of writers", in which he included Wyndham Lewis, T. S. Eliot, Huxley and Waugh. He found their criticisms and their lack of belief in progress "more damaging than anything that issues from the Individualist League or the Conservative Central Office" and characterises the neo-reactionary school by the "refusal to believe that society can be fundamentally improved. Man is non-perfectible, merely political changes can effect nothing, progress is an illusion." Orwell criticised these attitudes from a standpoint that was obviously not sympathetic, and yet he said, "The danger of ignoring the neo-pessimists lies in the fact that up to a point they are right. So long as one thinks in short periods it is wise not to be hopeful about the future."[25] It is a position close to the "short-term" pessimism that Koestler arrived at. During the War Koestler had many fewer outlets for comment than Orwell, but it seems clear that he was trying to make sense of similar anomalies. He was attracted by the features of British life that Orwell was reluctant to let go of. He recognised the opportunities the War provided for a social revolution that never happened. He condemned reaction yet drew back from the implications both of his previous commitment and of the fact that he had lost it. By 1945 his attitudes towards Communism, the War and the future coincided with Orwell's. Yet the conclusions he drew with reference to the action to be taken were at odds with Orwell's dogged determination to carry on the struggle.

If for Orwell the war years were a crucial phase in his development towards *Nineteen Eighty-Four* for Koestler they provided a sobering pause. For the first time since his withdrawal from the Party, and once Britain had survived the blitz, he found himself in relative calm. He, too, had tried to do his bit for the war effort, and lectured to the troops for the Army Bureau of Current Affairs. But, yet again, he did not have a more direct experience of battle. As victory approached he shared the left's disillusion. He had joined in the hope that 1940 would change the social and economic structure of the country. He had seen the grim year of 1942 as a challenge to the left to force its ideas between the cracks in the Government that crisis and lack of confidence revealed. The logic of his rejection of Communism hardened, and by 1945 his political outlook was firmly geared to the necessity of reserving commitment and pausing in action. Politically, the war years were the years in which he finally burnt himself out. Unlike Orwell he had no depth of moral belief to keep the sparks glowing.

9

A FAITH DEFEATED

The left was having to alter its ideas and Orwell was having to come to terms with disillusion. The country was tired, and Orwell was dismayed, with little buoyancy to sustain fresh hope. But in his capacity as propagandist Orwell felt it a moral duty to be encouraging. In his answer to reactionary criticisms of the left Orwell said that it should be made clear that socialism was not perfectionist, that socialists were aiming at improvement rather than utopia. In fact he is almost suggesting that the deliberate rejection of utopia would be a way of providing some kind of guarantee against totalitarianism. The absolutism of utopia seemed to demand absolute authority. It was no longer possible to think in terms of an English revolution, but Orwell was still able to see around him signs of movement towards a better situation. Class barriers seemed to be disappearing, and as long as this was in evidence things were proceeding in the right direction.

As victory became more certain, however, the old ways began to return. The iron railings that had been removed from the Islington squares, thus allowing children unhindered access, were being replaced. The left seemed to have no long term plans and could only criticise on immediate issues. The Government hesitated over the Beveridge Report, which had come out at the end of 1942, and, as peace approached, the Allies showed themselves quite willing to deal with fascists and reactionaries in liberated countries. And there were already signs that all was not going smoothly in the relationship between Russia and Britain and the USA. By the beginning of 1944 Orwell was predicting the cold war. Yet his growing belief in the possibility of the world splitting up into two or three permanently hostile blocks, and in the inevitability of totalitarianism outlasting Hitler did not bring to a halt his urgent appeals for action. He was dedicated to keeping alive the motives that had flourished during the Spanish war. He was one of the few men who had the resilience to even begin to think of doing this. He insisted that the fight against Fascism must not stop with the defeat of Hitler. Above all, he retained his belief in the strength of ordinary decency, and in the possibility of decency making democracy viable. He criticised James Burnham's *The Managerial Revolution* for ignoring the vital qualities of democracy—the basic error of the kind of thinking Burnham represented was a contempt for common humanity and a mythical belief in extremism. "A totalitarian society, it is felt, *must* be stronger than a democratic one : the expert's opinion *must* be worth more than the ordinary man's. The German army had won the first battles : therefore it must win the last one. The great strength of democracy, its power of criticism, was ignored."[1] Orwell was writing this with as much conviction as he later wrote *Nineteen Eighty-Four*, which showed precisely how a totalitarian society could be stronger than democracy. Yet his belief in the ordinary man —Winston Smith, an ordinary man, was at least aware of what was wrong, though he could do nothing about it—and his belief that men cannot be so morally worthless as to submit to the developments that pessimism allowed were as strong as they ever were, although his faith in the success of socialism was being chipped away.

From 1942 to 1943 there was little in the way of literature presenting a socialist case. The vast wave of books and pamphlets that spokesmen of the left produced with the beginning of the War died down. 1944 saw some resurgence, with an eye to the coming General Election, but the left was on the whole stifled or unsure of itself. The Government began to present its plans for peace, but Labour influence in the Coalition had its hands tied. The left's confidence received blow after blow. Moscow's behaviour over the tragic Warsaw Rising was dismaying. In Greece

Churchill performed a similar role by helping to suppress the Communist-led resistance movement. The forces of reaction were rallying, while the left still moved through the fog that had descended in 1942.

From 1941 Orwell had also been writing London Letters for the *Partisan Review*. This contained comment on literary and political activities in England and descriptions of the general mood. To some extent the London Letters provide the clearest documentation of Orwell's changing attitudes during the War, although they also show up some of his more wildly wrong predictions. They appeared at intervals of about four months, and represented a more solid assessment than he could manage in the shorter, more immediate and spontaneous pieces in *Tribune*. They were also written for an American audience, and were therefore deliberately explicit, carefully documented and explained. It is clear that Orwell enjoyed expressing his views to a fresh readership: he never tired of rephrasing and reiterating what he considered to be the basic and most urgent issues. The Letters reveal very precisely Orwell's view of England, for he was trying to clarify characteristic anomalies. He wrote in answer to questions about the freedom of the press:

> The position is that in England there is a great respect for freedom of speech but very little for freedom of the press. . . . This is a lowbrow country and it is felt that the printed word doesn't matter greatly and that writers and such people don't deserve much sympathy. On the other hand the sort of atmosphere where you daren't talk politics for fear that the Gestapo may be listening isn't thinkable in England. Any attempt to produce it would be broken not so much by conscious resistance as by the inability of ordinary people to grasp what was wanted of them.[2]

Orwell writes, as so often, with a mixture of affection and despair. He himself was a writer whose printed word did not matter greatly to the bulk of the public. And yet he is much attached to the qualities he describes. He writes here that he could not conceive of the Gestapo functioning around him at that time, yet elsewhere he criticises others for their inability to imagine what Nazism would mean in terms of ordinary life if there were a German invasion. And later London was to become the territory of the Thought Police.

The ambivalence of Orwell's own relationship with his country emerges strongly in these Letters. It is a mark of his honesty of outlook. Curiously, although he was often too much inclined to type-cast other people, to see them in terms of groups and allegiances, he did not necessarily sustain a consistent role himself. If he appeared inconsistent, he also deemed it pernicious to be bound by a rigid and dogmatic consistency. It is ironic that Orwell is so frequently accused of inconsistency when it is this very lack of being trapped by dogma and preconception, except with regard to people, whom he seemed to find genuinely difficult to understand, that makes Orwell so valuable a commentator. On the occasions when he does become blinkered by allowing a single idea to preside over his argument his writing is at its worst: as in the more unsatisfactory passages of *The Road to Wigan Pier*.

In the London Letters Orwell's natural habit of approaching subjects with startling freshness is much in evidence. He springs one ambush after another upon the conventional response. He makes predictions, but is ready to look at new evidence and reassess his judgments. Each new topic he tackles with a clean slate. His descriptions of the growth of the Common Wealth Party illustrate this. This was a movement of middle-class left wingers which was active in the last years of the War and won three by-elections. Each time he writes of it the picture has changed slightly, the image is coloured differently, public opinion has veered, the political situation involves new factors, and all this combines to produce a different response in Orwell and changes the direction of his anticipations. The important point is that he makes it quite clear that the situation and his own opinions have changed. He thus reflects not only his own views but the manner in which the evidence is shifting.

The earlier Letters are full of that same certainty of revolution that he articulates in *Tribune*. "The mass of the nation wants certain things that aren't obtainable under a capitalist economy and is willing to pay almost any price to get them."[3] But by the first issue of 1943 Orwell is becoming oppressed by the dreary situation he foresees:

> The British ruling class has never stated its real war aims, which happen to be unmentionable, and so long as things went badly Britain was driven part of the way towards a revolutionary stategy. There was always the possibility, therefore, of democratising the war without losing it in the process. Now, however, the tide begins to turn and immediately the dreary world which the American millionaires and their British hangers-on intend to impose on us begins to take shape.[4]

Orwell was not mistaken in his vision of a gloomy post-war Britain, though one may doubt that American millionaires were responsible—this was Orwell lashing out in an unknown direction, a tendency which he often could not suppress. Once the War was over there seemed to be no point in the grey austerity. It was no longer associated with the gallant effort for survival, with a sense of common sacrifice. Whale meat and rationed bread became symbols of the post-war Labour Government. Meanwhile in 1943 the park railings were being replaced and evening dress, which Orwell so much despised, was creeping back.

Two and a half years after his predictions of social change Orwell was tackling the question of why he and so many others had been wrong. He suggests that the fact that he started out with a misguided attitude, with a belief in "revolution or defeat", coloured his subsequent assessments, and made him "exaggerate the depth of the political crisis in 1942, the possibilities of Cripps as a popular leader and of Common Wealth as a revolutionary party, and also the socially levelling process occurring in Great Britain as a result of the war."[5] In fact, the 1942 crisis had been very real. It was largely the left itself that had been responsible for the missed opportunities. Orwell admits that he himself, although he had been reasonably accurate in his specifically military predictions, had been near to indulging in the kind of typically leftist political thought which he described as "a sort of masturbation fantasy in which the world of facts hardly matters".[6] His discussion of the explanation of non-objectivity is tinged with a bitterness that is more evident in his *Tribune* articles of this period. His reaction to this neglect of facts was to concentrate on the grimmest of those that presented themselves in 1945. The momentum of despair that brought him to *Nineteen Eight-Four* was gathering force. "People can foresee the future only when it coincides with their own wishes, and the most grossly obvious facts can be ignored when they are unwelcome,"[7] he wrote.

Orwell's picture of humanity was becoming a portrait of apathy and incapability overwhelmed by the mechanical power and military force of humanity's own creation. The effort to resist this tendency required a conscious struggle. "I believe that it is possible to be more objective than most of us are, but that it involves a *moral* effort."[8] Orwell continued to make the moral effort, and embarrassed and antagonised those who did not. He had again severed all contact with the orthodox left, though he still wrote for *Tribune*, and he must have felt, as war dissolved into cold war, that the moral effort was beginning to mean very little in terms of political and public achievement.

The end of the War brought a concern with new issues. A General Election was imminent, and up to the last moment Orwell did not believe that victory for the Labour Party was possible. In fact, the feeling for equality that war had encouraged and the votes of enquiring and disgruntled troops gave Labour a dramatic victory, a victory for which the left was not well prepared. Orwell's relief at the War's end had been soured by the demands for retribution which he vociferously condemned. While France on the one hand cried out for the blood of the quislings Britain had been making its own peace with reaction. Also, Orwell had spent two months in France and Germany as *Observer* correspondent, travelling in the wake of the advancing Allied armies. The devastation, the roaming, homeless populations, the growing hostility between Russia and the United States, contributed to his dark mood. His personal life, too, had been struck by tragedy : his wife died suddenly. He himself was suffering from the tuberculosis that finally killed him.

He had predicted cold war, had foreseen that totalitarianism would outlive Hitler. In the years after the War he saw nothing to encourage a different view. At home the Labour Government was struggling in the face of immense odds to patch up the gaping holes left by the War, without achieving, or even attempting, any of the fundamentals of socialism. After a year of witnessing these struggles Orwell commented : "Even allowing for the fact that everything takes time, it is astonishing how little change seems to have happened as yet in the structure of society. In a purely economic sense, I suppose, the drift is towards Socialism, or at least towards state ownership . . . but in the social set-up there is no symptom by which one could infer that we are not living under a Conservative government."[9] The old social inequalities that Orwell was so sensitive to had returned; war, in fact, had made no difference in the long run. What Orwell described as the "unconquerable, weed-like vitality of pre-war habits of mind" was returning. It was becoming necessary once again to expose oppression, economic and social inequalities and exploitation. The world of politics was as corrupt and irresponsible as it had been previously. More and more frequently Orwell found himself contrasting his enjoyment of simple pleasures—a good cup of tea, finding the first primrose—with the stale, grey, mechanised world. The odour of boiled cabbage which lingered in the doorway of Gordon Comstock's lodging and in Winston Smith's Victory Mansions seemed to have permanently infected the air Orwell breathed.

Orwell's disappointment grew more intense and the tone of

his writing grew more bitter. In the context of the Allied victory the symptoms of disintegration were even more sinister. The international situation darkened the horizon so thoroughly that Orwell at times could find no chinks of light at all. Everything seemed to be working out according to his most gloomy predictions; it is not surprising that *Nineteen Eighty-Four* appeared to be the logical end. Idealism had drifted into irrelevance; the flabbiness of action in the thirties and the hopefulness of the early years of the War had become a mockery. Orwell's writing at this time is full of remarks like "no thoughtful person whom I know has any hopeful picture of the future. The notion that a war between Russia and America is inevitable within the next few decades, and that Britain, in its unfavourable geographical position, is bound to be blown to pieces by atomic bombs, is accepted with a sort of vague resignation."[10] The situation was a dismaying one for socialists. Many had already withdrawn from the contest at the close of the previous decade. Now there seemed even less reason for carrying on. Many adopted, although without his reasoning, much the same attitude as Koestler was to come to—that in the short term action was useless, but that one nevertheless had a responsibility to keep awake to the political environment. The danger of this was that it could—and did—sink into a boneless liberalism. It was easy enough to take cover behind a literary hedge and allow analysis to become a substitute for action. Orwell had always been very conscious of the way in which an attitude of pessimistic resignation acted against socialist belief. He certainly did not feel that the time had come to alter the perspective of his commitment and constant polemic, but he was moved to characterise the socialist's predicament like this:

A socialist today is in the position of a doctor treating an all but hopeless case. As a doctor, it is his duty to keep the patient alive, and therefore to assume that the patient has at least a chance of recovery. As a scientist, it is his duty to face the facts, and therefore to admit that the patient will probably

die. Our activities as socialists only have meaning if we assume
that socialism *can* be established, but if we stop to consider
what probably *will* happen, then we must admit, I think, that
the chances are against us.[11]

This is Orwell's clearest statement of the socialist dilemma, a
statement that he had come to imply more strongly as the War
progressed. But it was a dilemma that had always existed and
that Orwell had always been partially conscious of. Fundamentally it is not rational theory that moves the socialist but a
kind of compulsion. And yet it is a compulsion that is generated
by a rational system of ideas as well as by the incapability to be
apathetic in the face of near disaster. It is the compulsion that
Winston Smith feels even in the extreme conditions of *Nineteen
Eighty-Four*, which Peter Slavek felt against odds of a different
kind, and which the Bolsheviks felt when victory was in their
hands. What Orwell does say explicitly is that, apart from the
well-meaningness of "ordinary decency", it is a compulsion that
is a basic part of the human make-up and has so far been able to
survive the versions of totalitarianism that this century has seen.

The fact that Orwell was sadly and bitterly aware of this
dilemma did not mean that he was moved in any way to turn to
the right. If anything, his awareness sharpened his concern for
humanity, and made him even more sensitive—perhaps over-
sensitive—to the petty injustices and the drab surroundings
that harried it. He was being pulled strongly in two directions:
he wanted to emphasise the importance of making the most of
the small things of life in order to lighten the immediate prospect; at the same time he could not allow the public to lose sight
of the vast dangers hanging over the world. He himself was
tempted to go into retreat—from the world if not from his commitment. He spent a great deal of time in the last years of his
life on the island of Jura in the Hebrides. But his conscience
would not allow him to abandon the role of chronicler and
prophet.

Koestler, having been on the move since the early thirties,

never had Orwell's opportunities for continuous comment on the political and social scene. While he documents his retreat from Communism in his autobiographies and other writings quite closely he has little to say about his own position in Britain. His unsettled past had meant that he could adjust, superficially at least, with great rapidity to the British way of life. It seems to have been at this time that he grew more self-conscious of his own attempts at fiction, and although it was later that he began to reveal a defensiveness in his remarks about his own novels the beginnings of this can be seen in what he has to say about the novelists of the thirties.

Most of Koestler's important writing of these years is collected in *The Yogi and the Commissar*, which was published in 1945 and represents fairly comprehensively his end-of-war mood. In "The Novelist's Temptations" he tackles the problem of the novelist in relation to political events. Although he sees the problem in terms similar to Orwell's, his phrasing of it is rather different, and he avoids the whole question of language, which Orwell found so central. Koestler criticises the documentary novelists of the pre-war period:

> It was a period in which novels read like dispatches by war correspondents from the Fronts of the class struggle. The characters seemed to be flat, two-dimensional beings, fighting their shadow battles against a lurid background. People in the pink novel had a class-dimension (length) plus, say, a sex-dimension (width); the third, the irrational dimension (depth), was missing or atrophied.[12]

Koestler pleads for a consideration of psychological factors, but in doing so, and in using such neat phraseology, he by-passes what clearly is the main issue here. It is not simply a question of the "irrational", which he tries so hard to incorporate into *Arrival and Departure*, but, more straightforwardly of personality. In the case of Peter Slavek we have him explained in depth but not expressed in depth. So often in Koestler we have personality explained only as it acts itself out in politics and sex. The

G

lesser aspects of life, the minor details that are such an essential part of Orwell's fiction, are neglected, or else a single detail is seized on and reiterated until its supporting and enlarging function is overwhelmed by its symbolic value. Koestler saw psychology in terms of major actions because the characters in his fiction are involved in major events. But this did not mean that their lives were not also lived on a more moderate level.

Koestler condemns also the novelist who is remote from the world of real events. The novelist writing in the thirties who ignored the facts of Nazism was as atrophied as the novelist who ignores the irrational element in human personality. He does not say that a novelist can only be good if he is concerned with political events—he does not take Edward Upward's line in *The Mind in Chains*—but he does insist that there must be an awareness of political events. He calls for an "all-embracing knowledge":

> The knowledge is not for actual use. . . . It is for use by implication. It has to act as a catalytic agent, as the saliva in the process of creative assimilation. Without it, the characters will be distorted and the story arbitrary like a Victorian plot. The act of creation presupposes omniscience.[13]

Arbitrariness of plot suggests a new and rather different area of discussion which Koestler does not pursue, and in fact it is not a very relevant phrase here. But Koestler can hardly be challenged when he insists that the novelist must have an intimate knowledge of the context of human life, and that this context, particularly in certain periods, is bound to include the world of public and political events. He says that the novelist must "locate its [the life of his characters] geometrical place in a co-ordinate system, the axes of which are represented by the dominating facts, ideas, and tendencies of the time."[14]

It is an easier job to indicate the proper balance of the novelist's position than to determine a mode of action for humanity in general. The main point here is that it is *possible* for the novelist to maintain a balanced position. His art allows it, even

though many are disinclined to make the effort. Orwell argues
that anyone who writes, who uses language as a medium of
expression, has a certain responsibility in the way he handles
language. Koestler sees the novelist as having a responsibility
allied to that which the intelligentsia as a whole should accept.
It was more natural for Koestler to see the problem in terms of
the intelligentsia, for he came from a background in which the
intelligentsia were a viable entity. Much of Orwell's isolation
arose from the fact that in Britain there was no such entity.
Koestler argues that the function of the intelligentsia is to be
continually aware of injustice of all kinds—the intelligentsia
ought to be discontented, restless and neurotic. This is the price
to be paid for sensitivity. It ought to be continually forcing
alternatives. The European intelligentsia of the pre-war years
failed because its status was eliminated. "The intelligentsia of
the Pink Decade was irresponsible, because it was deprived of
the privilege of responsibility. Left in the cold, suspended in a
vacuum, they became decadents of the bourgeoisie. It was nobody's fault; for they were the mirror, not the light."[15] And of
course later it was not only status that was eliminated. Koestler
does not explain precisely how it came to reflect rather than to
illuminate. But he does show how the revolutionary movement
disastrously involved the intelligentsia, encouraged the tendency towards imitation rather than influence, and left it
drained of its capacity to recognise its function. At the time of
writing it was impossible to be grandiose in one's demands of the
intelligentsia, or of any intellectually responsible group. "The
alternative for the next few years is no more 'capitalism or revolution' but to save *some* of the values of democracy and humanism or to lose them all; and to prevent this happening one has to
cling more than ever to the ragged banner of 'independent
thinking'."[16]

Koestler did not see the possibility of aligning independent
thinking with faith. In many ways his pessimism is much more
confining than Orwell's, for Orwell, however black the future,
was able to marshal his convictions in favour of carrying on.

Koestler allowed his experience of the past and view of the future to dictate his mood of the present. Orwell could always find something to respond to enthusiastically. Koestler gives no sign of this. For him independent thinking meant bolstering himself against belief. For Orwell it meant belief without submitting to that belief's authority.

Koestler's vision of his own function was as closely associated with his reaction to war-time and post-war Britain as was Orwell's, though he probably did not feel the changes so intimately. The comfortable, decent qualities of the British, the qualities that Orwell insists on, that had attracted him ceased to contain for him the positive energy that he looked for. The pattern of Koestler's disillusion resembled that of many of the left. Like them he believed that a real opportunity for social revolution had existed in 1940:

> If ever there was a chance for Socialism in Britain, it was in the period from Dunkirk to the fall of Tobruk. Popular discontent against the conduct of the war seemed at its peak. In a dozen or so by-elections the Government was defeated. The Government had been invested with the power of nationalising all individual property in the country; the transition to State-Socialism could have been achieved merely by political pressure, without revolution or civil war . . . the British ruling class, with dwindling exceptions, seemed prepared to live rather in a red Britain than under Nazi domination. . . . However, the working class lacked the political maturity to grasp its opportunity. Intelligent Tories have to this day not recovered from the surprise that capitalism survived the Dunkirk to Singapore crisis.[17]

As the War came to an end it was clear to him, as it was to Orwell, that victory was going to be a conservative victory:

> . . . the nearer victory comes in sight, the clearer the character of the war reveals itself as what the Tories always said that

it was—a war for national survival, a war in defence of certain conservative nineteenth-century ideals, and not what I and my friends of the Left said that it was—a revolutionary civil war in Europe on the Spanish pattern.[18]

Whether anyone really thought this kind of revolutionary war was possible in 1940 is doubtful. Koestler saw it as the war the European left had been anticipating throughout the thirties. But certainly the scale and scope of the War, the way in which it was fought, made it difficult for a revolutionary spirit to exist in battle as it had in Spain. The Nazis never set foot on British soil, and the War, in spite of the blitz and the struggle for survival, was never for the British so intimate as it was on the Continent. And Koestler, inevitably, saw it through the eyes of a Central European who had been face to face with the enemy.

By the time Koestler was writing this the perspective of politics had changed. The movement of the international climate into cold war seemed to place the political struggle beyond the people most directly involved. In Britain the Labour Government was uninspired. Koestler found the British people too resigned. They accepted austerity without complaint not because they understood its purpose or had any foresight, but because of what Koestler called in his later and final collection of political essays, *The Trail of the Dinosaur* (1955) a "puritan tradition, and lack of *joie de vivre*", and he wrote : "The people in the suburbs and working-class districts accept the bad life because they have never tasted the good life."[19] George Bowling's wife would certainly have been one of these.

Koestler recognised that Labour's 1945 victory could never have happened if the country had not had an accumulation of difficulties to face, but he demands that these should be tackled in an energetic and inspiring fashion. The worse the situation the more important it was to feel the Government's energy : "you can and must expect to give the people a message and an inspiration, to bring home to them the consciousness of the opening of a new era."[20] Few could have felt that the last years of the forties heralded a new era. Koestler's criticisms of the Labour Government were much the same as Orwell's. The basic lack was that there was no serious attempt to destroy the power of the old governing classes. Orwell insisted that there were three necessary initial reforms that were far more important than such things as the organising of a health service: the abolishing of public schools, titles and the House of Lords. Koestler would have agreed. In the long run Orwell was probably right. At the time few could have been convinced that they should barter free medical treatment in exchange for a socialist future.

But it was quite clear that the Labour Government was not making the most of its opportunities, and some of the reasons for this lay in the way its strength and ideas fizzled out in the second half of the War. The implications of its failure were extensive. Koestler wrote: "In the third year of the régime, it is becoming clear that it is squandering at a rapid pace the good will of the electorate, the benevolent neutrality of the Little Man, and the sympathy and hopes of the European Left."[21] This was a symptom of a more widespread disease that the peace emphasised, and that Koestler tried to analyse in his last novel, *The Age of Longing*. "The atmosphere of democracy has become a stale fug, and those who breathe it cannot be expected to be grateful for the air which it contains. The predicament of Western civilisation is that it has ceased to be aware of the values which it is in peril of losing."[22] Koestler did not at this stage venture into political prediction as Orwell did. But it is quite clear here that he anticipated the post-war confusion in Europe. Like Orwell, he saw that resistance to those very features of government over which the War had been fought was at its lowest.

By this time Koestler was much more concerned with placing himself exactly on the map of action and attitude than with making a positive contribution to the political struggle. In this perspective he formed his principle of "short term pessimism". He argued that he was, in the long run, optimistic about the future of the human race—that is, that he retained some faith in

human nature—but that one could only be a long-term optimist
if one was prepared to face all the most unpleasant facts of the
present and the immediate future. He says that the responsibility of people like himself is to form themselves into a "fraternity of pessimists". In spite of the fact that part of their pessimism would be an awareness of immediate issues, their function
is not to act but to keep a watchful eye on general developments,
and to recognise the point at which their interference or their
encouragement is required with regard to the long term. But at
what point the short term becomes long and immediate issues
lead into decisions for the future is not made clear, and Koestler's phrasing of the "pessimists'" precise duties is vague:

> What we need is an active fraternity of pessimists. . . . They
> will not aim at immediate radical solutions, because they
> know that cannot be achieved in the hollow of the wave;
> they will not brandish the surgeon's knife at the social body,
> because they know that their own instruments are polluted.
> They will watch with open eyes and without sectarian
> blinkers, for the first signs of the new horizontal movement;
> when it comes they will assist its birth; but if it does not come
> in their lifetime, they will not despair.[23]

There is a kind of arrogance in the argument here which is
underlined by the metaphorical phrasing. While suggesting that
his "fraternity" is superior in power and understanding, he in
fact nearly relegates it to impotence, if only because the impossibility of digesting history as it occurs leaves infinite scope
for vagueness and confusion. By the time a legitimate necessity
for action was recognised it might well be too late, and "the
fraternity of pessimists" would be liable to be so self-conscious
about their own lack of perfection and that of the instruments to hand that they would be perpetually frozen into inaction. Koestler's theory amounts to the opposite of Orwell's
insistence that socialism should not be seen as perfectionist: the
aim is to make things better, not to make things perfect. Koest-

ler suggests that the smaller issues, the inch by inch progress towards improvement, are not really important. But how is one to recognise an authentic horizontal movement? (He gives as examples of horizontal movements the League of Nations, the Second International, the official Churches. They all failed to fulfil their potential when crisis came.) It would have been possible to interpret Mussolini's Fascism in its early stages as a horizontal movement, and no doubt many did. It is quite clear that Koestler's theory could have no place in the minds of those who came to the political struggle after the War with enthusiasm but no experience. The short-term pessimist must not only have a principle to guide his actions, but also a vast body of experience and knowledge. For those, like Koestler, who had been through every degree of the European upheaval, the new faith might be fruitful. For a younger generation, or an isolated one, it could be disastrous. Many of those in Britain who retained their intellectual responsibility at the end of the War must have welcomed what Koestler had to say.

In a later essay Koestler appears to contradict some of the implications of short-term pessimism—and it was to be the contradictions that Orwell praised rather than the theory itself. When he writes of Palestine his tone alters. Here was a situation in which he at least could be quite clear that action was necessary. Although the fug of democracy offered no inspiration the desperate situation in Palestine during and just after the War engaged his most intense feelings. There, any kind of watchful aloofness was without doubt unacceptable. The struggle of the Palestinian Jews against the ban on immigration imposed by the British at a time when the gas chambers were at full power was an issue to which Koestler could not apply the principles of short-term pessimism. He tackled the subject most fully in *Promise and Fulfilment* (1949). In an essay, "Judah at the Crossroads", he argued the necessity of extreme action.

In *Thieves in the Night*, a novel about the Jews in Palestine, Koestler's hero, Joseph, joins one of the terrorist groups whose purpose was to persuade the British by force that immigration control must cease and to carry out reprisals for Arab attacks. The alternative was to watch while the leaky ships carrying refugees from Hitler were turned back to Germany. The terrorists felt that reprisal was a necessary part of self-defence. In "Judah at the Crossroads" Koestler attacked the kind of liberalism that automatically condemns extreme action of any kind:

> The pressure of totalitarian forces from outside and inside our Western civilisation has led to a tendency among liberals . . . to call any attitude of non-complacency "totalitarian". If you try to sort out logically a complex situation and to point out that it demands a choice between alternative lines of action, you will promptly be accused of painting in black-and-white. A certain amount of administrative and ideological muddle, a margin of tolerated confusion are indeed as essential to the functioning of a democratic society as lubricants and safety valves are to a machine. But the harsh, inhuman precision of totalitarian ideologies makes the liberal mind inclined to believe that the safety valves are all that matter, whereas pistons, pressure and energy are totalitarian as such.[24]

The theory of short-term pessimism obviates the necessity of choice. Here Koestler is clearly stating it. Not only is he concerned to show that there are situations in which violence is justifiable, if not necessary. The terrorists are not *ipso facto* "fascist" because they throw bombs into British administrative offices. It is the fact that a concern with the world of politics means a concern with modes of action, and that such a concern amounts to a commitment to choice, that Koestler emphasises. He presents his argument and the facts behind it more clearly in *Thieves in the Night* than in this short article. Here we are only too aware of the dangerous ground he is treading on. By what standards, in what perspective, is the justification for terroristic action assessed? The very nature of this kind of justification invites attack from the shocked liberal conscience. But Koestler does not base his appeal on an emotional plea for the ending of the persecution of his race. It is closer to a pragmatic defence of the action of a desperate people in their fight for existence. It was a situation in which the favourite British compromise was clearly not going to work.

In the years of the late forties Orwell composed his most extreme political statement: *Nineteen Eighty-Four*. In those same years Koestler was struggling to disengage himself from political commitment while still retaining his sense of political responsibility. He and Orwell both condemned the ineffectuality of the liberal intellectual. A major factor in the evolvement of their final positions was the discouraging political and social developments—or rather, lack of development—of the War and post-war years. The discouragement confirmed Orwell's determination: the blacker the future, the grimmer the struggle. And the grimmer the struggle the more important that he should be involved in it. The black future challenged Koestler's brisk and ingenious mind to formulate a position of wary responsibility that he himself could accept. It was primarily an intellectual position, and the most important influence behind it was Koestler's experience of Communism.

10

POST-WAR POSITIONS

Orwell and Koestler coincided in the publication of their main indictments of Stalinism. 1945 saw the appearance of both *The Yogi and the Commissar* and *Animal Farm*. Two of the most important essays in Koestler's book are concerned with anti-democratic developments in Russia since the death of Lenin and with what Koestler saw as the two extremes of action and inaction between which the political struggle seemed to be locked. He could not tear himself away from Communism. As long as he wrote about politics he was haunted by this major political experience of his life. In *The Yogi and the Commissar* he develops his theory of the Moscow Purges into an explanation of Communism in the 1930s and a description of its anomalies.

Having severed his connections with Communism, in the years following 1938 Koestler was preoccupied with describing and explaining its original attraction, and moving from this to a consideration of possible alternatives of attitude and action. The volumes of autobiography were a part of this search for simultaneous justification and atonement of guilt. He had found that political involvement inevitably brought him face to face with a whole series of opposites, between which it was impossible to make a choice while still preserving the value of commitment. The opposites could not be reconciled, but their distinctions could be deliberately blurred and disguised. It was possible to evolve elaborate methods of pretending they did not exist, or of hiding the fact that a choice had been made and that the consequent distortion of original purpose had therefore followed. It was with questions of this kind that *The Gladiators* and *Darkness At Noon* were concerned.

But now Koestler boils down his opposites into a single pair. In the book's first essay, "The Yogi and the Commissar", he presents the yogi, who ignores the world and is preoccupied with his own mind, and the commissar, who is dominated by material facts to such an extent that he cannot disentangle his own individuality from them. Koestler describes these two figures as representing the two extremes of a spectrum, the yogi the ultra-violet end, the commissar the infra-red. The position of humanity in general is constantly shifting, consciously or unconsciously, towards one extreme or the other. Looking back at the pre-war years he says: "Since the early 'thirties we are all travelling, more or less consciously, more or less willingly, towards the ultra-violet end."[1] This is a reaction against the "general displacement towards the Commissar or infra-red end" which took place in the nineteenth century. The danger is the possible loss of a sense of direction, or the ceasing to realise that one is moving at all and a compliance with a drift of which one is not aware. Koestler explains further:

The less consciously we drift with the wind the more willingly we do it; the more consciously the less willingly. Personally, I belong to the latter type; I wish one could still write an honest infra-red novel without an ultra-violet ending . . . no honest Socialist can write a survey of the Left's defeats without accounting for the irrational factor in mass-psychology. He who clings blindly to the past will be left behind; but he who abandons himself too readily will be carried away like a dry leaf. . . .[2]

A balance has to be preserved between consciousness of the drift and reaction against the drift. What Koestler in fact demands is a kind of omniscience, the kind of omniscience he also demands for the novelist. One must have a full understanding of the material features, the psychological features and the historical features of life. But his conclusion is that it is impossible to achieve, let alone maintain, the necessary mean. One is continually being pulled towards one or other of the spectrum's ends.

The essay is, of course, a highly personal one, backed by the intensity of Koestler's own experience. He is chiefly interested in the position of the artist and that of the revolutionary, the two positions that he himself had not been able to reconcile satisfactorily :

> . . . the artist shows the least resistance against being carried away; the revolutionary the greatest. Indeed the Commissar can be defined as the human type which has completely severed relations with the subconscious. This is the more remarkable as the constant danger under which he lives . . . is a constant temptation to communicate with those forbidden zones.[3]

It is the predicament that Rubashov becomes aware of, and the predicament that Malraux's heroes avoid, for in their case political commitment is founded on a communication between action and Koestler's "forbidden zones". Malraux allows them to combine both ends of the spectrum. Koestler's own personal attempt to resolve this predicament is so deliberate as to be rather synthetic. It is an attempt that could only be made with the assistance of hindsight.

Koestler shows that it is equally dangerous to allow either extreme to dominate one's life; the yogi's position is as stunted as the commissar's. Neither is more worthy, more morally justifiable, than the other. The commissar may conduct wholesale purges, but the yogi will look on complacently and do nothing to prevent the purges taking place. It is not possible to synthesise the viable features of each extreme, and the best that can be achieved is compromise, which is bound to be unsatisfactory, and perhaps useless, especially as it tends to involve the drifting of ignorance rather than knowledgeable adjustment. It is not possible to make a correct choice, and yet the issue cannot be avoided. At this stage in his life Koestler himself was veering towards the ultra-violet, if only because he was seeking explanations in a psychological framework. An understanding of material and historical circumstances does not automatically bring an understanding of humanity. Political action cannot succeed according to a genuinely human inspiration unless political actors understand the minds of men. The necessity of psychological understanding was to become Koestler's main preoccupation. He wanted to see it applied to politics. Through such arguments Koestler virtually forced on himself the role of an ineffectual but well-meaning sideliner rather than that of an active but destructive participant. Apart from the Palestine conflict, which by 1948 had changed its nature with the declaration of the independent Israel, Koestler has not since 1945 lent his voice to any major political issue.

In a later essay in *The Trail of the Dinosaur* (1955) Koestler expanded the argument that surrounds the yogi and the commissar by discussing the conflict between morality and expediency, and the impossibility of acting according to both concepts simultaneously:

> The fact that both roads lead to disaster, creates a dilemma which is inseparable from man's condition; it is not an invention of the philosophers, but a conflict which we face at each step in our daily affairs . . . it is a fallacy to think that the conflict can always be healed by that admirable British household ointment called "the reasonable compromise". Compromise is a useful thing in minor dilemmas of daily routine; but each time we face major decisions, the remedy lets us down.[4]

Expediency provides the energy for progress, morality the guide. Compromise can only halt progress altogether. Koestler presents us with yet another set of opposites which can neither be ignored nor resolved. He insists that synthesis is the necessary goal of our time.

Koestler's dialectical training is apparent in his approach to the paradoxes of action. He continually sees problems as involving sets of irreconcilable alternatives and choice being either impossible or disastrous. The alternatives remain static while the human mind fluctuates, clings first to one, then the other, or lapses into the irresponsibility of ignorance and indecision. There are two genuine alternatives, and one false. Koestler fills his writing with such neat but devastating paradoxes. As a method of articulating very real problems and conflicts it makes for clarity of expression and cogency of argument, but it can at the same time limit the area of the mind's activity. The clean-cut edges of Koestler's exposition can blind us to the fact that there may be different angles of approach that are just as legitimate and would lead to a wider territory of argument. We realise this when we see how Orwell handles the same kind of evidence.

Orwell in fact believed that Koestler was maintaining his positive commitment. In an essay which discussed *The Yogi and the Commissar* he said: "Koestler is generally assumed to have come down heavily on the side of the yogi. Actually, if one assumes the Yogi and the Commissar to be at opposite points of the scale, Koestler is somewhat nearer the Commissar's end. He believes in action, in violence where necessary, in government, and consequently in the shifts and compromises that are inseparable from government."[5] There is evidence for this in what Koestler has to say about Palestine, but little elsewhere. But Orwell is here making an important point, although it may not be widely applicable to Koestler's position at this stage: because of his commitment in Palestine Koestler could not disengage himself from "the shifts and compromises" of politics. His commitment virtually wiped out his own place in the fraternity of pessimists.

In his essay on Palestine Koestler lays as much weight on the necessity of making a choice as on his particular defence of the Palestinian terrorists. He does not deny the viability of the Arab case; he does insist that men have a responsibility to commit themselves. This has a direct connection with the picture of democracy Koestler has already painted. Democracy had become a haze which served to hide indecision, inadequacy, mistakes of all kinds which sometimes led to tragic consequences. Democracy had no positive energy left. "The understandable human weakness for evading painful decisions and responsibilities has come to be regarded as a virtue and the essence of democracy. The liberal in retreat does not ask for freeedom of choice but for freedom from choice."[6] This makes more sense of the demand for positive action than of the demand for short-term pessimism. Koestler condemns neither the yogi nor the commissar so much as the half-conscious compromiser, the man who retreats from facts and automatically condemns the actions that the facts inspire.

It is clear that Koestler was torn between taking a more violent line of action against the mass mediocrity he saw around him, and the knowledge that such an attitude was useless, that the only way out was to develop the omniscience he calls for and to recognise the proper time for action. But, as can be seen when we measure Koestler's Palestine views against his short-term pessimism, when the moment for action is seized the entire theory is shaken. Its principles no longer apply and the careful attitudes have to be ditched, presumably to be retrieved when the horizontal movement lapses into the well-worn contours. Koestler does not go into this. History seems to have justified his stance on Palestine; it is generally admitted that the terrorist groups played an essential part in the gaining of Israel's independence. So far Koestler has recognised no other issue which might challenge his theory, although perhaps the less experienced eye might have picked out and embraced several since the War's end.

Koestler still felt that part of his responsibility as a writer lay in utilising his pre-war experiences to the greatest extent possible. A long essay is devoted to showing how, even in the most material sense, Russia is far from being a socialist country. He details social and economic inequalities as well as going into the more obvious points concerning the suffering and confusion that resulted from such enormous reversals as the changing to a collective agrarian policy, the fluctuation in international alignments, the continual changes of line in cultural policy, and of course the Purges. Mistakes are inevitable, he argues, but they are not justifiable. Above all, the attempt to disguise and eliminate mistakes, the process Orwell describes in *Nineteen Eighty-Four*, is fatal:

> Detours on the road are unavoidable, and the only means to decide the broad direction of a movement is to watch it over a reasonable stretch of time and then draw the average curve of its oscillations. Subjective statements of its leaders are not of interest, and the question of their bona fides is historically meaningless. The only valid criterion is the cumulative effect of its achievements in various spheres.[7]

Koestler produces the now familiar argument that the results are due not only to the detours, not only to the Stalinist perversion, but to the quality of the original aims. "The Russian Revolution has failed in its aim to create a new type of human society in a new moral climate. The ultimate reason for its failure was the arid nineteenth-century materialism of its doctrine. It had to fall back on the old opiates because it did not recognise man's need for spiritual nourishment."[8]

The Yogi and the Commissar completes Koestler's rejection of Marxism. But it neither indicates the adoption of a right-wing stance nor a belief in the impossibility of socialist achievement. "The Russian experiment neither proves nor disproves the possibility of Socialism; it was an experiment carried out under the most unsuitable laboratory conditions and hence inconclusive."[9] One might say that revolution is almost bound to occur only when the laboratory conditions *are* unsuitable. Even the 1945 Labour Government, as Koestler himself pointed out, was only voted in because the country was in a bad way and the odds therefore against it making a success of putting things right. While Orwell was dubious about the possibility of socialism but believed that one must continue to act as if it were possible, Koestler, while withdrawing from action, considered not only that socialism could be a viable force, but that it offered the only means of clearing the democratic fug and filling in the chasm in humanity created by the first half of the century. Like Orwell, Koestler singles out as humanity's most significant loss the end of the possibility of a belief in immortality :

> The age of enlightenment has destroyed faith in personal survival; the scars of this operation have never healed. There is a vacancy in every living soul, a deep thirst in all of us. If the Socialist idea cannot fill this vacancy and quench our thirst, then it has failed in our time. In this case the whole development of the Socialist idea since the French revolution has been merely the end of a chapter in history, and not the beginning of a new one.[10]

Koestler pins all hope on a revival of socialism, but this was before the end of the War. "The balance of Europe can only be restored through a revival of the values on which Western civilisation is based. But this is a task beyond the powers of the conservative rearguard, and can only be achieved if the socialist movement sheds its illusions and regains its vigour and independence, both in the national and international sphere."[11] Koestler wrote this before it became apparent that Britain would have and lose the opportunity to take the first steps towards this revival. He wrote it before room for the flexing of political ideas had been squeezed out. He is never precise about the exact nature of the socialism he visualises. He rejects Marxism, or at least Marxist-Leninism. He despises the British Labour Party. He says very little about individual politicians he might have admired. Rosa Luxemburg was one, but it is unlikely that Koestler believed that if her criticism of Lenin had carried more weight the course of the Russian Revolution would have been greatly affected. The most he tells us about his post-Marxist concept of socialism is that it must be inspiring and energetic; it is as if he sees socialism as being more important as a force than as an achievement. It must break away from the "phantom creed" of Communism and pursue a truly independent course. Koestler is precise in his analyses but considerably less detailed in his criticisms and statements of belief than Orwell. He can locate his position in a vista of large forces, but is unable to make contact with the small, ordinary details with which Orwell is constantly in touch. And so, although his argument is never abstract, it is usually without the solidity and intimacy that is characteristic of Orwell's writing.

In the book's final essay Koestler returns to his opening theme. He has discussed some of the groups of opposing forces and indicated where synthesis might be possible. Here he sums up, again in general terms, the major challenge :

> The basic paradox of man's condition, the conflict between freedom and determinism, ethics and logic, or in whatever symbols we like to express it, can only be resolved if, while thinking and acting on the horizontal plane of our existence, we yet remain constantly aware of the vertical dimension. To attain this awareness without losing the other is perhaps the most necessary and most difficult task that our race has ever faced.[12]

Koestler ends by demanding the synthesis of the yogi and the commissar. There is the suggestion throughout the book that only men with his kind of experience, who have been irrevocably involved in one extreme and forced to recognise the value of the other, have any chance of achieving this synthesis. *The Yogi and the Commissar* is an attempt to warn and rally the remnants of his own generation. This underlines the disparity of attitudes : the intensity of commitment and the resignation to disaster, the hatred of totalitarianism and the contempt for vague democracy, the urgency and the patience. Koestler is working out a *modus vivendi* for battered, exiled, instinctive revolutionaries like himself.

Koestler's final political words were contained in *The Trail of the Dinosaur*, but they do not represent a significant development from 1945. He returns to a number of the same themes. But it would be a mistake to separate his more direct political discussion from his last two works of fiction, one of which at least is intimately concerned with the politics of action. *Thieves in the Night* (1946) is set in pre-war Palestine. The victims of Hitler who made their way to the country, then under British mandate, found that strict immigration controls, imposed to appease the Arab population, prevented their setting foot on the promised land. The situation is reflected in the thoughts of Joseph, the novel's central character, who ponders the power this barren country has over his race:

> The Arabs are in revolt, the British are washing their hands of us, but the Place is waiting: fifteen hundred acres of stones of all sizes on top of a hill, surrounded by Arab villages, with no other Hebrew settlement for miles and a malaria swamp thrown in into the bargain. But when a Jew returns to this land and sees a stone and says, This stone is mine, then something snaps in him which has been tense for two thousand years.[13]

The "Place" is the settlement of Ezra's Tower, the founding and growth of which the book chronicles. Most of the settlers are refugees from Europe presented, as Koestler presents Peter Slavek, as typical products of the upheaval. Their minds are driven by Things to Forget and Incidents which cannot be named. Their roots have been destroyed, except for those that lie in Palestine. From the outset Koestler is not asking us, or is not able to ask us, to look at a collection of individuals with particular problems. He is investigating a syndrome. He marshals his characters into various representative positions and lines of argument, briskly stamps them with an easily recognisable personality, and uses them as voices in his debate.

In many cases we do not see these personalities at work. The *kibbutz* leader, Reuben, is described as "a kind of neutral person-

ality which offered no points for attack and made him the
socially ideal type for collective life."[14] but we only see this
"neutral personality" functioning as a moderate tone of voice.
Reuben has no relationships. His function in the community
and his function in the debate are made clear, but we look for
something more than mere statement.

The debate itself is concerned with the legitimacy of terrorism. Britain is preventing immigration while Jews are being
harried in Europe. Illegal immigrants who are caught are de-
ported. The Arabs are terrorising the Jews and the British are
making only feeble efforts to control them. Some of the settlers
are entirely bound up with the day-to-day problems of Ezra's
Tower. Their jobs require absolute dedication and superhuman
effort. Others, the intense and serious Simeon, and finally Joseph
himself, see the founding of a single *kibbutz* in terms of its relevance to the community as a whole, to Palestine and to the
political situation in Europe. As we are shown the early stages
of construction this fundamental disparity comes into evidence.
Bauman, the leader of a group of *Haganah*, the illegal but not
terroristic Jewish defence force, says "we cannot afford to see
the other man's point".[15] For him the solution is beyond the
realm of decency. One must be deliberately blind to objectivity.
He has trained himself and others to use force in the most
effective way.

The debate is sharply focused when the young settlement receives its first attack from the neighbouring Arab village. Early
in the novel Koestler presents the Arab viewpoint. The land for
Ezra's Tower has been legally purchased but the Mukhtar resents the Jews' presence—"his love for the hills and his country
was genuine . . . he would defend it against the intruders with
cunning, courage and ruse, with smiles and treachery"[16]—
although his village, Kfar Tabiyeh, is squalid and riven with
internal feuds. The sight of the efficient Jews building and
ploughing and transforming land that had been his for generations disgusts him.

The varieties of British attitudes are also presented. There are officials who sympathise with the Jewish settlers but whose official capacity prevents them taking any action. There are those who find the Arabs charming and likeable and the Jews neurotic and offputting. There are those who have no time for either side. Koestler also introduces an outsider's view, through the observations of Dick Matthews, an American journalist. He witnesses the first stages of the construction of Ezra's Tower with reluctant admiration. He could not like the people, but he was forced to recognise their achievements. Joseph, too, is an outsider. He is only half Jewish, he is English, and has therefore neither been through the European experience nor has he any concrete reason for allegiance to the resettlement of Palestine. Like Matthews, his admiration is reluctant. Like Matthews, he finds many of his comrades exasperating. He has no patience for their attitudes and neuroses, but he wants to contribute to their achievement. Reuben says of him: "You are engrossed in Judaism, but don't like the Jews. . . . You have lived with us for six years and still we are objects to you, not subjects."[17]

Koestler uses Joseph's hostility and his position as outsider as a technique of persuasion. Joseph's commitment in spite of his critical attitude and his emotional revulsion is more tenacious and more striking. It is backed by Matthews' ultimate position as apologist for the Jews. Joseph's hostility is not expressed through relationships but is conveyed in his diary : another useful technique. It allows Koestler to use Joseph as an instrument of direct comment—the diary furnishes the chronicle, which is present in both *The Gladiators* and *Darkness At Noon*—and to present an insight into the mind of his central character which, as is demonstrated in *The Age of Longing*, he was not able to handle satisfactorily through the mutual relation of personalities, or even through the reaction of personalities and events.

Joseph is the debate's centre. It is his function to be worked upon by each point of view and to make a firm decision in favour of one or the other. But it is not merely the argument that works on Joseph. In fact, ultimately, as in the case of Peter Slavek, circumstances force impulse to take over from reason.

In the first discussion of the rights and wrongs of terrorism Simeon says, "We have to encounter terror by terror".[18] That night the Arabs from Kfar Tabiyeh attack Ezra's Tower, as if to reinforce his point. But for most of the settlers such attacks are an accepted part of the hazards of construction. They do not think in terms of reprisal, but concentrate on making themselves invulnerable.

The outside world encroaches on their endeavour. Koestler establishes the political context by using official reports, newspaper cuttings, reports of Commons debates. This adds up to a brisk and even-toned presentation of events, and is balanced by the minor details of *kibbutz* life. In no other novel does Koestler devote so much space to conveying the quality of the life of his characters. Here, we are given a precise and lively picture. Joseph's diary brings together the two elements. As he grows more restless with communal life his eyes are more frequently turned outwards. The fact that he is given a job that takes him to the cities and gives his life new scope encourages this tendency, and our attention is directed away from the particular problems of a single commune and towards the increasing tension between Arab, Jew and British mediator.

The first step in Joseph's progress towards terrorism comes when Simeon leaves the *kibbutz* to join Bauman's gang—now a group dedicated to terroristic activities. It is not easy for Joseph to sympathise. His commitment is not so absolute that he can forget his origins although he can condemn them:

. . . if at least I could hate as Simeon does! But after all I am half English myself. Spoiled and pampered by the safety of our island, uninvaded for a millennium while other countries served as battlefields, we could afford to muddle and bungle through the ages and develop the mystic belief that our bungling is some higher God-inspired wisdom. We will plunge ourselves and the rest of the world into a disaster worse than anything in history; and when we scramble out of it we will make humorous remarks about our own stupidity—blissfully unaware that, though we pay for our own mistakes, we shall never be able to pay for the horrors into which we have dragged the others, who are dead and buried and unable to share the joke.[19]

Joseph is hampered in his ability to come to a decision by his lack of experience of extremity. He is faced with a situation of an entirely different quality from anything he has known before. He condemns Britain, but is not able at this stage to follow the logic of this condemnation. Again, Koestler's hero is confronted with the necessity of choice. But it needs the murder of Dina to shock Joseph into making a decision.

Joseph's relationship with Dina fills out his personality. She is a fragile and sympathetic character—by far the most likeable of Koestler's female characters—calm in spite of her neurosis, and has a softening influence on the hard intellectual edges of the other characters. Her murder by the Arabs drives Joseph to Bauman. He can no longer resist his will to action. Bauman explains his position. "To see both sides is a luxury we cannot afford."[20] Violent circumstances challenge man to grapple with them according to their own terms, and Bauman accepts this challenge. He talks of the "logically unassailable doctrine of the post-Genevan world. Whether the doctrine was propounded by the strong aiming at conquest, or by the weak aiming at survival, was merely a difference in degree, not in kind. For ultimately the strong too was animated by fear and insecurity, and ultimately the weak had to resort to the same violent and detestable means. It was a global infection against which the only defence was to get contaminated oneself."[21]

Like Rubashov Bauman sees his actions as being demanded by circumstance. But in fact Koestler comes much nearer to convincing us when he sticks to the particular events in Palestine without framing them with a general apologia. Joseph makes no attempt at this kind of intellectual justification. He gives way to the compulsion to act, and this we can understand more readily. He is not allowed to take part in the reprisal against the

mukhtar, but his commitment becomes no longer merely emotional, nor merely a sense of communal loyalty. He now has to
be prepared to face the consequences of illegal action and he
cannot retreat from violence:

> This was no time for soul-searching. Who was he to save his
> integrity while others had their bodies hacked to pieces? In
> the logic of the ice-age tolerance became a luxury and purity
> a vice. There was no way to escape the dilemma. To wash
> one's hands and let others do the dirty job was a hypocrisy,
> not a solution. To expose oneself was the only redeeming
> factor.[22]

But Joseph does manage a *modus vivendi* between his now
divided responsibilities. He continues to spend half his time at
Ezra's Tower while he secretly supports the terrorists. Ezra's
Tower remains withdrawn from the conflict. Joseph is therefore preserving a refuge for himself. Although there is no demonstration of how Bauman's gang furthers the purpose of the Jews,
and although the novel ends in uncertainty as far as political
events are concerned, Joseph is let off more lightly than most of
Koestler's heroes. He has no pretensions to being a revolutionary
hero. Koestler conceives him rather as *un homme moyen intel-
lectuel* than as a man entangled in historic forces. Perhaps this is
why he is able to satisfy both conscience and compulsion with
relative ease. The novel ends in an atmosphere of desperate acts
but not of despair. Koestler believed that the situation in Palestine provided opportunities for appropriate action, action with
some hope and purpose behind it. There are horizons in *Thieves
in the Night* that exist in no other of Koestler's novels.
But *Thieves in the Night* is also much nearer straight documentary than the other novels. Some critics found this, in itself,
a serious defect:

> The journalistic novel exploits nonfiction in order to enable
> the writer to avoid the more difficult challenges of fiction

proper, while on the other hand it uses fiction to make the shaping, manipulation, and adulteration of nonfiction easier. Where the genuine artist starts from a personal, particular experience, the journalist-novelist starts from a general, public one, whose automatic cogency relieves him of the necessity of making it cogent by means of art.[23]

The assumption here is that public events have no place in fiction, that they are intrinsically less important than private experience, and that they automatically infect fiction with an alien product that interferes with its proper content; in other words, that it is a damaging contradiction to make fact the basis for fiction.

In each of his novels, except perhaps in *The Age of Longing*, Koestler is concerned with the relationship between men and political events, and this necessitates a discussion of the facts of these events. In *The Gladiators* and *Darkness At Noon* he demonstrates the progress of revolution. In *Arrival and Departure* his characters are rooted in devastating political events, in *Thieves in the Night* he deals with persecution and rebellion. In all of these his subject is the mutual influence of men and history, and in handling it his task is, precisely, the making of public experience cogent—for history does not necessarily have a natural shape and meaning—by means of art. He must make for, in John Grierson's words, "the creative treatment of actuality". The above passage, from a review by Clement Greenburg, finds the writing of documentary fiction a means of escaping the difficulties of both journalism and fiction. In fact, it is the undertaking of the difficulties of both with the added problem of their fusion to handle.

The fusion Koestler achieves is not without flaws. Again, he overdoes the emphasis on the psychological explanation of personality, and the Incident that provides the motive for Joseph's immigration verges on the ridiculous. Such an emphasis splits the level of the novel, and the psychological examination interferes with the political demonstration without humanising it.

The humanising factor is provided by the novel's texture, made richer by the detailed illustration of daily life. These are details which Koestler omits in, for instance, *Arrival and Departure*, and their presence in *Thieves in the Night* adds to both the scope and the depth of the novel. It is not so angular a work. The sharp corners of political conflict are smoothed by the intimacy of daily life: the conflict becomes intimate also.

Joseph himself is responsible for most of the remaining jagged edges. The thread of self-analysis which his diary contains interrupts the more important function of the diary as a vehicle for drawing together the public and the private, general events and individual behaviour. We are less interested in Joseph's private troubles than in the Palestinian situation, and this is as it should be. We can accept Joseph's personality and actions without the rather artificial and self-conscious examination of motive. It is in this examination, rather than in the presentation of events, that Koestler's language, in T. R. Fyvel's phrase, "seems to assault the intellect".[24] Koestler's antithetical, hammer-blow style works powerfully when he is dealing with facts, but is very often clumsy when he employs it to fashion personality.

It is when Koestler is trying hardest to preserve the balance between events and individuals that we are most conscious of discrepancy. The carefully planned movement of emphasis from the public to the personal, from political argument to individual feeling becomes almost perfunctory. The dinner at which the Assistant Chief Commissioner, Dick Matthews, a Jewish professor and an Arab politician are brought together is an example. There should be tension in this balance—and at times Koestler does achieve it—but often there is merely opposition. In spite of this *Thieves in the Night* is more immediately moving than anything else Koestler wrote. His own emotional involvement must partly account for this. In Koestler's case subjectivity enhances rather than hinders the novel's achievement. On the final pages, when men and women from Ezra's Tower are on their way to help found a new settlement their courage and pathos leap to life. Koestler allows them a brief moment of extrovert glory.

And Joseph for the first time admits that his predicament is a shared predicament, and his alien attitudes dissolve in the communal effort.

Thieves in the Night was Koestler's last committed novel. The Palestinian issue was the last major issue over which Koestler took a stand. His final novel, *The Age of Longing*, published five years later, deals with, and suffers from, the aftermath of commitment. He brings together a group of disillusioned and weary individuals, who still have a lingering itch for action, and faces them with the threat of invasion, which is represented more intimately by the brash, single-minded official at the enemy country's embassy. The action takes place in Paris and the threatening state is Russia. The novel is a failure, largely because Koestler has moved away from the representation of any kind of action, and the physical threat is entirely unreal. His characters have come to a physical and intellectual standstill: they brood over the past and shrug their shoulders at the future. The only real answer and the only real threat lie in the sexual encounter of Hydie, a lapsed Catholic American girl, and Nikitin, the Russian. The fierce conflicts of political and historical standpoints have dwindled to the confrontation of a bored American, motivated, as far as one can tell, by an irresponsible curiosity, without faith and without love, and a dogmatic, narrow and intolerant Russian.

None of the characters is sympathetic. (Koestler himself seems to dislike them all.) The plot is static—there is neither action nor argument to move it. Koestler's characteristic weaknesses are laid bare without a stitch of concrete circumstance or demonstrable thesis to cover them. The result is that the overemphasis of psychological detail is a great deal more intrusive than in previous novels. Both Hydie and Nikitin are supplied with "Incidents" that are intended to provide clues to their behaviour. Koestler relies heavily on a presentation of the past as clinical data in his characterisation. But there is no precise or alive demonstration of the links between Hydie's alcoholic mother and her loss of faith, or between Nikitin's instinctive act of betrayal in the Komsomol and his detached vindictiveness towards Hydie. These facts are like so many loose threads; they are not worked into the main weave of the novel. As with both Joseph and Peter they are not necessary to our understanding of Hydie or of Nikitin. It is almost as if Koestler would have us believe that any kind of impulsive, out of the ordinary, or even just energetic action is impossible without some childhood trauma.

Nikitin is another, if less powerful, Gletkin. He despises the revolutionary spirit of 1917. "They were all of the past; what had they done to be so proud of themselves anyway? Conspired and thrown bombs and fought partisan actions—all romantic, outmoded stuff. They had not built a single factory, had no inkling of production and the Plan."[25] His function is to hammer home the fact that such faith as this "age of longing" can offer is rigid and inhuman, concerned with machines and not with men. But Nikitin himself, for all his coldness and awkwardness in the face of any situation which his calculations cannot handle, is the most energetic of the novel's characters. He has a vitality that Julian, the disillusioned Marxist poet, Boris, the refugee and the others lack. Clearly such men as Nikitin and Gletkin hold a strange fascination for Koestler. Nikitin is handsome, potent and controlled. "In his shirt, which brought out his straight, muscular shoulders, he was very good-looking. His face had a simple directness, simplicity without guile; only his slightly slanting grey eyes were markedly expressionless—one-way pupils that took the light in, gave nothing out."[26] Neither conscience nor experience will allow Koestler to favour the commissar rather than the yogi, but in *The Age of Longing*, when he is presenting an atmosphere of faded ideas, drab expectations and bleak irresponsibility such sympathy as he has is inclined towards Nikitin.

The attempt to give the novel a hard philosophic core is not successful. (It would have counteracted the strength of Nikitin.) The characters group and regroup aimlessly, deliver random remarks as contributions to the exposition of the intellectual climate. They have behind them an accumulation of tragedies, but cannot help each other, or even feel any warmth towards each other. Nikitin is alone with his creed and his sense of duty. He is very conscious of his solitary position and is cautious and unresponsive. The others resent the strength that this gives him : they are both envious and disgusted. Hydie is enraged by humiliation, but it is not caused by her consciousness of his solidity and her lack of direction. It is a sexual humiliation, which is in fact so artificially contrived that even this carries very little convincing weight. Afterwards she rationalises : "I hate him because of what he does and believes and stands for. Just as I fell for him because—because he was sure of himself and had a belief, a certitude which none of you have. Because he is *real*, which none of you are. And now I know he must be fought tooth and nail *because* he is real."[27] Hydie's rationalisation is an understanding, but an understanding that would not have led to action if resentment and injured pride had not motivated her. Her action—an unsuccessful attempt to murder Nikitin—is inappropriate and absurd.

Koestler is attempting to describe a flawed society. Unfortunately the defects of personality and social circumstance that he handles infect the quality of the novel. Hydie's irrelevant behaviour merely damages the plot without illuminating the argument. Koestler's weary characters cannot support the book's glib pronouncements. Under any circumstances the state of disillusion is difficult to manage. In *The Age of Longing* the bitterness and the shoulder-shrugging is empty, not backed by any solid experience. We look for detail that is not extreme and melodramatic, but which would give a substantial background of normal life. In attempting to translate his own convalescence from the demands of political commitment into fiction Koestler has failed. When he tackled the problem directly, without disguising the fact that he was writing about himself, his own experiences and his own attitudes, he was directly relevant and persuasive. *The Yogi and the Commissar* was written six years before *The Age of Longing*. In the intervening years

POST-WAR POSITIONS

Koestler lost a great deal of his intensity and his touch became less sure.

Orwell had only four and a half years after the War in which to make his position clear. He did it devastatingly and unequivocally in *Animal Farm* and *Nineteen Eighty-Four*. Whether there would have been any significant change after *Nineteen Eighty-Four* is impossible to say. After the War Orwell's journalistic output slackened off considerably, so we have virtually just these two novels as his final statements. Koestler devoted a large part of *The Yogi and the Commissar* to an indictment of Stalinism, both directly and by implication. Orwell's own condemnation, *Animal Farm*, was short, simple and direct. It was the first of Orwell's books to make money.

A year after the War's end Orwell was writing:

Exactly at the moment when wealth might be so generally diffused that no government need fear serious opposition, political liberty is declared to be impossible and half the world is ruled by secret police forces. Exactly at the moment when superstition crumbles and a rational attitude towards the universe becomes feasible, the right to think one's own thoughts is denied as never before.[28]

This is the mood of both Orwell's last novels. At the same time they were both efforts at countering these tendencies. *Animal Farm* was written at a time when Stalin was still Britain's ally. In Orwell's eyes British politicians and public alike had developed a dangerous admiration for a figure who represented a totalitarian state not so far removed from Hitler's. Orwell had great difficulty in getting the book published. It was rejected by at least three publishers, and Victor Gollancz, to whom it was offered, even went the length of advising other publishers to turn it down. It was finally accepted by Secker and Warburg, but by the time it was brought out, in August 1945, Britain and Russia were no longer allies in war but enemies in peace. In the United States, ironically, the book was rejected by at least eight publishers, and was not brought out there until the end of 1946.

In his introduction to the Ukrainian edition of *Animal Farm* Orwell tells us something of the way it came to be written. He makes his propagandist purpose quite evident. "It was of the utmost importance to me that people in Western Europe should see the Soviet régime for what it really was." But he also says : "I would not condemn Stalin and his associates merely for their barbaric and undemocratic methods. It is altogether possible that, even with the best intentions, they could not have acted otherwise under the conditions prevailing there."[29] Orwell is directing his attack against those who persisted in the belief that Russia was the home of socialism. He was convinced that this belief had a crippling effect on the socialist movement in Britain. "Nothing has contributed so much to the corruption of the original idea of socialism as the belief that Russia is a socialist country and that every act of its rulers merits excuse, if not imitation." This is the starting point of *Animal Farm*.

Animal Farm crystallises the ideas present in the Ukrainian edition's introduction into a plain, English and allegorical version of *Darkness At Noon*. V. S. Pritchett describes the book as "the traditional English fable"[30] and there is certainly something almost homely about Orwell's treatment. He avoids the problem of digesting an experience that is second-hand. He attempts neither realism nor interpretation. He allows the facts, shaped and coloured by allegory, to speak for themselves. The satire too moves within the allegory, which uses the English countryside and farm beasts familiar to him. The allegorical method far from reducing what he has to say to the coldness of symbols gives the book a warmth and texture which Orwell rarely achieved. The animals are never mere representations. They have a breathing individuality that is lacking in most of Orwell's human characters. There are no barriers between Orwell and his understanding and affection for his characters, no reticence, no distracting complications, no sociological points to be made. Boxer, the cart horse, for instance, does not simply represent a Stakhanov figure. He is attractive in his own right, and the incident in which the pigs arrange for him to be taken to the glue factory is one of the most moving passages in the whole of Orwell's writing.

Nor is Orwell's handling of his animal characters sentimental. It is simple. Relationships are presented on their simplest levels. This makes the bewildered reaction to the pigs' power, the involvement of belief in political expedience, even more shattering. The absence of barriers in the method of characterisation can also be felt in the overwhelming logic of the story's development. The pigs' assumption of leadership after the initial revolt, the process of corruption gently underlined, the banishing of Snowball, the Trotsky figure—each incident melts into the overall development. There are no jerks, no sudden piling up of emphases, in the book's superbly controlled movement. The distortion of the original commandments and the animals' inability to challenge the leadership occur inevitably. Without venturing into analysis or explanation Orwell presents a compact and detailed statement of the corruption of revolution.

The allegory is very precise in its use of the major figures and incidents of the Russian Revolution. It expresses quite nakedly and with a complete lack of intellectual argument those aspects of Stalinism that most disturbed Orwell. At the same time the humbleness and warmth of the narrative give an attractive obliqueness without turning the direction of the satire. We can feel compassion for Orwell's creatures in a way that we cannot for Winston Smith, for the stark narrative of Nineteen Eighty-Four stuns our capacity for reaction. But Animal Farm is equally relentless in its message. The relentless quality is partly contained in the even tone of the language. In the midst of describing hardship and disaster it does not vary—it matches the pathetic doggedness of the animals themselves. In no other work does Orwell so successfully resist the temptation to launch into barely relevant side issues. The measured amalgam of straightforward vocabulary and colloquial phrase has a strange power, perhaps because Orwell writes with a complete lack of

H

self-consciousness, as if he were describing recognised facts, and without the pretense of inserting himself into the animals' minds:

> Meanwhile life was hard. The winter was as cold as the last one had been, and food was even shorter. Once again all rations were reduced, except those of the pigs and the dogs. A too rigid equality in rations, Squealer explained, would have been contrary to the principles of Animalism. In any case he had no difficulty in proving to the other animals that they were *not* in reality short of food, whatever the appearances might be. . . . The animals believed every word of it. Truth to tell, Jones and all he stood for had almost faded out of their memories. They knew that life nowadays was harsh and bare, that they were often hungry and often cold, and that they were usually working when they were not asleep. But doubtless it had been worse in the old days. They were glad to believe so. Besides, in those days they had been slaves and now they were free, and that made all the difference, as Squealer did not fail to point out.[31]

Orwell identifies himself with the animals while maintaining his distance, in the same way as he identified himself with tramps or the unemployed. His sympathetic detachment reinforces the plain strength of the prose. The words are simple, the sentences short, many with only a single clause. The simplicity gives an authentic quality to the writing. As in so much of Orwell's writing he does not erect clusters of words and phrases which come between him and his reader and disguise meaning rather than illuminate it. Adjectives like "harsh and bare", "cold", "hungry" do all the work that is needed without embroidery, although they are the kind of adjectives that often become removed from their plain meanings.

Part of the success of Orwell's writing in *Animal Farm* lies in the familiarity of most of his details. He is dealing with a locality and a gathering of animals which he not only knew but for which he had a great affection. He had always found pleasure in the country and in what he knew of farming. This pleasure generates its own warmth. Perhaps it also helps to account for the lack of self-consciousness, a quality that Orwell often found difficult to achieve in his fiction. And it is not insignificant that Orwell spent most of his writing life in London, which he disliked, and much of what he wrote was about London and city life.

A fairly modest first impression of *Animal Farm* was printed : 4,500 copies. It is some indication of the book's success that a second impression of 10,000 was printed soon after. But there was no consistent reaction to the book. Those for whom Russia's part in the War had bolstered a faith little damaged by events preceding it did not receive the book kindly. Kingsley Martin decided that it was not to be taken seriously. "If we read the satire as a jibe at the failings of the USSR and realise that it is historically false and neglectful of the complex truth about Russia, we shall enjoy it and be grateful for our laugh."[32] The politically sensitive stated categorically that the allegory did not work, though it was not explained precisely in what way it failed. Others praised both the quality and the aptness of the allegory, and one critic eulogised the book as "the finest political parable of our time".[33] But whatever the critics said, Orwell was suddenly a successful writer. *Animal Farm* was a best seller in dozens of different languages. Its immortality cannot now be challenged, for it is firmly entrenched in the GCE Ordinary Level syllabus.

Animal Farm confirmed the finality of Orwell's break with the orthodox left. Again, many sections of the left were embarrassed. The reaction against Orwell became sharper and more bad tempered as the book's success became apparent. The earlier judgments that he was honest and well-intentioned but misguided could no longer be held. Koestler had wounded the conservative right, the weak-kneed liberal, and the rigid Stalinist with equal vehemence by his intellectual sharp shooting. By making a plain statement without attempting to cover himself Orwell laid himself open to criticisms that he was doing more to damage socialism than to condemn totalitarianism. With the publication of *Nineteen Eighty-Four* he had to face a flood of accusations that he had abandoned every vestige of socialist belief, and he had to face also the cries of welcome from the political right, who claimed him as a powerful ally.

II

POST-WAR PROPHECY

There had been hints of *Nineteen Eighty-Four* in the very beginning of Orwell's writing career. Most of the themes had preoccupied him from about 1942. The book is a sign of the intensity with which he reacted against both the conditions of post-
war Britain and the deadlock of the international situation. It is
also an accumulation of all those aspects of life that Orwell felt
most desperately about. A further consideration is the effect his
illness was having on him, for the years in which he was writing
Nineteen Eighty-Four were also the years in which his illness
was at its most serious and debilitating.

The emotions and attitudes of the book had been present for
many years, certainly present in *Wigan Pier* and *Keep the
Aspidistra Flying*, if not earlier. He mentioned in his wartime
Notebooks his long-held belief that the future would be "catastrophic", and it was clear throughout the War that he saw the
future in extreme terms. He continually warned against complacency about totalitarianism: "the fallacy is to believe that
under a dictatorial government you can be quite free *inside*.
Quite a number of people console themselves with this thought,
now that totalitarianism in one form or another is visibly on the
upgrade in every part of the world."[1] And in 1945 he prophe-
sied the development which is the heart of *Nineteen Eighty-
Four*:

> . . . we have before us the prospect of two or three mon-
> strous super-States, each possessed of a weapon by which
> millions of people can be wiped out in a few seconds, dividing
> the world between them. It has been rather hastily assumed

that that means bigger and bloodier wars, and perhaps an actual end to the machine civilisation. But suppose—and really this is the likelier development—that the surviving great nations made a tacit agreement never to use the atomic bomb against one another? Suppose they only use it, or the threat of it, against people who are unable to retaliate? In that case we are back where we were before, the only difference being that power is concentrated in still fewer hands and that the outlook for subject peoples and oppressed classes is still more hopeless.[2]

This vision was not entirely Orwell's own. James Burnham predicted much the same development in *The Managerial Revolution*, a book whose assumptions Orwell disagreed with, yet which contained a number of ideas he admired. By the time *Nineteen Eighty-Four* was published the cold war was a reality, and Orwell's description of the politics of power blocs was extraordinarily apt.

There had, of course, been other anti-utopian works of fiction before *Nineteen Eighty-Four*. In January 1946 Orwell had written a short piece in *Tribune* on Eugene Zamyatin's book *We*, which he had read in a French edition. The book had been written in 1920 by a Russian exile. It was a prophecy of totalitarianism based on, Orwell thought, "not any particular country but the implied aims of industrial civilisation". Orwell was impressed by the book because its concept of totalitarianism was founded on what he considered an essential element of the dictatorial state. Zamyatin, he says, had "an intuitive grasp of the irrational side of totalitarianism—human sacrifice, cruelty as an end in itself, the worship of a Leader who is credited with divine attributes".[3] This concept became an essential part of the creed of Ingsoc. It was a concept that Orwell had clearly been helped to formulate by Koestler's *Darkness At Noon* and Jack London's *The Iron Heel*. It was the aspect of the totalitarian state that was most difficult to combat. It could not be answered with intellectual argument, and its very nature tended to overwhelm logical explanation. Koestler, in fact, did not really attempt to explain or even to present the divinity of No. 1.

The events in *Darkness At Noon* take on the aura of ritual, but it is a ritual of the mind, not of the emotions. There is no cruelty for its own sake—this we tend to associate more with the Nazi régime—nor emotional build-up of the infallibility of No. 1. Yet the possibility is suggested. In *The Iron Heel* the Oligarchy's grasping for material wealth is transformed into a lust for power for its own sake, and the people's demands for social justice become an uncontrolled passion for revenge. Both these portrayals helped to form Orwell's understanding of authoritarian rule.

There is little indication that Orwell derived any wider influence from Zamyatin's book, although he greatly admired its ingenuity. *We* is constructed through a series of impressionistic pictures, studded with glittering detail, but leaving a sense of incompleteness. We get a sharp impression of contrast between the clean, bright city, built almost entirely of glass, and the slave-like existence of its inhabitants. Life is not dirty and colourless as in *Nineteen Eighty-Four*, but it is organised out of all humanity. The revolt in *We* is haphazard and imprecise. There are no explanations; we do not understand how it happens. Its aims and its inspiration are unclear; the impressionistic style ceases to be satisfactory. The mood and tone of *We* is far removed from *Nineteen Eighty-Four*. In its details it is far more distant from contemporary reality, particularly from Russia immediately after the Revolution. Its purpose appears to be much less particular, even less deliberate, than Orwell's.

But as a description of a dictatorial society Orwell found *We* much more satisfactory than Huxley's *Brave New World*, published in 1930. His chief criticism was that *Brave New World's* ruling group had neither energy nor purpose:

. . . no clear reason is given why society should be stratified in the elaborate way that is described. The aim is not economic exploitation, but the desire to bully and dominate does not seem to be a motive either. There is no power-hunger, no sadism, no hardness of any kind. Those at the top have no strong motive for staying at the top, and though everyone is happy in a vacuous way, life has become so pointless that it is difficult to believe that such a society could endure.[4]

Orwell's criticism directly opposes that which is sometimes made of *Nineteen Eighty-Four*: that a state founded solely on power for its own sake could not survive. But Orwell saw in the kind of sadism displayed by the Nazis an irresistible energy. The purposeless advances in science described in *Brave New World* provided no substitute. Science made physical power unnecessary, and the ultimate result is bound to be the dispensing with human beings altogether. This has very nearly happened in *Brave New World*. And when humanity no longer exists in the way we know it science becomes meaningless. Orwell insists that totalitarianism derived its energy from the exploitation of human beings, even though their major qualities were bludgeoned into dormancy.

Orwell's theory of the energy of power was closer to Jack London than to any of the books that paralleled his forecast of totalitarianism. London gives a violently savage picture of dictatorial methods and of mass reaction to them. (He himself may have been influenced by Frank Norris's *The Octopus*, a book more directly founded on contemporary reality than *The Iron Heel*.) Orwell says that London understood "just how the possessing class would behave once they were seriously menaced".[5] *The Iron Heel* shows the extremes to which the passion for power could lead. Published in 1908 it was a strangely apt foretaste of what was to occur not in America but Europe. Orwell tempered such ferocity with the particular details he had learned from Koestler and others who described the process of interrogation and produced a mixture of sadism and cold logic. He did not think *The Iron Heel* an entirely good book, but he admired it because it did contain a feature missing, or mistakenly envisaged, in other books of prediction. "The book is chiefly

notable for maintaining that capitalist society would not perish
of its 'contradictions', but that the possessing class would be
able to form itself into a vast corporation and even evolve a sort
of perverted Socialism, sacrificing many of its principles in
order to preserve its superior status."[6] Orwell does not tell us
very much of Ingsoc's developments, but he clearly indicates,
through Goldstein's theories, that this is how he visualised its
coming to power.

But it was from his experience of contemporary London that
Orwell drew the inspiration for the opening pages of *Nineteen
Eighty-Four*. It was an experience that had also conditioned his
writing of *Keep the Aspidistra Flying* and we can recognise a
number of similar details:

It was a bright cold day in April, and the clocks were striking
thirteen. Winston Smith, his chin nuzzled into his breast in
an effort to escape the vile wind, slipped quickly through the
glass doors of Victory Mansions, though not quickly enough
to prevent a swirl of gritty dust from entering along with him.

The hallway smelt of boiled cabbage and old rag mats. At
one end of it a coloured poster, too large for indoor display,
had been tacked to the wall. It depicted simply an enormous
face, more than a metre wide: the face of a man of about
forty-five, with a heavy black moustache and ruggedly handsome features. Winston made for the stairs. It was no use
trying the lift. Even at the best of times it was seldom working, and at present the electric current was off during day-
light hours. It was part of the economy drive in preparation
for Hate Week.[7]

There are two streams of description in this passage—the
familiar details of drabness, the dust, the smell, the out-of-order
lift, and the individual words that disturb the familiarity and
introduce a foreign and troubling note. The clock strikes thirteen, the building has a glass door, hardly compatible with the
smell of cabbage, the poster is a metre wide. The phrase "Hate

Week" removes all doubt that this is not the Britain of 1948. By the end of the paragraph there are further details that are important hints of the major themes and contrasts of the novel:

> The flat was seven flights up, and Winston, who was thirty-nine and had a varicose ulcer above his right ankle, went slowly, resting several times on the way. On each landing, opposite the lift shaft, the poster with the enormous face gazed from the wall. It was one of those pictures that are so contrived that the eyes follow you about when you move. BIG BROTHER IS WATCHING YOU, the caption beneath it ran.[8]

We are told only two things about Winston, but we already see him as a frail and undistinguished man, completely dominated by his surroundings. Even against these relatively minor facts of life in Airstrip One—the stair, the poster, the lift—Winston has no authority. On the first page he is as powerless as on the last. The force of the poster grows from sentence to sentence. At first, apart from the size, it seems inoffensive, but its recurrence on each landing, the apparent movement of the eyes, lead to the starkness of the caption which baldly sums up the condition of life in 1984.

The remainder of the book enlarges this caption. On the final page everything else is subservient to it. But we have already been warned not to be surprised at anything that might follow. We know at once that Winston is a frail creature, robbed by the state of any vitality he might have had, brought to subjection by the stairs as much as by any direct wielding of authority. He has no chance of developing his vague and inarticulate revolt against the Thought Police and the telescreens that eliminate any kind of private life, and he understands this from the beginning. He is a part of the dreary, colourless background of which he is so conscious.

Winston's uneasiness at life in Oceania is aggravated by his nostalgia for a half-remembered past. It is a nostalgia very similar to George Bowling's, and the years immediately after the Second World War take on the colouring of those just before the First. The dim scenes and impressions in Winston's memory encourage him to indulge in an instinctive feeling that the quality of life has not always been the same, and in fact *should* not be as Ingsoc has made it. In his diary Winston feels his way towards revolt. It is a half-willed reaction against the Thought Police, against "the bombed sites where the plaster dust swirled in the air and the willow-herb straggled over the heaps of rubble"[9] and above all against the Party's power over the past.

The basis of Ingsoc's revolution is the manipulation of language. The Thought Police, terror and torture are instruments of preserving order; Newspeak is a means of controlling the thoughts and inclinations that inspire disorder. Syme, Winston's colleague, describes the aim of Newspeak: "In the end we shall make thought-crime literally impossible, because there will be no words in which to express it. Every concept that can ever be needed will be expressed by exactly *one* word, with its meaning rightly defined and all its subsidiary meanings rubbed out and forgotten."[10] The manipulation of language is essential to the manipulation of history, as Orwell became so much aware of at the time of the Spanish Civil War. The Party that holds the key to forcing belief upon the public is in a position to force a certain interpretation of history. In the case of Ingsoc it is not an interpretation that is forced, but the complete destruction of history.

There is a further aspect of the manipulation of language that Orwell deals with in his appendix to *Nineteen Eighty-Four*, "The Principles of Newspeak". He made the point that the principle of abbreviation, which Newspeak adopts extensively, was a characteristic feature of political language in the first half of the century. He says:

In the beginning the practice had been adopted as it were instinctively, but in Newspeak it was used with a conscious purpose. It was perceived that in thus abbreviating a name one narrowed and subtly altered its meaning, by cutting out most of the associations that would otherwise cling to it. The words *Communist International*, for instance, call up a composite picture of universal brotherhood, red flags, barricades, Karl Marx and the Paris Commune. The word *Comintern*, on the other hand, suggests merely a tightly-knit organisation and a well-defined body of doctrine. It refers to something almost as easily recognised, and as limited in purpose, as a chair or a table. *Comintern* is a word that can be uttered almost without taking thought, whereas *Communist International* is a phrase over which one is obliged to linger at least momentarily. In the same way, the associations called up by a word like *Minitrue* are fewer and more controllable than those called up by *Ministry of Truth*.[11]

Orwell reveals here not only an understanding of the way in which political language could be made to work, but the basis of the authenticity of Ingsoc's control. It is this that Winston begins to grasp as he discovers hints of a world that Ingsoc has tried to obliterate.

Winston's rebellion begins when he buys the notebook in which he keeps his diary. It comes to represent his boyhood, of which he is only half-conscious. He tries to force it back into his memory. But as in the process of writing his memories begin to clarify he realises the impossibility of communicating from one generation to the next:

For whom, it suddenly occurred to him to wonder, was he writing this diary? For the future, for the unborn. His mind hovered for a moment round the doubtful date on the page, and he fetched up with a bump against the Newspeak word *doublethink*. For the first time the magnitude of what he had undertaken came home to him. How could you communicate with the future? It was of its nature impossible. Either the future would resemble the present, in which case it would not listen to him: or it would be different from it, and his predicament would be meaningless.[12]

The frailty of Winston's position is underlined. He can find no intellectual support for his instinctive revolt. Ingsoc has brought history to a standstill, and has wiped out the relevance of such actions as writing down one's private thoughts. The only function Winston's diary can perform is to provide the means of betrayal to the Thought Police.

Certainty of failure is in front of him, yet Winston moves on to the next stage in his rebellion, his affair with Julia. When he first encounters her he takes her for what she seems, a blind, hearty worshipper of Big Brother. But in fact Julia is also involved in an instinctive revolt, a revolt against the Party's control of private pleasure. "The aim of the Party was not merely to prevent men and women from forming loyalties which it might not be able to control. Its real, undeclared purpose was to remove all pleasure from the sexual act. Not love so much as eroticism was the enemy . . ."[13] For Julia revolt entails cheating the Party of this control. She does not seek an intellectual basis, she is not concerned with the past. Her affair with Winston entirely satisfies her urge to revolt.

Winston shares her feelings, but his revolt is not contained by them. For him sex represents an energy that can be both creative and corrupting. "Who knew, perhaps the Party was rotten under the surface, its cult of strenuousness and self-denial simply a sham concealing iniquity. If he could have infected the whole lot of them with leprosy or syphilis, how gladly he would have done so!" He believes in the "animal instinct, the simple undifferentiated desire: that was the force that would tear the Party to pieces."[14] But just as it is a force that could perhaps corrupt the Party from within and also act against it from without, it can both stimulate the instinct to rebel and deflect it. Julia does not feel the need for revolt in a larger sphere than that of private pleasure. Winston seeks restlessly for a means of striking a blow against the perversion of language and history.

Winston's attempt to piece together some impression of the past leads him to the district inhabited by the proles, the majority of the population kept in a condition of complete sup-

pression as a necessary and uncomplaining labour force. To
Winston the proles are a seething mass of energy which, properly directed, could break the Party's grip. He soon discovers
that they are not aware of their own potential. It is a problem
that Rubashov also ponders : there can be no revolution without
the people's consciousness of their condition, and they cannot acquire this consciousness with revolution. Hope lies
in the proles, Winston says. But the condition of the proles is
hopeless.

The old, crumbling part of London works on Winston's
memory. He finds a junk shop with a room above it filled with
curiosities from the past. His instinctive feeling for history returns. The room "had awakened in him a sort of nostalgia, a sort
of ancestral memory. It seemed to him that he knew exactly
what it felt like to sit in a room like this, in an arm-chair beside
an open fire with your feet on the fender and the kettle on the
hob . . ."[15] It is again the *Wigan Pier* nostalgic interior. Winston's visit to the country with Julia has a similar quality : it is
much happier than the outing of Gordon and Rosemary. But the
moments of warmth and comfort, or of light relief, are brief.
They are just long enough to hint that life could be better.
Winston's more usual surroundings are these :

A low-ceilinged, crowded room, its walls grimy from the contact of innumerable bodies; battered metal tables and chairs,
placed so close together that you sat with elbows touching;
bent spoons, dented trays, coarse white mugs; all surfaces
greasy, grime in every crack; a sourish composite smell of bad
gin and bad coffee and metallic stew and dirty clothes. Always
in your stomach and in your skin there was a sort of protest,
a feeling that you had been cheated of something that you
had a right to.[16]

The disgust here outdoes that in the scenes of physical torture.
This was Orwell recoiling from a scene that he himself could
have experienced in many of its details. Scenes of contrast with

this kind of thing occur seldom, but they have an important function. They are, of course, a stimulus to Winston's revolt, but they also provide small areas of warmth and reality that help to convince us of the genuineness of the love of Winston and Julia. The room above the junk shop with its decay and its rats becomes an interior in which they can build their own world. Compared with the outside reality it is pleasant and comfortable. They make real coffee and eat real bread with real jam. The food has a solid substance which the syntheic canteen stew has not.

Winston's contact with O'Brien is the third stage in his revolt. Julia, in spite of her philosophy of "the clever thing was to break the rules and stay alive all the same".[18] accompanies him on his visit. O'Brien is a more difficult and puzzling character than any other Orwell created. He is physically unattractive, yet has an outgoing charm—"a large, burly man with a thick neck and a coarse, humorous, brutal face. In spite of his formidable appearance he had a certain charm of manner. He had a trick of resettling his spectacles on his nose which was curiously disarming . . ."[18] Early in the novel the charm predominates. Winston feels that O'Brien will be sympathetic to his unease. He interprets the tiniest gesture in favour of what he wants to believe. But always he has a sense that O'Brien will destroy him, a kind of perverse knowledge that he can trust O'Brien because he will be responsible for his cure.

When O'Brien becomes Winston's torturer this duality comes into its own. O'Brien is both his destroyer and his saviour. Winston hates him for the pain which he inflicts and yet clings to him for the very reasons that he hates the Party, because he represents an absolute that is constant and unchangeable, which can remove all life's complications. Something of Winston's attitude is reflected in the way in which Orwell draws the character of O'Brien. There is both admiration and disgust in the portrayal. The duality can be explained a little by Orwell's own attitude to Hitler. Although Nazism appalled him he understood Hitler's power of attraction. "The fact is there is something deeply appealing about him. One feels it again when one sees his photographs. . . . It is a pathetic, dog-like face, the face of a man suffering under intolerable wrongs. In a rather more manly way it reproduces the expression of innumerable pictures of Christ crucified. . . . One feels, as with Napoleon, that he is fighting against destiny, that he *can't* win, and yet that he somehow deserves to. The attraction of such a pose is of course enormous; half the films that one sees turn upon some such theme."[19] Of course, there is no suggestion that O'Brien will lose in the end, yet we do feel Orwell's admiration for him, that he half intends that O'Brien deserves to win, that it is better for Winston that O'Brien does win. O'Brien has a physical presence quite unlike Hitler's; it is more like Stalin's, but it is also like that of *The Iron Heel*'s hero Everhard. Everhard also has great physical strength—"He was a superman, a blond beast"—but he is the novel's hero and an attractive character, a man associated with "nobleness of purpose and heroism of effort".[20] It may be that Everhard was Orwell's inspiration for O'Brien's attractive ugliness; it is a type that occurs throughout Jack London's fiction. It is not only the pathetic attraction of Hitler, but the attraction of solid physical strength, that contrasts sharply with Winston's meagreness.

Koestler's Gletkin and Nikitin are very similar, and yet we are not conscious of a duality. Nikitin's attraction, his strength and what he stands for in the Party are all one and the same thing. Gletkin seems to have physical strength because he has power. If anything we lose the sense of O'Brien's personal strength when we see him wielding instruments of torture. In exhibiting O'Brien's apparent change of character there is a change also in the quality of the characterisation. His fullness of personality and presence fade as he shrinks to a mere machine for torture and justification. We never see Gletkin in any other role. O'Brien loses a dimension, yet it is important that all the elements of his personality remain, as Winston still sees him as combining charm and brutality. At the same time the transformation of O'Brien from man to machine provides an important part of the horror of the torturing scenes and ultimately of the horror of 1984. Part of Orwell's contention is that conditions could arise under which men are stripped of all personality and become emotionally and intellectually impotent. The complete picture of O'Brien is less abhorrent and more horrifying than Koestler's picture of Gletkin. Gletkin's attraction can only be intellectual. He does not have O'Brien's capacity to induce emotional faith and reliance and therefore cannot destroy such feelings.

Against the power of O'Brien we have to measure the quality of Winston's love, for it is his relationship with Julia that is the final test of his revolt. In his first long scene with Julia, in her country hideout, there is an aggressive hardness about their relationship in spite of the calmness of their surroundings. They are not able to lose themselves in the temporary safety of their short time together. Winston is conscious of this:

In the old days, he thought, a man looked at a girl's body and saw that it was desirable, and that was the end of the story. But you could not have pure love or pure lust nowadays. No emotion was pure, because everything was mixed up with fear and hatred. Their embrace had been a battle, the climax a victory. It was a blow struck against the Party. It was a political act.[21]

Winston realises that he has at last acted against the Party, and from that moment he cannot detach his love for Julia from his revolt. They become identical. The quality of his love is contained in the quality of his revolt, and ultimately they both prove to have been equally inadequate.

We can never exactly distinguish between Winston's failure and the Party's success. A stronger personality might have carried him further; but the Party denies the possibility of such a personality, except where it can fully utilise the strength—as in the case of O'Brien. In the junk shop scenes the relationship of Winston and Julia is real and intimate. They are lulled into relaxation. They give each other's personalities a chance that they never before had. They luxuriate in their privateness and in the sense of the past that the room generates. Winston remembers his mother as possessing "a kind of nobility, a kind of purity, simply because the standards that she obyed were private ones".[22] Thinking themselves secure from the Thought Police Winston and Julia make a start in the search for standards. But the purity and nobility are beyond them :

> The terrible thing that the Party had done was to persuade you that mere impulses, mere feelings, were of no account, while at the same time robbing you of all power over the material world. When once you were in the grip of the Party, what you felt or did not feel, what you did or refrained from doing, made literally no difference. Whatever happened you vanished, and neither you nor your actions were ever heard of again. You were lifted clean out of the stream of history. And yet to the people of only two generations ago, this would not have seemed all-important, because they were not attempting to alter history. They were governed by private loyalties which they did not question. What mattered were individual relationships, and a completely helpless gesture, an embrace, a tear, a word spoken to a dying man, could have value in itself. The proles, it suddenly occurred to him, had remained in this condition. They were not loyal to a party or a country or an idea, they were loyal to one another. . . . The proles had stayed human.[23]

Against such odds Winston's love is nullified. It can never have value as an end in itself. The qualities that might have enabled him to resist betrayal have been extinguished from all humanity except the proles, and the proles do not know how to utilise such qualities.

Winston's perception and fear are matched against an irrational belief in himself. He believes that the Party cannot touch his inner feelings. "What you say or do doesn't matter : only feelings matter. If they could make me stop loving you—that would be the real betrayal."[24] "If you can *feel* that staying alive is worth while, even when it can't have any result whatever, you've beaten them."[25] Of course, they do make him stop loving Julia and kill his belief that staying alive is worth while. Even while Winston is saying this he knows that every part of himself and Julia are vulnerable to the Party. Their betrayal of each other is already inevitable.

The duality of Winston's attitude to O'Brien is complemented by the duality of his love. It is emphasised by the gulf that has always existed between himself and Julia. Julia's private rebellion is enough for her—she falls asleep while Winston is reading Goldstein aloud. He resents Julia's attitude, yet will not admit that it represents a serious difference between them. He has little more than their relationship to sustain his revolt.

He finds intellectual sustenance in the work of Goldstein, *Nineteen Eighty-Four's* Trotsky figure. The book contains lengthy extracts from Goldstein's writings. This serves to explain a situation that for most of the novel has been more emotionally real than intellectually probable. Goldstein's theories are developments of many of the ideas that had been characteristic of Orwell's thinking for some years; they also ingeniously echo the tone and phrasing of the writings of Trotsky himself. They explain that the invincibility of Ingsoc rests on two foundations: the perversion of language and the fact of perpetual war. War on a limited scale is an ideal way of controlling the energies of the population:

The essential act of war is destruction, not necessarily of human lives, but of the products of human labour. War is a way of shattering to pieces, or pouring into the stratosphere, or sinking in the depths of the sea, materials which might otherwise be used to make the masses too comfortable, and hence, in the long run, too intelligent. Even when weapons of war are not actually destroyed, their manufacture is still a convenient way of expending labour power without producing anything that can be consumed.[26]

War is being used as a means of controlling the population of the State's own territory rather than of destroying or conquering enemy territory. It is a concept that Orwell frequently touched on, and, for us now, perhaps represents the most valuable warning the book contains. The connection that he draws between a totalitarian society and atomic war is still very relevant. It is worth quoting at length from an article by Erich Fromm, written in 1961, in which he explains this relevance:

> Orwell's picture is so pertinent because it offers a telling argument against the popular idea that we can save freedom and democracy by continuing the arms race and finding a "stable" deterrent. This soothing picture ignores the fact that with increasing technical "progress" (which creates entirely new weapons about every 5 years, and will soon permit the development of 100 or 1000 instead of 10 megaton bombs), the whole society will be forced to live underground, but that the destructive strength of thermonuclear bombs will always remain greater than the depth of the caves, that the military will become dominant (in fact, if not in law), that fright and hatred of a possible aggressor will destroy the basic attitudes of a democratic, humanistic society. In other words, the continued arms race, even if it would not lead to the outbreak of thermonuclear war, would lead to the destruction of any of those qualities of our society that can be called "democratic", "free", or "in the American tradition".[27]

Fromm goes on to say that *Nineteen Eighty-Four* "is simply implying that the new form of managerial industrialism, in which man builds machines which act like men and develops men who act like machines, is conductive to an era of dehumanisation and complete alienation, in which men are transformed into things and become appendices to the process of production and consumption".[28] Orwell's theory of Oceanic society is perhaps more feasible than its reality—and yet, of course, they cannot be separated. Fromm sharply indicates the force of the connection between a dehumanised society and perpetual war, or preparation for war. As well as the more concrete links, perpetual war can be exploited as a continual crisis which demands continual sacrifice on the part of the individual on behalf of the state. The creed of Ingsoc is not in itself sufficient to sustain the adulation of Big Brother and thereby the order of society. There needs to be a monstrous threat from outside to enable the machinery of authority to function with complete efficiency inside. And if the threat does not exist it has to be created. This situation is not merely an intellectual one. The basic elements were apparent in the heightened period of the cold war, and can be seen now in, for example, China's exploitation of American intervention in Vietnam, or the United States' similar use of the threat of Communism in Latin America.

It is clear, both from Goldstein and from Orwell's previous writings, that he was entirely conscious of the implications of the structure of Oceanic society and the division of the world, and of its basis in contemporary reality. It is this that maintains the book's relevance long after we have ceased to speculate as to what particular details of life in *Nineteen Eighty-Four* will match those in 1984.

The reading of Goldstein is, as it were, the book's theoretical climax. What follows is concerned with the arrest and torture of Winston, his betrayal of Julia and his acceptance of Big Brother. His defeat has been implied from the first pages. Orwell builds it up into a second climax of horror and disgust. Physical torture is an accepted factor in the methods of sustaining a totalitarian régime, and Orwell was clearly determined to present elaborate details, although he himself had had no experience of imprisonment or torture. It is here that we feel the strain on Orwell's imagination. Pain is used as therapy. The enforcing of the Party's perverted logic into Winston's mind is seen as a cure. O'Brien is the surgeon. Orwell tries to indicate precisely the relationship between degrees of pain and the breaking down of Winston's resistance, and in the earlier stages he is successful. The process is quite different from the interrogation of Ruba-

shov. There are other factors involved. Winston's regard for
O'Brien is not destroyed—he wants to believe that O'Brien is
holding up five fingers, although he can only see four. But Winston's intellect will not accept what his emotions and imagination are eager to embrace. It is O'Brien's task to cut out the section of resistance in Winston's brain, and to replace it by an
absolute faith that has nothing whatever to do with logic in the
truth of what the Party states. He succeeds, and Winston actually sees five fingers:

> He saw five fingers, and there was no deformity. Then every-
> thing was normal again, and the old fear, the hatred, and the
> bewilderment came crowding back again. But there had been
> a moment—he did not know how long, thirty seconds per-
> haps—of luminous certainty, when each new suggestion of
> O'Brien's had filled up a patch of emptiness and become abso-
> lute truth, and two and two could have been three as easily as
> five, if that were what was needed.[29]

Winston's relief at finding a moment of "luminous certainty"
is a part of the general inclination in humanity to have life made
easier by absolute faith. By this time circumstances are just too
difficult for Winston to apprehend. He realises that the only
way in which life—if he is allowed to live—will be endurable is
by accepting blindly everything that O'Brien suggests. He wills
himself to this acceptance, but has to know first why the Party
needs to have this power over him. O'Brien explains. "Power is
not a means to an end. One does not establish a dictatorship in
order to safeguard a revolution; one makes the revolution in
order to establish the dictatorship. The object of persecution is
persecution. The object of torture is torture. The object of power
is power."[30] As Winston perceived there is no question of right
or wrong involved in this, no discussion of ends and means.
Rubashov's dialogue is irrelevant. Even the necessity of justification has been removed. The Party has achieved its aim so effectively that the intellect is blunted and the emotions are channelled into hysteria.

O'Brien insists that Ingsoc has created a Party which has a vitality and force that is entirely independent of individuals. Human life is not its sustaining energy—it sustains human life, or destroys it, at will. O'Brien says: "You are imagining that there is something called human nature which will be outraged by what we do and will turn against us. But we create human nature."[31] Finally, O'Brien himself is no different from Winston, except that he is more thoroughly under the Party's control.

One level of Winston's resistance remains, and at this stage he himself is only half aware of it. He slowly finds that he can quite naturally articulate the Party's slogans. He can easily dismiss the occasional doubts—"What knowledge have we of anything, save through our own minds? All happenings are in the mind. Whatever happens in all minds, truly happens."[32] But torture has not been able to break the thread of his memory, and memory leads him back to Julia. He still loves Julia. He realises that "It was more difficult than accepting an intellectual discipline. It was a question of degrading himself, mutilating himself. He had got to plunge into the filthiest of filth."[33] The final stage in the torture, the final degradation, is Room 101.

In Room 101 Winston has to face being eaten alive by rats, of which he has an uncontrollable, hysterical fear. His betrayal of Julia is violent and final. "For an instant he was insane, a screaming animal. Yet he came out of the blackness clutching an idea. There was one and only one way to save himself. He must interpose another human being, the *body* of another human being between himself and the rats."[34] The human being he calls upon is Julia. At this moment Winston relinquishes complete control of himself to the Party. He is cured. He himself denies, wipes out, his final personal loyalty and there ceases to be any hope for him as an independent human being.

The remaining pages of the book return us to the drab atmosphere of the opening. Winston has become a feeble, gin-soaked creature. He encounters Julia who has been put through the same process of rehabilitation. The only emotion they are capable of is hatred, and even that is half-hearted. But the announcement of a military victory stirs Winston to tears: he loves Big Brother.

Orwell himself was not happy about Room 101. He was searching for a climax to the devastation of human individuality, and although he does succeed in communicating the reality of the rats, he does not convince us that they represent the ultimate in horror. In a letter to Julian Symons he wrote, in answer to criticisms of this scene, "You are of course right about the vulgarity of the 'Room 101' business. I was aware of this while writing it, but didn't know another way of getting somewhere near the effect I wanted."[35] Some kind of climax was obviously necessary. We know throughout the book that the Party will defeat Winston, and therefore the end must be something more than the mere working out of our expectations. We need to be shocked. Clearly, Orwell's own lack of experience reduced the range of detail he could communicate. It would have been too risky to rely on second-hand accounts for the final stage in the horror. Typically, perhaps, he chose to exploit a commonplace, a fear that his readers should have been able to feel much more intimately than Gestapo methods. And there is no logical reason why rats should not be so terrible as complicated machines of torture. In theory the switch from machine-made horror to natural horror should have been effective, but Room 101 does not stun quite in the way it should. Part of the failing lies in Winston's own reaction: the active side of the horror is convincing, the reactive side we suspect of being forced. Winston's response is very specific and in no particular way connected with the nature of the torture. He is neither totally irrational in his hysteria nor is his mind in control of what he says. The result is unsatisfactory. It is of course hard to assess a passage of writing conceived entirely in terms of extremes, for it is in the very nature of an extreme situation that anything is both possible and probable. But Orwell, in forcing so much to rely on this incident, is perhaps overloading with particularity a scene which would have been more successful as a general climax of horror.

An evaluation of a novel like *Nineteen Eighty-Four* must be undertaken in terms of the effect which it had, of whether the message was received as it was delivered. To this extent characterisation is instrumental. On the whole we feel no particular attraction for Winston or Julia. We are interested in the nature of their revolt. However, if the instruments are flawed the purpose cannot be achieved with complete success. Many critics based a rejection of *Nineteen Eighty-Four* on a failure of characterisation. Tom Hopkinson and Christopher Hollis for instance. At the same time some, notably Irving Howe, went to some length to illustrate how the nature of the society Orwell describes precisely determines the personalities dominated by it. This could be developed as a blanket excuse for any apparent flaw in the novel; it is necessary to recognise that those details which result from the picture of society also contribute to it. Winston is in many respects a more rounded and sympathetic character than most of Orwell's creations. His conflict is more genuine and less perverse than that of Gordon Comstock. He is less preoccupied with himself and with the meaning of his own personal revolt. His affair with Julia, though its foundations may be shaky, is more immediate and more intimately presented than that of Gordon and Rosemary in *Keep the Aspidistra Flying*. The difficulties Gordon has to overcome flatten his personality as it flattens his resistance. Until the final pages Winston's personality is rounded by his revolt. In his case the way in which he faces impossibility gives him depth of character, and although Julia remains rather mindless she becomes a part of this depth. The growth of Winston's consciousness is closely geared to the realities of life in a situation where an improbable vision would have been the more natural reaction. His characterisation is not hampered by small obsessions. Ultimately, of course, Winston achieves far less than Gordon and becomes completely lifeless, without even Gordon's truculence. But Winston emerges favourably from a comparison with almost all Orwell's pre-war characters.

Nineteen Eighty-Four had an electrifying effect on the public.

A first impression of over twenty-six thousand copies was printed. Compared with the fifteen hundred copies sold of *Homage to Catalonia* and *Animal Farm*'s first impression of 4,500 this marked a vast change in the anticipated public response. Reviewers who had previously been more critical than approving acclaimed the book. V. S. Pritchett wrote : "The faults of Orwell as a writer—monotony, nagging, the lonely schoolboy shambling down the one dispiriting track—are transformed now he rises to a larger subject" and "The heart sinks but the spirit rebels as one reads Mr. Orwell's ruthless opening page. . . ."[36] The *Times Literary Supplement* reviewer wrote : "the last word about this book must be one of thanks, rather than criticism : thanks for a writer who deals with the problems of the world rather than the ingrowing pains of individuals, and who is able to speak clearly and with originality on the nature of reality and the terrors of power."[37] In contrast, one reviewer dismissed the book as being "stale news".[38]

It is important to note in what light *Nineteen Eighty-Four* was praised, for in this lies our judgment of success. In Britain it was not, on the whole, immediately received as a blow struck for Conservatism. In the United States, however, many reviews, particularly in provincial and religious newspapers, hailed the book as a weapon to be used on behalf of the right. And it was, of course, reviled by Communists. It is clear that Orwell did not intend *Nineteen Eighty-Four* as a statement of his rejection of socialist principles. It would have been entirely inconsistent with his writing career if he had not found a more direct method of articulating any change in attitude. There is no indication in the work of the last years of his life that the motives for writing the book were other than those already described. Crudely put, Orwell's message had always been "keep humanity human", and he spent his life in trying to show how Conservative values involved a denial of the right of fulfilment to a large section of humanity. He deplored Soviet society precisely because of its corruption of socialist principles. On the other side, he deplored the still remaining dictatorships of Franco and Salazar, so often apologised for by the right in Britain. It meant little to Orwell in what name men acted. It was the quality and the consequences of their actions that he judged.

Orwell's compulsion to present his beliefs honestly and without compromise put him in a vulnerable position, from which he could not extricate himself by means of good faith. The root of the book's vulnerability is described by Isaac Deutscher:

> A book like *1984* may be used without much regard for the author's intention. . . . Nor need a book like *1984* be a literary masterpiece or even an important and original work to make its impact. Indeed a work of great literary merit is usually too rich in its texture and too subtle in thought and form to lend itself to adventitious exploitation. As a rule its symbols cannot easily be transformed into hypnotising bogies, or its ideas turned into slogans. The words of a great poet when they enter the political vocabulary do so by a process of slow, almost imperceptible infiltration, not by a frantic incursion. The literary masterpiece influences the political mind by fertilising and enriching it from the inside, not by stunning it.[39]

It cannot be denied that *Nineteen Eighty-Four* can be dangerous, and can become something quite different from what Orwell intended, in the hands of those who wish to exploit it. But the implications of Deutscher's remarks, and they are substantiated in the remainder of his article, are more than this. He suggests that *Nineteen Eighty-Four* is an undistinguished book, that because of its immediate impact and its popularity it cannot be good in literary terms. We do not have to go far to find examples of great novels that were received immediately, made a "frantic incursion", into the public consciousness; Scott and Dickens provide many. It is a fallacy that the influence of literary greatness must necessarily be slow and subtle. The immediate does not necessarily preclude the long-lasting.

No work of literature is so subtle that it can prevent parody, and the kind of exploitation that Deutscher warns against is a species of parody. Of course language is powerful; it is also just too fragile to prevent distortion. Deutscher suggests that the symbols and ideas of Orwell's novel are superficial because they can be "transformed into hypnotising bogies" and "turned into slogans". As Orwell was writing precisely about slogans and hypnotising bogies and their effects on ordinary human life this becomes rather a cheap point. Most of Deutscher's remarks are in general true, but not necessarily, and to array them as a list of rules against which *Nineteen Eighty-Four* must be tested is bound to be misleading.

Yet Deutscher makes an important and legitimate political point, and a political novel must be able to stand up to political criticism. He warns that it is impossible to control the way in which a book is used, and because of this, whatever Orwell's intentions, *Nineteen Eighty-Four* can be described as a weapon for the right if it is used as such. There is no doubt that it has been used as such. However strongly we point out that this is not a legitimate use of the novel, that all the evidence points to a different interpretation, Deutscher's point remains crucial. However, he states his criticism in such a way that it almost becomes possible to reverse his argument, and say that the form of the novel necessarily invites a certain flexibility of interpretation which a mere political tract does not, and therefore it is to the credit of *Nineteen Eighty-Four* that it can be variously understood. In fact, Deutscher is directing an attack against the novel as a genre used for propagandist purposes, basing it on reasons rather different from those of the literary critics. He criticises political fiction because it is less explicit than direct political expression.

Deutscher's most significant point is the making of a distinction between different processes of influence. It is evident in the reaction to the book that its effect was indeed to stun, and that it still stuns now. Orwell had established a relationship between different elements of society and of political endeavour which no one had before perceived. But it is also clear that the shocking impact does not preclude a perfectly cogent response. The power of the book to stun lies in its power to force readers to see the connections Orwell makes. It would otherwise have as fleeting an effect as an indifferent horror film, whose influence drops away as soon as one leaves the cinema.

Nineteen Eighty-Four stunned its readers into perception in the same way as a man suffering from amnesia can be stunned into remembering the past. The response to the book was not dulled, although it was at times misdirected. And it is important that the book still legitimately retains its force, and is still relevant, as Erich Fromm has shown. The vocabulary it injected so precipitately into the English language also remains. Big Brother is almost as famous as Falstaff or Frankenstein. The initial impact relies on whether tension is maintained. Orwell is not so much concerned with building up supense as with shifting without warning the levels and the quality of the intensity, and in turn blurring and clarifying the edges between hope and despair. Sometimes they are in savage conflict, as when Winston begins to keep his diary, sometimes terror seems to melt away, as when Winston and Julia go to the country. Although the frame around the characters' existence is in fact rigid, it appears to be constantly shifting.

Orwell himself admitted that *Nineteen Eighty-Four* was affected by his illness. The book might have been less artistically troubling if there had been greater scope for the shifts in tension. On the other hand, it is probable that Orwell's illness gave the book the uncompromising urgency which helped to force it into the public's mind. The exaggeration of some of the claims made for the book, on either side, is a symptom of the exaggerative quality of parts of it. But never had Orwell been so irresistible.

12

TWO MODES OF ISOLATION

The problem of a meaningful documentary was essentially one of communication, a problem not so much of what the facts were as of how they were transmitted. Much of the documentary, in both fictional and factual form, of the 1930s was of its very nature propagandist. The interest in the social conditions of life was a reforming interest. Motives had developed from the unguided reaction to the First World War—partly a compulsive recording of events and physical suffering, partly a feeling that people, posterity, ought to be made acquainted with the monstrosities of modern war—to a positive desire that conditions must be changed. This development in documentary matched the development in political involvement. But it occurred in this particular way only in a small section of society. The middle-class intelligentsia struggled to handle facts that concerned, once the First War was behind them, a class that they did not know, in some cases did not wish to know, but felt it a duty to approach.

Many tried to make this approach through the written word rather than through direct contact. Most of the poets and writers concerned did not solve the problem of how to communicate to a section of society that was not familiar with the language and conventions they used. Most of them did not attempt to solve it. One of Orwell's main objectives was to eliminate all extraneous and misleading matter from his writing, to use conventional phrasing only when it was meaningful, to be straightforward and intelligible. In fact, he was trying to evolve a classless language. Koestler had no such concern. His style is intellectually challenging rather than smoothly comprehensible and he uses the language of the educated, stimulated mind. This suggests that he was more confident of his audience. In the context of the European struggle he was almost a romantic, certainly a heroic, figure to English eyes. He and those like him were perhaps the nearest the post-First War imagination could come to Byronic figures, although they did not appeal to the heart so much as to the mind. Koestler's books sold considerably better than Orwell's pre-1945 publications. While Orwell tried to force language as near to reality as it would go, Koestler developed a series of picturesque formulae, a code of expression, through which he represented and argued.

Koestler saw himself sometimes in the role of prophet outcast, a Cassandra compelled to continue to warn although no one would listen. But in fact he was well received and widely read. He was more secure as an author and, one suspects, as an individual than Orwell. He dramatised himself in a way that was utterly foreign to Orwell's concept of his own role as a writer. Self-dramatisation was Koestler's method of communication. Dominating the discussion in, for instance, *The Yogi and the Commissar* are the facts and experiences of the life of Arthur Koestler. He presented his life as an example that could teach and help the understanding of a certain period of history. He had made mistakes. These mistakes could be partially justified if they could be used to illustrate and interpret history. Action, drama and physical suffering coloured the political events he wrote of. His writing was spiced with a sense of danger and urgency that was also intimate. This smoothed the lines of communication.

Orwell tackled the problem of language and communication with his usual directness. His experiences of political intrigue in Spain had deepened his preoccupation with the meaning of words. His primary concern had always been the representation of reality, and to achieve this he was not content merely to render the facts and let the facts speak. As Orwell was so intensely aware, facts did not speak, however hard the writer tried to ventriloquise. Response had to be raised by something more than statement. He had to assume that he was writing against an immunity to words, an inclination on the part of his readers to resist unpleasantness. When he is dealing with the facts of tramping or the liquidation of POUM Orwell does not rely on artificial emphasis, which could serve to muddle communication. He handles shocking circumstances with deliberate understatement and forces attention through apparent incongruity. But there are times when he suddenly makes an outrageously sweeping statement—he does this frequently in the second part of *Wigan Pier*—in a breathtakingly uncompromising fashion. This kind of thing is part of a different, more dubious, technique of persuasion. He seems to have used it quite deliberately, and it can be impressively refreshing, and even funny. The making of bare, challenging, half-true statements was simply one of Orwell's instruments of assertion, but it was a rash technique to employ : it could result in his audience being shocked into attention or into merely shrugging their shoulders. It is in fact a common technique of propagandists, and Orwell most often used it when he was attempting a desperate retaliation. In his hands the weapon was often more potent, for he retained the nakedness that we see in his understatement. Instead of adding meaningless decorations to his prose that weakened the argument and confused the issue, his language was stripped bare, strengthened occasionally by a lively and precise metaphor.

Orwell's tendency to overstate his case is illustrated in his argument that a writer should be in contact with political events. In order to show that a writer *ought* not to cut himself off from politics Orwell stated that he *could* not. In a sense he is right, but he does not explain in what sense. He was not willing to compromise himself by the expression of opinions he had no faith in, but he was ready to go any lengths to communicate what he thought was true, without appearing to recognise that in so doing he sometimes came near to distorting the truth. *Nineteen Eighty-Four* is an obvious example, though legitimately handled. He recognised a possible danger and transformed it into a certainty. His continual forecasts of the growth of totalitarianism are on similar lines. There was plenty of evidence that democracy would not survive, and Orwell translated this evidence into the impossibility of survival.

It seems at times that Orwell is committing the very dishonesties that he continually attacks. He condemns propaganda, insists that writers who are primarily interested in creed rather than humanity are bad writers, that politics are corrupting, "a mass of lies, evasions, folly, hatred, and schizophrenia". But Orwell himself is an avowed propagandist and uses propagandist techniques, although with clarity and refinement and a genuine understanding of the power of language. It is perhaps impossible to prove that Orwell was a propagandist who did not tell lies. It is, however, evident that while the more blatant party-liners obscured the facts through vagueness and euphemism whenever it was convenient, Orwell illuminated the facts through his precise presentation of detail. He was concerned with being true only to his own vision, not to any external orthodoxy. In his own words, "In our time it is broadly true that political writing is bad writing. Where it is not true, it will generally be found that the writer is some kind of rebel, expressing his private opinions and not a 'party-line'. Orthodoxy, of whatever colour, seems to demand a lifeless, imitative style."[1] Orwell was himself a rebel, and it is this and his use of language that isolate him from his fellow propagandists.

In his essay "Politics and the English Language" Orwell demonstrates the connection between inaccurate writing and some of the worst features of political behaviour. Because so many political writers, however well meaning, have bad writing habits—use vague abstractions, stale metaphors, stock and meaningless phrases—it makes it easier for writers whose aim is to deliberately mislead to get away with it. They use the language that is to hand, which has grown from a mixture of slovenliness, lack of interest and the development of a technique of deliberate lying. In another essay, "The Prevention of Literature", Orwell writes: "Political writing in our time con-

I

sists almost entirely of prefabricated phrases bolted together like the pieces of a child's Meccano set. It is the unavoidable result of self-censorship. To write in plain, vigorous language one has to think fearlessly, and if one thinks fearlessly one cannot be politically orthodox."[2] The fear of offending at least one of a number of authorities encourages the inclination to let one's language, and therefore one's meaning, look after itself.

Orwell particularly attacks the use of sloppy abstractions, often a result of simple laziness. Words cease to be selected for their meaning. They are at hand, ready-made in association with other words, and their use transforms the concrete into the densely abstract. He illustrates his criticisms with a number of examples, and suggests that part of the explanation for slack writing is that political writers do not really care what they are saying in terms of meaning and are only concerned with producing a particular result. "The great enemy of clear language is insincerity. Where there is a gap between one's real and one's declared aims, one turns as it were instinctively to long words and exhausted idioms, like a cuttlefish squirting out ink."[3] As long as motives such as these exist writing will continue to deteriorate, and so will political honesty. As long as language is used laxly misleading political propaganda will thrive.

Simone Weil attacks the inaccurate use of language in much the same way as Orwell. She is a writer who occupied in France a position similar to Orwell's in England. She belonged to no group, was governed by no orthodoxy and fashioned her own alienated creed. On the subject of the dangerous use of words she writes this:

. . . when empty words are given capital letters, then on the slightest pretext, men will begin shedding blood for them and piling up ruin in their name, without effectively grasping anything to which they refer, since what they refer to can never have any reality, for the simple reason that they mean nothing. In these conditions the only definition of success is to crush a rival group of men who have a hostile word on their banners; for it is a characteristic of the empty word that each of them has its complementary antagonist. It is true, of course, that not all of these words are intrinsically meaningless; some of them do have meaning if one takes the trouble to define them properly. But when a word is properly defined it loses its capital letter and can no longer serve either as a banner or as a hostile slogan; it becomes simply a sign, helping us to grasp some concrete reality, or concrete objective, or method of activity. To clarify thought, to discredit the intrinsically meaningless words, and to define the use of others by precise analysis—to do this, strange though it may appear, might be a way of saving human lives.[4]

Simone Weil goes a stage further than Orwell. She links the meaning of words not just with political behaviour but with political action. Orwell sees the danger in terms of the atrophy of the mind, Simone Weil in terms of literal death. She suggests that no cause is worth fighting for. But they both have the same fundamental concern with the corruption of language and the corrupting power of language. Language stupidly used could be destructive.

The connection between politics and language creates a vicious circle. Sloppy language encourages corrupt and dangerous politics and corrupt politics produce sloppy language. It is in the interests of many to keep the circle unbroken. Orwell had discussed this problem in several of his *Tribune* pieces before he wrote this essay. It became an intimate part of his horror at the rewriting of history. On one occasion he shows how words lose all their meaning through imprecise usage in precisely the way Simone Weil pointed out:

. . . the word Fascism is almost entirely meaningless. In conversation, of course, it is used even more widely than in print. I have heard it applied to farmers, shop-keepers, Social Credit, corporal punishment, fox-hunting, bull-fighting, the 1922 Committee, the 1941 Committee, Kipling, Ghandi, Chiang

Kai-Shek, homosexuality, Priestley's broadcasts, Youth Hostels, astrology, women, dogs and I do not know what else.[5]

General imprecision renders genuine attempts at definition useless, and of course influences the quality of the political struggle. It was this mess of vagueness and deliberate malice that Orwell was trying to penetrate with his own technique.

It was bad writing that Orwell condemned rather than propaganda in itself. It was this that allowed him to be an expert propagandist. He recognised the necessity of the Labour Government's publicising itself adequately, to make clear what it was doing and what it intended to do. He frequently criticised its incompetence and its failure to make any real contact with the public, and attributed this failure partly to the neglect of publicity. He wrote during the war: "It seems clear that it pays to tell the truth when things are going badly, but it is by no means certain that it pays to be consistent in your propaganda. British propaganda is a good deal hampered by its efforts not to be self-contradictory."[6] These are certainly not the words of one who viewed propagandists with a moral aloofness.

Orwell was angered at the clumsiness of many propagandists, but realised that part of the problem was the fact that in most cases the public believed what it wanted to believe and different sections of the public would accept their chosen area of propaganda regardless of the manner in which it was expressed. In order to communicate it was necessary to overcome the barriers of uncritical acceptance and unconsidered rejection. Orwell's attack on the tendency of prose to move away from the concrete is naturally bound up with his attempts to reach an audience. It was not until *Animal Farm* that he produced a book that sold really well, and that was a success precisely because it coincided with the public's rejection of Stalin.

In his essay "Why I Write" Orwell discusses the connection between language and political purpose with reference to his own work:

What I have most wanted to do throughout the past ten years is to make political writing an art. My starting point is always a feeling of partisanship, a sense of injustice. When I sit down to write a book I do not say to myself "I am going to produce a work of art". I write it because there is some lie I want to expose, some fact to which I want to draw attention, and my initial concern is to get a hearing. But I could not do the work of writing a book, or even a long magazine article, if it were not an aesthetic experience.[7]

Here Orwell sums up his commitment to precision of language. It was an aesthetic experience for him to use words with accuracy. To have done otherwise would have offended not only his conscience but his very profound sense of artistic integrity. It is interesting that Koestler blames "a feeling of partisanship" for the faults of his fiction, while Orwell has based his principles of writing upon it.

Orwell's thoughts about the writer and politics are reflected in his comments on social and political novelists. He praises Henry Miller for his ability to portray everyday experiences and to reveal the inner workings of the mind, in spite of the fact that he has no concern whatever, rather a flamboyant unconcern, for political events. On the other hand he criticised Upton Sinclair for writing mere "political tracts", "a sort of Socialist adaptation of the old-style religious tract in which the young man who is on the road to ruin hears a striking sermon and thereafter touches nothing stronger than cocoa".[8] Orwell says that Sinclair's novels are plotless and the characterisation non-existent. Sinclair was a novelist as much concerned as Orwell with the detailed communication of facts, and considering the vast sweep of his subject matter he was extraordinarily knowledgeable and accurate. He, like Orwell, made it his business to find things out. His *World's End* series covers very nearly every facet of political and social activity in Europe and America from before the First World War until after the Second, and although we can quarrel with the streak of sentimentality that runs through his characterisation it is hard to attack the very digestible way in which he presents his facts.

Sinclair's technique was very different from Orwell's, and Orwell was clearly not in sympathy with it. Orwell plunges his characters into the midst of some grim and pernicious set of circumstances and uses them as subjective instruments of exposure. Sinclair allows his characters to wander through a vast variety of experience, opening their eyes gradually. And as their eyes open so do ours: at least, that is the object of the exercise. The *World's End* novels are centred on the character of a sensitive, intelligent, moneyed and very likeable young man who acts as witness of events and sounding board of opinions while gradually moving towards political commitment. (Sinclair's *Oil!* (1927) has a similar pattern.) The essence of Orwell's novels is that the alternatives facing his characters are equally gloomy. Sinclair leaves nothing to the imagination in his exposure of ghastly conditions, but the almost cheerful laxness of his prose counteracts the gloom. His language is cluttered, his sentences often ponderous, a curious mixture of the colloquial and the stylised, but Sinclair himself had the qualities of a virtuoso (though he continually repeated characters and situations) and his many novels were popular and, in some cases at least, effective as propaganda. Orwell clearly admired Sinclair: "It is good history, if mediocre fiction", he says of the *World's End* books. He was a man of prodigious output who never ceased in his efforts to follow his commitment. But Orwell suggests that Sinclair spoils his case by casting his propaganda in a fictional framework. Orwell's sensitivity towards the adulteration of literature by propaganda probably explains why he himself refrained from attempting to deliver a directly political message in his novels except in the form of allegory and science fiction.

Orwell had no lively tradition of radical writing to sustain him. In the United States the pattern that Orwell's life followed, the pattern of the middle-class intellectual embracing an essentially working-class experience, was a fairly common occurrence. Dos Passos, Eugene O'Neill and Hemingway all followed it. Parallel to this was the experience of the working-class, self-educated man writing his way to the top—the experience of Jack London. It seems almost impossible that a book like Alexander Saxton's *The Great Midland* (1948), a novel about industrial Chicago between the Wars with powerful characterisation and rigorous exposure of oppression, could ever have been written in this country. *The Great Midland* spans the experience of opposed classes. British writers just did not have this breadth of experience behind them. Orwell was an exception, and yet even he was never for any length of time healthily out of touch with his own class, as a writer like Alexander Saxton was. Orwell does not seem to have been familiar with many American writers; he was more at home with the European novelists—Koestler, Malraux, Silone. It was the European political experience that he looked to. Inevitably Spain meant more to him than the savage industrial battles of America. He was used to political novels that were an interweaving of violent action and theoretical argument, and although he was clearly influenced by these when he wrote *Nineteen Eighty-Four* he rejected that mode of political writing. His particular gifts would have been well suited to the American tradition of radical writing which, until the end of the 1930s, had such a lively existence. Sustained by such a tradition he might have explored the possibilities of the novel as a means of propaganda to a far greater extent.

Orwell could not help but admire the few proletarian writers of the thirties, the documentaries of slum living and unemployment, the criminal underworld and imprisonment, such as *The Big Wheel* by Mark Benney (1940) or B. L. Coombes' books. Yet he found many of them strangely insulated and unaware, perhaps understandably, of a broader picture of political conflict. He himself had so rapidly isolated the growth of Fascism as the dominant issue that, although he never for a moment lost touch with domestic issues and conditions, he felt that anyone sensitive to social conditions should be sensitive to major political issues. He detected, too, a note of acceptance that tempered the bitterness and the starkness of the facts and was obviously not conducive to political action. He says of *The Big Wheel*: "Its distinctive mark is its acceptance of the lumpen-proletariat outlook, its assumption that the world of narks, pimps, eightpenny kids, punchdrunk boxers and rival race-groups is as eternal as the pyramids."[9] The central drive of Orwell's propaganda was his determination to make people discontented, either with their own lot or with society in general, and to force on them such an awareness of deprivation that they would be prepared to take action against it.

It was, ultimately, Orwell's striving for clarity of expression, for communication, that made him so valuable as witness and commentator. It is the source of both his originality and his isolation. No other writer used language so uncompromisingly and to such good effect. Few writers were so personally committed to each word they set down, and suffered so much from this commitment. Few were prepared or able to devote the same care to a description of toads mating in a pond as to the details of miners working underground. Neither subject warranted sloppiness or inaccuracy or an essentially different attitude. Orwell received a letter complaining that, because he discussed Woolworth's rose bushes in "As I Please", he was a "bourgeois sentimentalist". He certainly did not believe that the battle against Fascism necessitated an inattention to roses. And his contention that the revitalisation of language would bring about a regeneration of political behaviour applied to smaller things also.

There were times, though, when anger, bitterness or desperation deflected Orwell from his aim of clarity to the extent of momentarily blinding him to all considerations apart from the effort to communicate. The intense strain of the struggle to make contact with the public's Achilles' heels at times gave his prose an obsessive tone. He cared too much about the things he wrote of to compromise it by restraint, and this could mar the fine balance of his prose and blunt his most powerful weapon. He saw the power of understatement but sometimes not of a simpler holding back. It was presumably this kind of over-committed writing that led V. S. Pritchett to say: "Excellent pamphleteer though he was Orwell was patently crabbed, bleak and sweeping; he was strongly marked by the crank's vanity in being the only just man. He is not humourless but his laughter is negligent and offhand."[10] There were certainly times when Orwell's mood and outlook were bleak, and when his statements were sweeping. The bleakness, at least, was at times justified and not in itself a literary failing. But his prose rarely lost its deft touch, and his vanity, if it existed, was of a painful and lonely kind. The more he criticised and attacked the more severely was he cut off from the bulk of humanity and the more bitterly he felt the distance between his writing and the people he addressed. It seems that his very isolation was a source of his strength, and it is ironic that when in the last five years of his life his work was accepted by the public, it was also misused.

The characteristics that Pritchett condemns are admired by Koestler, who identified this source of his strength. He writes: "his uncompromising intellectual honesty was such that it made him almost inhuman at times. There was an emanation of austere harshness around him which diminished only in proportion to distance, as it were: he was merciless towards himself, severe upon his friends, unresponsive to admirers, but full of understanding sympathy for those on the remote periphery."[11] Considering that Koestler wrote as an admirer and perhaps as a friend there is something impressively accurate about this statement. It seems so much more in tune with the intensity of Orwell's moral outlook than Pritchett's slightly patronising summing up. The qualities Koestler mentions drove Orwell into exile from society, an exile that one would guess was partly a result of an inability to make contact with others and to make himself known to others. Such a position inevitably prevented relaxation. He tried to establish a viable position for himself as a social being by creating a morally indispensable role rather than by finding himself a niche that was bolstered by human relations. One critic has written: "Orwell's dominant concern is to find a place for himself in society—the main spring of his work is to find an honest political outlook for a person of just *his* particular environment, education, beliefs and emotions. The desire to fit this one square peg into the framework of existence and to demand everyone else's attention while he does so, is, with Orwell, almost an obsession."[12] This is only half the story, and only half true. It is detaching motive from style, and we have seen that an understanding of Orwell's relationship with his facts as expressed through his style is essential to the understanding of the whole body of Orwell's work. Orwell both accepted and rejected the European tradition of the political writer offering himself as an *exemplum*. He did choose to communicate political belief via his own experience, but it was the experience that was important, not himself.

Isaac Deutscher finds another kind of obsession. He sees Orwell as a rationalist facing the irredeemable irrationality of human existence. The Moscow Trials represented the culmination of human irrationality:

> Orwell pursued reality and found himself bereft of his conscious and unconscious assumptions about life. In his thoughts he could not henceforth get away from the Purges. Directly and indirectly, they supplied the subject matter for nearly all that he wrote after his Spanish experience. This was an honourable obsession, the obsession of a mind not inclined to cheat itself comfortably and to stop grappling with an alarming moral problem. But grappling with the Purges, his mind became infected by their irrationality. He found himself incapable of explaining what was happening in terms which were familiar to him, the terms of empirical common sense. Abandoning rationalism he increasingly viewed reality through the dark glasses of a quasi-mystical pessimism.[13]

One has to remember Deutscher's own unorthodox position as revisionist admirer of Trotsky, but even bearing this in mind it is hard to find direct evidence for what he says although we can see that it is partially relevant. In fact, such a "quasi-mystical pessimism" does not dominate, for instance, "As I Please", nor is it present in *Animal Farm*, which in spite of its thesis of defeat is Orwell's most unclouded piece of writing. He wrote directly very little about the Purges and he seems to have accepted Koestler's interpretation of them. He makes passing references and condemns the English left wingers who were too nervous or too bound by orthodoxy to question their necessity. But he himself digested and placed them rapidly precisely because they did make sense according to his experience of Soviet Communism. He had gained that experience in Spain, and it was Spain that was crucial in Orwell's development. From that time he never doubted that the worst was true because he was continually preparing for the worst. There is nothing mystical about *Nineteen Eighty-Four*—it was simply his final preparation. It was not a lack of rationality that led him to be weighed down by pessimism but, if anything, an overdeveloped sense of the rational. Just as Koestler saw the Moscow Purges as an instance of the supremely logical development of a creed Orwell saw *Nineteen Eighty-Four* as the logical extension of certain aspects of society and politics. It is the kind of extension on which the best science fiction is based. In Orwell's book it has a different quality, because he was also making a desperate attempt to issue a serious and legitimate warning.

The swing from chronicler to prophet was a gradual though natural one. Prophecy is a form of interpretation, and in Orwell's case the compulsion to prophesy was encouraged by his instinct for self-preservation, or rather for the preservation of democracy and humanity. In many particulars his picture of the future was a presentation of the dreariest and most depressing features of contemporary life with all the escape hatches bolted. The astonishing thing is that Orwell was able to imagine in so much detail and with so much force such a situation. His ability was in part due to the fact that he had an exaggerated feeling that the situation was already in some respects a reality—an essential feeling for the most convincing prophets. And again, the quality of his interpretation, that complete lack of hindrance by vague and extraneous detail, the penetration and the single-mindedness—the characteristics that are described as both "honest" and "obsessive"—is a result of the quality of his language.

Koestler's experiences with the Communist Party inevitably shaped his response to the use of language In his book *The Writer and the Commissar* G. Paloczi-Horvath says: "In Communist Party life language is an important and precise instrument—and an extremely dangerous one. At the same time, language has a ceremonial role and it must be used according to the proper ritual." The Party member has to learn to recognise the most minute inflections of policy. "For the commissar the slightest verbal change in a basic formula or ceremonial expression has a supreme importance. The actual situation of power within the top leadership can be fathomed from these slight changes. And the success, even the life of the commissar . . . largely depends on his ability to fathom those changes. The commissar fears and respects formulae."[14]

This formalisation of language occurred in most political organisations. The repeated phrase, the watchword, the rapid and almost inevitable superficial summing up of a complex political issue—these features are so much a part of our political language that we hardly notice them. As Orwell pointed out the well-worn cliché could be dangerous as well as tedious, and not merely in the sense of the commissar offending against orthodoxy. Orwell also showed the part played by the abbreviation of words in ceremonial expression. This rigid control over life that the Communist Party exerted by means of language is reflected in Koestler's own description of the effect of his Communism on his methods of argument and expression. "My vocabulary, grammar, syntax, gradually changed. I learnt to avoid any original form of expression, any individual turn of phrase. Euphony, gradations of emphasis, restraint, nuances of meaning, were suspect. Language, and with it thought, underwent a process of dehydration, and crystallised in the ready made schemata of Marxist jargon."[15] This is precisely the process that Orwell is describing in his creation of Newspeak, and that he attacks in "Politics and the English Language". Newspeak represents the most thorough dehydration of language that is possible.

Koestler describes the CP method of argument as a "dialectical tom-tom":

> Repetitiveness of diction, the catechism technique of asking a question and repeating the full question in the answer; the use of stereotyped adjectives and the dismissal of an attitude or fact by the simple expedient of putting words in inverted commas and giving them an ironic inflection . . . through its very tedium produced a dull, hypnotic effect. Two hours of this dialectical tom-tom and you didn't know whether you were a boy or a girl, and were ready to believe either as soon as the rejected alternative appeared in inverted commas.[16]

The dialectical method has left its stamp on Koestler's writing. He shook off the dogma that was the cause of the distortion but the process continued to affect him. The blatant techniques of *Spanish Testament* linger in *The Yogi and the Commissar*, and can even be detected in *The Act of Creation*, his latest book. The language and the phraseology have changed, but the construction of sentences and the representation of ideas remains similar. The pairing, confronting and attempted synthesis of opposites recurs, and often provides the central conflicts of his novels. In *Thieves in the Night* Joseph becomes a synthesis of the passive liberal and the aggressive terrorist, with Dina and Simeon acting as catalysts. In *The Act of Creation* Koestler is continually describing processes which follow this pattern. This suggests either the powerful influence of the dialectical method, or the fact that Koestler's natural style (its development is hard to follow through four different languages) accommodated itself easily to the process Koestler describes above.

The language of the Communist Party was frequently used in

order to disguise reality. Koestler, in spite of his advantage in experience over Orwell, wrote at a greater distance from experience. His own life provides the terms of reference of his argument, but continual reference to his life comes between his argument and his audience. His continual reliance on metaphorical expression results in the toning down of reality :

> Among the great Powers, Britain, thanks to the obstinacy of her traditions and the great inertia of her body social, is probably the most capable of developing an oasis-climate. Interregnums are downward slopes of history; and at this point of our journey the brakes of the train are more important than the engine. During the last century our ethical brakes were more and more neglected, until totalitarian dynamism made the engine run amok. In plain language, that means that if I have to choose between living under a Political Commissar or a Blimp, I unhesitatingly choose Blimp.[17]

This is taken from Koestler's essay "The Fraternity of Pessimists", and the entire essay is constructed around a series of metaphorical representations. In it Koestler does not develop an argument, he balances symbols. The result is a glut of metaphor. This can only appeal to the intellect, and then only on a certain level. His symbolic language is in itself very accurate and very ingenious so far as it goes, but this again detracts from the facts it is based on. There are too many factors that the representation cannot accommodate. The whole of British history is clinched in a single phrase. We cannot help wondering whether, if Koestler had chosen a symbol other than an engine without brakes, he would have come to some other conclusion, that his alternatives might have been different or a choice not forced. When he says "In plain language" he introduces the reduction of the problem to its simplest possible terms. He is writing algebraically.

This can be a useful and dramatically persuasive means of argument. But it is probably at the root of many of the more

serious criticisms of Koestler's writing. Harold Rosenberg criticised Koestler's glibness :

> Because of the intelligence, and particularly the *relevance*, of
> his novels, it is easier to praise Koestler than to indicate the
> correct proportion of his lack. His thinking tackles boldly
> some of the most real dramatic situations of our time. And it
> never forgets the personal sufferings of those who are caught
> up in them. At the same time there is a pervading glibness in
> Koestler, the journalist satisfying himself with devices aiming
> at the reader's opinions. This glibness is not altogether a vice,
> since it permits him to put down quickly and cleanly events
> whose meanings a more painstaking investigation might not
> reveal for a long time or might even find to be out of reach
> entirely. Haste is especially important for the chronicles of
> political conscience, since the background of the drama
> changes so rapidly today that details of doubt recorded about,
> say, Spain in 1935 no longer have the same point if described
> in 1943.[18]

Rosenberg here puts his finger on an important aspect of political fiction which most critics neglect—the necessity of
rapidity. But in doing so he himself fails to say that the political
novelist is not only interpreting a contemporary situation to a
contemporary audience, but history to succeeding generations.
But this does not really interfere with the pertinence of Rosenberg's point. Koestler's boldness in coming to grips with "real
dramatic situations" is partly a result of the uncompromising
character of the dialectical method. His glibness is due to the
same method's ability to skate over what it is chosen to ignore,
and this, in its turn, is due to the most dubious characteristic of
the dialectic—the fact that thesis and antithesis are artificially
and arbitrarily selected and set against one another. As Rosenberg indicates, at times it is important to allow deliberate rejection to be legitimate, but the dialectic imposes rejection. Koestler can be devastatingly convincing. But at the same time a fre-

quent and natural reaction is one of profound distrust. It was not only his handling of political evidence that provoked, in many cases, a hesitant critical response, it was the language of political description that he employed. Two *TLS* reviewers emphasise different difficulties of Koestler's style. One says, in a review of *The Yogi and the Commissar*, "with all his boldness of mind Mr. Koestler . . . is frequently both evasive and a little cheap. The embellishment of his argument, to begin with, can only be described now and then as intellectually precious. Relishing cleverness as he does he indulges in too obviously clever phrase-making, ignoring the danger that this may not only dull the edge of sincerity but prevent clear thinking."[19] The reviewer of *Thieves in the Night* detected "a faint incongruity between the intensity of Mr. Koestler's views and the borrowed calm of his style of expression".[20] The calm and the clever suggest opposition. For one the tough, acute, antithetical style, the vocabulary chosen from a wide range of technical, psychological and political knowledge formed a barrier against understanding. For the other it muted reality.

Koestler was much further from solving the problem of communication than Orwell. The use of language was not for him so intimate an experience. This is clearly partly due to the fact that he twice changed his language of literary expression, from Hungarian to German and from German to English, and also had a brief period of writing in French. As well as this he had to learn and unlearn that anonymous language of inter-class and international communication invented by the Communist Party. This lack of intimacy influenced the quality of his propaganda : it is much more negative than Orwell's. He attacks a faith that deluded him, but the only alternative he offers is essentially without positive energy. For a man who was so deeply involved in political experience, who was so widely known as a political writer, there is remarkably little in the nature of constructive proposal in his writing. This again may be due to the destruction his responses suffered in the CP. Orwell was constantly offering proposals, some unrealistic, some trivial, but always actively constructive. There seems to be here a very basic difference in the quality of imagination: Koestler did not know how to make imaginative and creative use of his experience. Orwell, with his greater imaginative powers, was in many respects more vital and more immediate in his handling of politics.

Neither successfully solved the problem of the propagandist response to their own propaganda. John Lewis wrote a pamphlet which simply dismissed the evidence in *The Yogi and the Commissar* as being fabricated—and not even by Koestler himself.[21] There were similar reactions to *Darkness At Noon*, to Orwell's *Animal Farm* and *Nineteen Eighty-Four*. The result of the attempt to communicate with those for whom the message was not urgent was deadlock. In the confrontation of two opposing systems of belief language becomes powerless. As Koestler wrote of the Communist working within a closed system, "He can prove anything he believes, and he believes anything he can prove".[22] Koestler showed in *Darkness At Noon*, Victor Serge showed in *Memoirs of a Revolutionary*, how the control of orthodoxy paralysed growth. Koestler was conscious of the paralysis of language, but he found this a problem of expediency rather than of morality. Sartre wrote: "The function of a writer is to call a spade a spade. If words are sick, it is up to us to cure them. Instead of that, many writers live off this sickness. In many cases modern literature is a cancer of words."[23] For Orwell this cancer was an essentially moral disease: without morality language could not function properly.

In many minds the two words morality and propaganda are implicitly contradictory. Orwell himself leaned towards the view that propaganda was inherently immoral, but we have seen that he explained why he found most propagandist writing dishonest in a very precise way. Koestler discussed propaganda as such only with reference to Communist propaganda, and both he and Orwell insisted that it was the control of orthodoxy that made Communist propaganda such a supreme example of immorality, although moral and immoral were not words that Koestler frequently used. We have to keep both the political and literary aspects of the morality of propaganda in mind when we discuss it, both the use of language in politics and the use of politics in language. But to begin with the context provided by a social philosopher is useful. The following quotations are taken from Reinhold Niebuhr's *Moral Man and Immoral Society*. They provide an essential background to the discussion:

> Politics will, to the end of history, be an area where conscience and power meet, where the ethical and coercive factors of human life will interpenetrate and work out their tentative and uneasy compromises. The democratic method of resolving social conflict, which some romanticists hail as a triumph of the ethical over the coercive factor, is really much more coercive than at first apparent. The majority has its way, not because the minority believes that the majority is right . . . but because the votes of the majority are a symbol of its social strength.[24]

> A social conflict which aims at the elimination of these injustices [social and racial inequalities] is in a different category than one which is carried on without reference to the problem of justice. In this respect Marxian philosophy is more true than pacifism. If it may seem to pacifists that the proletarian is perverse in condemning international conflict and asserting the class struggle, the latter has good reason to insist that the elimination of coercion is a futile ideal but that the rational use of coercion is a possible achievement which may save society.[25]

> A distinction must be made, and is naturally made, between the propaganda which a privileged group uses to maintain its privileges and the agitation for freedom and equality carried on by a disinherited group.[26]

Propaganda is so frequently condemned largely because of its coercive character. It is regarded as an illegitimate weapon, in some respects a less legitimate weapon than bombs and tanks—for example, the American reply to Communist propaganda in Latin America has on occasion been the use of arms. Propaganda can be described as dishonest, but arms cannot lie. Propaganda is mistrusted precisely because it is unanswerable on its own terms. And it is mistrusted also because the propaganda put out by a conventionally described democratic Government is invariably seen as something other than propaganda : in the eyes of the average citizen propaganda always comes from the enemy, and if something can be identified as propaganda then whoever is behind it is an enemy. The hero of Sillitoe's *Saturday Night and Sunday Morning* reflects this.

Orwell and Koestler both had an intimate experience of the effects of propaganda and both condemned it for a variety of reasons. They both recognised the perversion of language that commitment to an orthodoxy brought. Orwell found that this perversion infected the quality of political action. Koestler admitted that his own commitment, even when it was no longer rigid, blurred the potential of his fiction. Yet both writers remained compulsive, intense propagandists. Orwell was as committed to propaganda as he was to his beliefs, but the roots of his beliefs were throughout his life deeply moral. Although Koestler's preoccupations were predominantly concerned with historical movement—he rejected Marxism because it did not work, although he was prepared to base his appeal on a more emotional sense of morality—they were tempered by an ethical sensitivity. In fact, the confrontation of historical inevitability with individual morality was at the very centre of his fiction. He and Orwell were trying to find weapons that were both moral and effective against immoral society.

Both writers would have seized on Niebuhr's distinction between kinds of propaganda as an essential one in their battle. If we are to recognise the rebel, the spokesman of a "disinherited group", the fighter against the majority as anything more than an antic figure we must accept this distinction also. It is an acceptance of the morality of conscience. Genuine belief must be allowed to speak. If it is not genuine, those who think they can recognise it for what it really is must be allowed to fight it. This is the essence of democracy. The tragedy of democracy is that it can throw up a Hitler as easily as it can throw up a Stanley Baldwin, whom Orwell once so aptly described as "a hole in the air".

In spite of the fact that Koestler presented himself as typical of his generation, and on this founded his very confident stance, he was like Orwell an outcast. He was an exile from his own country, an exile from the faith that had sustained his ancestors, an exile from the faith that had sustained himself over an important period of his life, an outsider in the country he chose to adopt. He did not speak on behalf of a "disinherited group" so much as of a disinherited individual—himself.

Both Orwell and Koestler saw propaganda as being a "coercive factor" and they used it as such. They were continually concerned with working out a mode of action that could be both ethical and aggressive. Niebuhr shows that the context of "democracy" does not necessarily provide a sufficient or genuine yardstick as a measure of the ethics of propaganda. He demonstrates that there are certain inequalities that are fundamentally immoral if measured by any rational system of belief, and that conflict on behalf of erasing these inequalities is more moral than other kinds of conflict. In other words, those who are fighting for racial equality in the United States are more moral than the supporters of South Africa's *apartheid*. The argument about whether propagandist methods of conflict are in themselves immoral—an argument which neither Orwell nor Koestler uses—becomes irrelevant. If Niebuhr's principles are accepted, and of course ruling groups are less likely to accept them than the disinherited, propaganda used in the struggle for a more rationally moral situation is justifiable.

Orwell's conception of propaganda in relation to the use of language has already been discussed. If the propagandist methods used by Koestler and Orwell are morally acceptable— it is too early to determine whether they are historically justifiable—their ultimate defence rests on whether they were compatible with the literary forms in which they were used, and on whether they in fact produced results. An approach to the work of Orwell and Koestler that does not place it in a social and historical context is not an adequate one. Literary compatibility cannot be discussed at a distance from the events with which the literature is concerned.

In the search for the most appropriate framework for propaganda Orwell was clearly more successful than Koestler. He adapted the traditions of literary documentary to his own purpose and achieved a standard of personal chronicle that has not been surpassed as a vehicle for the communication of belief. In his two attempts at casting political comment and prophecy in a fictional form, *Animal Farm* and *Nineteen Eighty-Four*, his public success was remarkable and, in the case of the former, his literary integrity has rarely been questioned. Koestler was able to shape real events into the form of fiction, but he did not have the imaginative powers to prevent continual criticisms that the form he chose was inappropriate. To some extent the form can be justified by the novels' achievements. There is a great deal of evidence to suggest that Koestler's two most overtly propagandist works, *Darkness At Noon* and *Thieves in the Night*, were widely influential and were also his best fiction. When he chose to write directly of personal experiences his writing was at its least propagandist—or perhaps self-propagandist rather than committed.

In many ways Orwell and Koestler were antithetical. Their personalities and the way their personalities intruded upon their writing, were obviously so. Their experience and their understanding of events, and the translation of this understanding into literary terms, were also very different. Joseph Wood Krutch, as other critics have done, places Orwell and Koestler side by side. "Arthur Koestler is, of course his [Orwell's] only rival claimant to the title of spokesman par excellence for the doomed generation. But Orwell has the advantage of a richer culture and a less melodramatic method, while Koestler seems to have been born yesterday and . . . is unaware that thought existed before Freud, Marx and Stalin."[27] Koestler may have the more acute sense of historical movement—some have accused Orwell of having none at all—but Orwell has the more sensitive understanding of the past. These differing cultural supports influenced their response to the present. Orwell placed literature and experience in a tradition which permeated his whole being. But he was also acutely conscious of its decay and breakdown. Zionism and Marxism were Koestler's substitutes for tradition. They necessitated an understanding of the processes rather than the quality of history.

Koestler will continue to be an important writer because of his position as symbol and spokesman of an area of action that had never encroached so nearly on to the grounds of common experience. Orwell will always be important because of his solitary voice, but more than this, because of the quality of his writing. If it is suggested that these are not sufficient grounds on which to lay claim to Orwell's historical as well as his literary significance, here is Conor Cruise O'Brien summing up his crucial contemporary influence. Having insisted that the genuine intellectual must—and did—accept the truth of much of what Orwell said, he goes on to say:

There can be little doubt that Orwell did change the minds of quite a few people through whom he changed the minds of many others. He cleared out a great deal of cant, self-deception, and self-righteousness, and in doing so shook the confidence of the English left, perhaps permanently . . . the cant of the left, that cant which has so far proved almost indispensable to the victory of any mass movement, was almost destroyed by Orwell's attacks. . . . His effect on the English left might be compared with that of Voltaire on the French nobility: he weakened their belief in their own ideology, made them ashamed of their clichés, left them intellectually more scrupulous and more defenceless.[28]

This may be an exaggerated claim, but the most trustworthy critics (that is, those who are not dogmatically committed to beliefs that oppose Orwell's) accept the morality even if not the message of Orwell's writing. I have tried to show that both this morality and its acceptance are rooted in the quality of Orwell's language, and that this quality is an embodiment of the mind and personality of the man himself as far as we can know him. In the case of Koestler it is not possible to come to so compact a conclusion. The variety and the intensity of his experience was such that the quality of his thought has been battered by rigorous exposure. His commitment determined the nature of his interests and the depth of his response, and to some extent dulled the sharpness of his original passionate reactions and excited reasoning. Koestler underwent a gradual process of withdrawal that began some time before he left the Communist Party. Orwell fought to come closer to the source of the evils of modern society, and, as O'Brien shows, did a great deal of damage on the way. At his death all the signs pointed to a continuation of his severe and relentless commitment.

Orwell and Koestler chronicled an area of action and reaction that continues in barely modified—in some cases intensified—form in the present day. It is fashions of response that have changed rather than the realities of political struggle. What they have written is of more than historical interest. As long as authoritarian governments and social inequalities, both within and outside democracies, continue to exist they will continue to be relevant, perhaps even politically or morally effective. The argument that *Darkness At Noon* or *Animal Farm* have no value beyond the events that inspired them, or that the value of *Nineteen Eighty-Four* is negated because it is now clear that society is not going to be like that in the near future, is cheap and facile. Orwell warned that history could be rewritten under one's very eyes. The evidence that these two writers have set down is something of a guarantee against this.

NOTES

1 *Limping after Reality*

1 "Arthur Koestler", *Horizon*, May 1947
2 "The Case for Responsible Literature", *Horizon*, May 1945
3 *What is Literature?*, Methuen & Co. Ltd., 1949, p. 14
4 *Writers and Politics*, Chatto & Windus Ltd., 1965, Introduction, p. xx
5 *Outline, an autobiography and other writings*, Faber & Faber Ltd., 1949, p. 210
6 *A Passionate Prodigality*, MacGibbon & Kee Ltd., 1965 (first published in 1933), pp. 280-1
7 *The Thirties*, The Cresset Press Ltd., 1960, p. 44
8 "A Marxist Interpretation of Literature", *The Mind in Chains*, C. Day Lewis, ed., Frederick Muller Ltd., 1938, p. 52
9 *I Am My Brother*, Longmans Green & Co. Ltd., 1960, p. 17
10 *These Poor Hands*, Victor Gollancz Ltd., 1939, p. 7
11 "Barcelona", *The Condemned Playground*, Routledge & Kegan Paul Ltd., 1945, p. 186
12 *The Thirties*, pp. 120-1
13 Quoted in *First Year's Work by Mass-Observation*, Charles Madge and Tom Harrisson, ed., L. Drummond, 1938, p. 60
14 Notes, *Collected Poems*, Faber & Faber Ltd., 1966

2 *From Paris to Wigan*

1 "Why I Write", *England Your England*, Secker & Warburg Ltd., 1953, p. 13
2 *The Road to Wigan Pier*, Secker & Warburg Ltd., 1959 (first published in 1937), p. 180
3 ibid., pp. 181-2

4 *Down and Out in Paris and London*, Secker & Warburg Ltd., 1949, p. 6
5 ibid., p. 20
6 *Vagrancy*, Penguin Books Limited, 1963, p. 27
7 *Down and Out in Paris and London*, p. 153
8 *Letters from Jack London*, King Hendricks and Irving Shepard, ed., MacGibbon & Kee Ltd., 1966, p. 137
9 *The People of the Abyss*, Arco Publications Ltd., 1962 (first published in 1903), p. 7
10 *Letters from Jack London*, pp. 136-7
11 "George Orwell and *The Road to Wigan Pier*", *Critical Quarterly*, Spring 1965
12 *The Road to Wigan Pier*, p. 18
13 ibid., pp. 87-8
14 "George Orwell and *The Road to Wigan Pier*"
15 *The Road to Wigan Pier*, p. 19
16 "Orwell Reconsidered", *Partisan Review*, Winter 1960
17 *The Road to Wigan Pier*, foreword, p. xvii
18 ibid., pp. 210-11
19 *Left News*, March 1937
20 *The Jungle*, Penguin Books Limited, 1965, p. 132

3 The Extreme Experience

1 *Under the Crust*, The Bodley Head Ltd., 1946, pp. 126-7
2 ibid., p. 53
3 *The Road to Wigan Pier*, p. 24
4 ibid., pp. 24-5
5 *Miner's Day*, Penguin Books Limited, 1945, p. 14
6 *Charity Main*, George Allen & Unwin Ltd., 1964, p. 18
7 ibid., p. 40
8 *The Road to Wigan Pier*, p. 23
9 ibid., p. 24
10 *Alamein to Zem Zem*, Faber & Faber Ltd., 1946, p. 17
11 loc. cit.
12 ibid., p. 51
13 *Scum of the Earth*, Wm. Collins Sons & Co. Ltd., 1955, p. 188
14 ibid., p. 79
15 ibid., p. 70
16 ibid., p. 71

4 Orwell and the Middle Class

1 "Culture, Progress and English Tradition", *The Mind in Chains*, p. 255
2 *A Clergyman's Daughter*, Secker & Warburg Ltd., 1960 (first published in 1935), pp. 193-4
3 "Inside the Whale", *England Your England*, p. 109
4 *New English Weekly*, 1 August 1935
5 *Angel Pavement*, William Heinemann Ltd., 1950, p. 160
6 *Keep the Aspidistra Flying*, Secker & Warburg Ltd., 1954 (first published in 1936), pp. 30-1
7 ibid., p. 173
8 ibid., p. 175
9 ibid., p. 255

5 The Necessity of Action

1 *Homage to Catalonia*, Secker & Warburg Ltd., 1951 (first published in 1938), p. 3
2 ibid., p. 26
3 *The Owl of Minerva*, Rupert Hart-Davis Ltd., 1959, p. 40
4 *Homage to Catalonia*, p. 18
5 *The Owl of Minerva*, p. 39
6 *Homage to Catalonia*, p. 207
7 ibid., p. 36
8 ibid., p. 65
9 ibid., p. 160
10 "The Spanish Tragedy", *New Statesman*, 30 April 1938
11 *The Invisible Writing*, Hamish Hamilton & Wm. Collins, 1954, p. 333
12 *Spanish Testament*, Victor Gollancz Ltd., 1937, p. 133
13 ibid., p. 343
14 *Arrow in the Blue*, Hamish Hamilton & Wm. Collins, 1952, pp. 99-100
15 ibid., p. 242
16 *The God that Failed*, Richard Crossman, ed., Hamish Hamilton Ltd., 1950, p. 26

6 The Revolutionary Hero

1 The Gladiators, Macmillan & Co. Ltd., 1948 (first published in 1939), p. 94
2 Conspiracy of Silence, Hamish Hamilton Ltd., 1951, p. 1
3 Communism and the French Intellectuals, Andre Deutsch Ltd., 1964, p. 128
4 Quoted in ibid., p. 128
5 Quoted in loc. cit.
6 New Statesman, 4 January 1941
7 "Soviet Myth and Reality", The Yogi and the Commissar, Jonathan Cape Ltd., 1945, p. 148
8 Darkness At Noon, Jonathan Cape Ltd., 1940, p. 61
9 ibid., pp. 21-2
10 The Gladiators, p. 163
11 Darkness At Noon, p. 99
12 ibid., pp. 99-100
13 ibid., p. 166
14 ibid., p. 227
15 ibid., p. 246
16 Man's Estate (La Condition Humaine), Penguin Books Limited, 1961, p. 5
17 ibid., p. 219
18 Bread and Wine, Victor Gollancz Ltd., 1964 (first published in 1937), p. 288
19 The Invisible Writing, p. 267
20 loc. cit.
21 Arrival and Departure, Jonathan Cape Ltd., 1943, p. 118
22 ibid., p. 68

7 The Third Dimension

1 The Case of Comrade Tulayev, Hamish Hamilton Ltd., 1951, p. 111
2 ibid., p. 134
3 Darkness At Noon, p. 65
4 The Rebel, Penguin Books Limited, 1962, p. 21
5 The Act of Creation, Hutchinson & Co. Ltd., 1964, p. 346
6 Arrow in the Blue, p. 218
7 "Arthur Koestler", Critical Essays, Secker & Warburg Ltd., 1946, p. 130

8 *A Faith to Fight For?*

1 14 March 1938, quoted in *Encounter*, January 1962
2 *Encounter*, 8 June 1937
3 ibid., 14 December 1938
4 *Coming Up For Air*, Secker & Warburg Ltd., 1948 (first published in 1939), p. 34
5 "Inside the Whale", *England Your England*, p. 97
6 ibid., p. 99
7 ibid., p. 103
8 ibid., p. 98
9 ibid., p. 104
10 From the publisher's announcement
11 *The Lion and the Unicorn*, Secker & Warburg Ltd., 1941, p. 14
12 ibid., p. 47
13 ibid., p. 95
14 loc. cit.
15 ibid., pp. 10-11
16 ibid., p. 96
17 ibid., pp. 98-9
18 "Fascism and Democracy", *The Betrayal of the Left*, Victor Gollancz Ltd., 1941, p. 208
19 ibid., p. 214
20 "Boys' Weeklies", *Critical Essays*, p. 70
21 "The Proletarian Writer", *The Listener*, 19 December 1942
22 "The Frontiers of Art and Propaganda", ibid., 29 May 1941
23 Quoted in *I Am My Brother*, p. 93
24 "Thomas Hardy Looks at War", *Tribune*, 18 September 1942
25 "As I Please", ibid., 24 December 1943

9 *A Faith Defeated*

1 London Letter, *Partisan Review*, 1941, no. 4
2 loc. cit.
3 ibid., 1942, no. 4
4 ibid., 1943, no. 2
5 ibid., 1945, no. 1
6 loc. cit.
7 loc. cit.

8 loc. cit.
9 ibid., 1946, no. 3
10 loc. cit.
11 "Towards European Unity", Partisan Review, 1947, no. 4
12 "The Novelist's Temptation", The Yogi and the Commissar, p. 29
13 ibid., p. 32
14 ibid., p. 33
15 "The Intelligentsia", ibid., pp. 78-9
16 ibid., p. 84
17 "The Fraternity of Pessimists", ibid., p. 108
18 "Knights in Rusty Armour", ibid., p. 102
19 "Land of Virtue and Gloom", The Trail of the Dinosaur, Wm.
      Collins, 1955, p. 27
20 ibid., p. 29
21 ibid., pp. 38-9
22 "The Fraternity of Pessimists", The Yogi and the Commissar,
      p. 111
23 "The End of an Illusion", ibid., p. 218
24 "Judah at the Crossroads", The Trail of the Dinosaur, pp. 138-9

10 Post-War Positions

1 "The Yogi and the Commissar", The Yogi and the Commissar,
      p. 13
2 loc. cit.
3 ibid., p. 14
4 "The Challenge of Our Times", The Trail of the Dinosaur, p. 13
5 "Catastrophic Gradualism", Politics, September 1946
6 "Judah at the Crossroads", The Trail of the Dinosaur, p. 139
7 "Soviet Myth and Reality", The Yogi and the Commissar, p. 135
8 ibid., p. 200
9 ibid., p. 191
10 "The End of an Illusion", ibid., p. 226
11 ibid., p. 222
12 "The Yogi and the Commissar—II", ibid., p. 255
13 Thieves in the Night, Macmillan & Co. Ltd., 1946, pp. 6-7
14 ibid., p. 55
15 ibid., p. 37
16 ibid., pp. 27-8
17 ibid., p. 169

18 ibid., p. 57
19 ibid., pp. 161-2
20 ibid., p. 296
21 ibid., p. 295
22 ibid., p. 300
23 Clement Greenberg, *Partisan Review*, 1946, no. 5
24 T. R. Fyvel, *Tribune*, 25 October 1946
25 *The Age of Longing*, Wm. Collins, 1951, p. 145
26 ibid., p. 14
27 ibid., p. 375
28 "As I Please", *Tribune*, 29 November 1946
29 Introduction to the Ukrainian edition of *Animal Farm*, quoted in *George Orwell: some material towards a bibliography*, Diploma in Librarianship thesis, London University, 1953
30 *New Statesman*, 15 August 1953
31 *Animal Farm*, Secker & Warburg Ltd., 1945, p. 88
32 "Soviet Satire", *New Statesman*, 8 September 1945
33 Reginald Reynolds, *Forward*, 24 November 1945

11 Post-War Prophecy

1 "As I Please", *Tribune*, 28 April 1944
2 "You and the Atom Bomb", ibid., 19 October 1945
3 "Freedom and Happiness", ibid., 4 January 1946
4 loc. cit.
5 "Prophecies of Fascism", *Tribune*, 12 July 1940
6 Jack London, *Love of Life*, Elek Books Ltd., 1946, Introduction, p. 9
7 *Nineteen Eighty-Four*, Secker & Warburg Ltd., 1949, p. 5
8 loc. cit.
9 ibid., p. 7
10 ibid., p. 54
11 "The Principles of Newspeak", ibid., p. 307
12 *Nineteen Eighty-Four*, p. 11
13 ibid., p. 67
14 ibid., p. 127
15 ibid., p. 98
16 ibid., p. 61
17 ibid., p. 133
18 ibid., p. 14

19 Reviews of *Mein Kampf, New English Weekly*, 21 March 1940
20 *The Iron Heel*, Laurie Ltd., 1947, p. 15
21 *Nineteen Eighty-Four*, p. 128
22 ibid., p. 165
23 ibid., p. 166
24 ibid., p. 167
25 ibid., p. 168
26 ibid., p. 192
27 "Afterword on *1984*", *Orwell's Nineteen Eighty-Four*, Irving
      Howe, ed., Harcourt, Brace & World, Inc., 1963, p. 207
28 ibid., p. 209
29 *Nineteen Eighty-Four*, p. 259
30 ibid., p. 265
31 ibid., p. 270
32 ibid., p. 279
33 ibid., p. 282
34 ibid., p. 286
35 Quoted by Julian Symons in "Orwell, a reminiscence", *London
      Magazine*, September 1963
36 *New Statesman*, 17 June 1949
37 "Power of Corruption", *Times Literary Supplement*, 10 June 1949
38 Robert Kee, *The Spectator*, 17 June 1949
39 "*1984*—The Mysticism of Cruelty", *Orwell's Nineteen Eighty-
      Four*, p. 197

12 Two Modes of Isolation

1 "Politics and the English Language", *Shooting an Elephant*,
     Secker & Warburg Ltd., 1950, p. 95
2 "The Prevention of Literature", ibid., p. 125
3 "Politics and the English Language", ibid., p. 97
4 "The Power of Words", *Collected Essays*, Secker & Warburg Ltd.,
     1961, p. 156
5 "As I Please", *Tribune*, 24 April 1944
6 loc. cit.
7 "Why I Write", *England Your England*, pp. 13-14
8 "Propaganda in Novels", *Tribune*, 13 September 1940
9 "Life in London's Underworld", ibid., 23 August 1940
10 *New Statesman*, 15 August 1953

11 "A Rebel's Progress", *The Trail of the Dinosaur*, p. 102

12 T. A. Birrell, "Is Integrity Enough?", *Dublin Review*, Autumn 1950

13 "*1984*—The Mysticism of Cruelty", *Orwell's Nineteen Eighty-Four*, p. 201

14 *The Writer and the Commissar*, The Bodley Head Ltd., 1960, p. 10

15 *The Invisible Writing*, p. 26

16 *The God that Failed*, p. 56

17 "The Fraternity of Pessimists", *The Yogi and the Commissar*, p. 112

18 "The Case of the Battered Radical", *Partisan Review*, 1944, no. 1

19 *Times Literary Supplement*, 12 May 1945

20 ibid., 26 October 1946

21 *The Philosophy of Betrayal*, Metcalfe & Cooper Ltd., 1945

22 *Arrow in the Blue*, p. 253

23 *What is Literature?*, p. 210

24 *Moral Man and Immoral Society*, Scribners, 1932, p. 4

25 ibid., p. 235

26 ibid., p. 245

27 *Saturday Review*, 23 April 1953

28 *Writers and Politics*, p. 32-3

K

BIBLIOGRAPHY

ARTHUR KOESTLER

Fiction

The Gladiators, Macmillan & Co. Ltd., 1949, first published in 1939
Darkness at Noon, Jonathan Cape Ltd., 1940
Arrival and Departure, Jonathan Cape Ltd., 1943
Thieves in the Night, Macmillan & Co. Ltd., 1946
The Age of Longing, Wm. Collins, 1951

Autobiographical

Dialogue with Death, Hutchinson & Co. Ltd., 1966, first published
  in 1940
Scum of the Earth, Wm. Collins, 1955, first published in 1940
Arrow in the Blue, Hamish Hamilton and Collins, 1952
The Invisible Writing, Hamish Hamilton and Collins, 1954

Political

Spanish Testament, Victor Gollancz Ltd., 1937
The Yogi and the Commissar, Jonathan Cape Ltd., 1945
The God that Failed (ed. Richard Crossman), Hamish Hamilton Ltd.,
  1950
The Trail of the Dinosaur, Wm. Collins, 1955

Historical and Scientific

Promise and Fulfilment, Macmillan & Co. Ltd., 1949
Insight and Outlook, Macmillan & Co. Ltd., 1949
The Lotus and the Robot, Hutchinson & Co. Ltd., 1960
The Sleepwalkers, Hutchinson & Co. Ltd., 1961

The Act of Creation, Hutchinson & Co. Ltd., 1964
The Ghost in the Machine, Hutchinson & Co. Ltd., 1967

Play

Twilight Bar, Jonathan Cape Ltd., 1945

GEORGE ORWELL

Fiction

Burmese Days, Secker & Warburg Ltd., 1949, first published in 1934
A Clergyman's Daughter, Secker & Warburg Ltd., 1960, first published in 1935
Keep the Aspidistra Flying, Secker & Warburg Ltd., 1954, first published in 1936
Coming Up for Air, Secker & Warburg Ltd., 1948, first published in 1939
Animal Farm, Secker & Warburg Ltd., 1945
Nineteen Eighty-Four, Secker & Warburg Ltd., 1949

Documentary and Political

Down and Out in Paris and London, Secker & Warburg Ltd., 1949, first published in 1933
The Road to Wigan Pier, Secker & Warburg Ltd., 1959, first published in 1937
Homage to Catalonia, Secker & Warburg Ltd., 1951, first published in 1938
The Lion and the Unicorn, Secker & Warburg, 1941
The Betrayal of the Left (ed. Victor Gollancz), Victor Gollancz Ltd., 1941

Mainly Literary

Inside the Whale, Secker & Warburg Ltd., 1946
Critical Essays, Secker & Warburg Ltd., 1946

Shooting an Elephant, Secker & Warburg Ltd., 1950
England your England, Secker & Warburg Ltd., 1953
Collected Essays, Secker & Warburg Ltd., 1961

Articles and Reviews Quoted, not included in the above collections

New English Weekly, review, 1 August 1935
   review, 21 March 1940
New Statesman, 'The Spanish Tragedy', 30 April 1938
The Listener, 'The Proletarian Writer', 19 December 1942
   'The Frontiers of Art and Propaganda', 29 May 1941
Partisan Review, London Letter, 1941, no. 4
   1942, no. 4
   1943, no. 2
   1945, no. 1
   1946, no. 3
   'Towards European Unity', 1947, no. 4
Politics, 'Catastrophic Gradualism', September 1946
Tribune, 'Prophecies of Fascism', 12 July 1940
   'Life in London's Underworld', 23 August 1940
   'Propaganda in Novels', 13 September 1940
   'Thomas Hardy Looks at War', 18 September 1942
   'As I Please', 24 December 1943
   'As I Please', 24 April 1944
   'You and the Atom Bomb', 19 October 1945
   'Freedom and Happiness', 4 January 1946
   'As I Please', 28 November 1946

A SELECTED LIST OF CRITICAL WORKS WITH DIRECT BEARING
ON ORWELL AND KOESTLER

Atkins, John : *Arthur Koestler*, Neville Spearman Ltd., 1956
   George Orwell, John Calder Ltd., 1954
Howe, Irving, ed. : *George Orwell's Nineteen Eighty-Four*, Harcourt,
   Brace and World Inc., 1963
O'Brien, Conor Cruise : *Writers and Politics*, Chatto and Windus
   Ltd., 1965
Rees, Sir Richard : *George Orwell, Fugitive from the Camp of
   Victory*, Secker & Warburg Ltd., 1961

Thomas, Edward: *George Orwell*, Oliver and Boyd Ltd., 1965
Voorheese, R.: *The Paradox of George Orwell*, Purdue University Studies, 1961
Woodcock, George: *The Crystal Spirit*, Jonathan Cape Ltd., 1967

ARTICLES AND REVIEWS QUOTED IN THE TEXT

Birrell, T. A.: 'Is Integrity Enough?' *Dublin Review*, Autumn 1950
Fyvel, T. R.: review, *Tribune*, 25 October 1946
Greenberg, Clement: review, *Partisan Review*, 1946, no. 5
Hoggart, Richard: '*George Orwell and The Road to Wigan Pier*', *Critical Quarterly*, Spring 1965
Kee, Robert: review, *Spectator*, 17 June 1949
Krutch, Joseph Wood: review, *Saturday Review*, 23 April 1953
Martin, Kingsley: 'Soviet Satire', *New Statesman*, 8 September 1945
Pritchett, V. S.: 'Arthur Koestler', *Horizon*, May 1947
review, *New Statesman*, 17 June 1949
review, *New Statesman*, 15 August 1953
Reynolds, Reginald: review, *Forward*, 24 November 1945
Symons, Julian: 'Orwell, a reminiscence', *London Magazine*, September 1963
Wollheim, Richard: 'Orwell reconsidered', *Partisan Review*, Winter 1960
'Power of Corruption', *Times Literary Supplement*, 10 June 1949

INDEX